EGON SCHIELE
LANDSCAPES

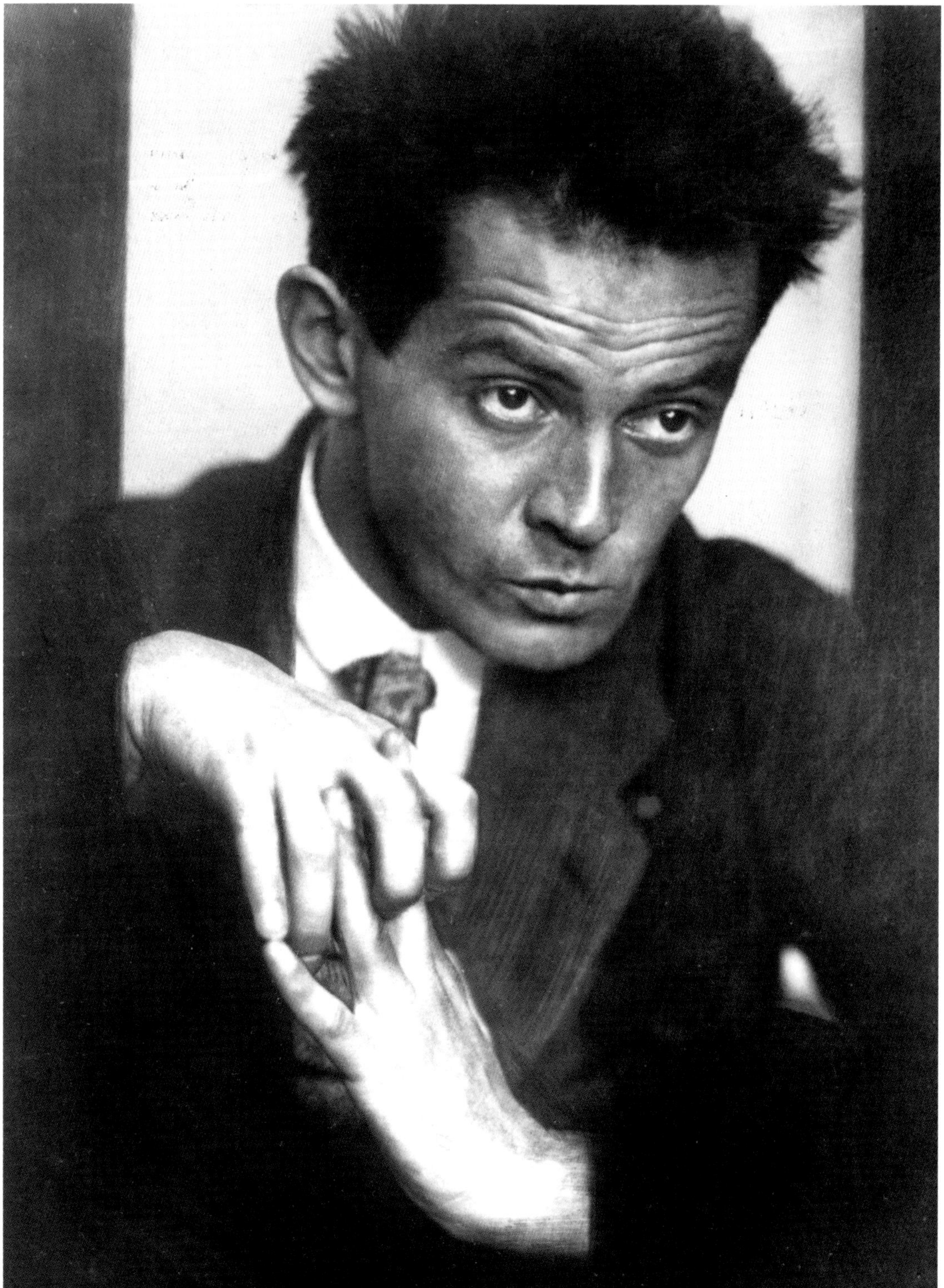

EGON SCHIELE
LANDSCAPES

Rudolf Leopold

LEOPOLD MUSEUM
VIENNA

PRESTEL
MUNICH · BERLIN · LONDON · NEW YORK

Acknowledgements

Rudolf Leopold, Vienna

Albertina, Vienna
Egon Schiele Museum, Tulln on the Danube
Kunsthaus Zug, Sammlung Kamm
Kunsthaus Zürich
Landesmuseum Mainz
MUMOK, Museum Moderner Kunst Stiftung Ludwig, Vienna
Musée d'Art et d'Historie, Geneva
Museo Thyssen-Bornemisza, Madrid
Museum der Moderne – Rupertinium, Salzburg
Neue Galerie Graz
Niederösterreichisches Landesmuseum, St. Pölten
Oberösterreichesche Landesmuseen, Linz
Österreichische Galerie Belvedere, Vienna
Sammlung Eberhard Walter Kornfeld (E. W. K.), Bern
Städeliches Kunstinstitute und Städtische Galerie, Frankfurt
Stiftsmuseum Klosterneuburg
Tiroler Landesmuseum Ferdinandeum, Innsbruck
Tyssen-Bornemisza Collections, Zurich
Wien Museum, Vienna
and many private collectors

First published on the occasion of the exhibition
"Egon Schiele. Landscapes" held at the Leopold Museum, Vienna
17 September 2004 to 31 January 2005

Publisher for the Leopold Museum Privatstiftung: Rudolf Leopold
Managing director: Peter Weinhäupl

Front cover: Egon Schiele, *Setting Sun* (detail), 1913 (see p. 123)
Back cover: Egon Schiele, *Island Town* (also known as *Krumau Town Crescent II*; detail), 1915
Frontispiece: Egon Schiele (photo by Anton Josef Trcka), 1914
Page 6/7: Egon Schiele, *Houses and Laundry* (also known as *Two Blocks of Houses with Washing Lines*) 1914

Photo credits: Picture material has been kindly made available and lent to us by museums and collections mentioned in the captions; further material originates from Prof. Dr. Rudolf Leopold, Vienna:
pp. 14, 38, 40, 44, 46, 48, 50, 56, 60, 64, 68, 70, 72, 76, 80, 88, 92, 108, 110, 112, 114, 124 (above), 127, 132, 134, 138, 140, 142, 152, 160, 166, 168, 176, 190, 204 (1st, 3rd, 4th picture from left), 205 (1st, 3rd, 5th picture from left), 207 (1st, 2nd, 3rd picture from left); Albertina, Vienna: p. 204 (2nd picture from left), 205 (3rd picture from left), Wien Museum, Vienna: p. 205 (4th picture from left).

The names of towns, locations, streets etc. are in accordance with the German edition of this book.

The Library of Congress Control Number: 2009942476
British Library Cataloguing-in-Publication Data: a catalogue record for this book is available from the British Library. The Deutsche Bibliothek holds a record of this publication in the Deutsche Nationalbibliografie; detailed bibliographical data can be found under: http://dnb.d-nb.de

Prestel books are available worldwide. Please contact your nearest bookseller or one of the addresses below for information concerning your local distributor.

Verlagsgruppe Random House FSC-DEU-0100
The FSC-certified paper Chinese Golden
Sun matt art is produced by mill Yanzhou
Tianzhang Paper Industry Co., Ltd.,
Shandong, PRC.

Prestel, a member of Verlagsgruppe Random House GmbH

Prestel Verlag
Königinstrasse 9
80539 Munich
Tel. +49 (0)89 24 29 08-300
Fax +49 (0)89 24 29 08-335

Prestel Publishing Ltd.
4 Bloomsbury Place
London WC1A 2QA
Tel. +44 (0)20 7323-5004
Fax +44 (0)20 7636-8004

Prestel Publishing
900 Broadway, Suite 603
New York, N.Y. 10003
Tel. +1 (212) 995-2720
Fax +1 (212) 995-2733

www.prestel.com

Bookbinding by Conzella, Pfarrkirchen

Project management by Victoria Salley
Copyediting by Jürgen Schönwälder, Jon Smale, Munich
Design and production by Cilly Klotz
Production: Selen Bulut
Origination by Repro Ludwig, Zell am See
Printed and bound by C & C Printing
Translated from German by John Gabriel
Printed in China

ISBN 978-3-7913-4458-4

CONTENTS

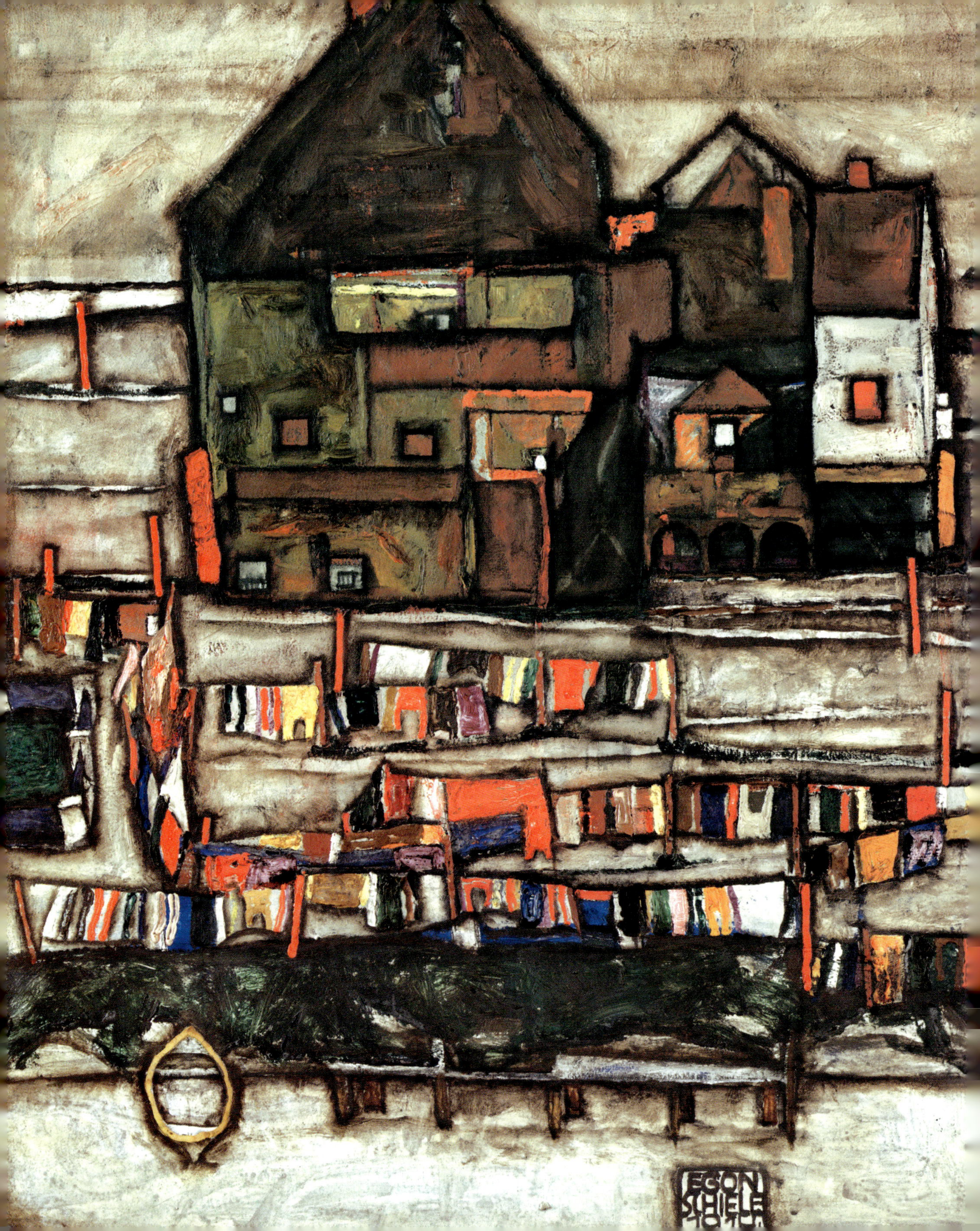
EGON
SCHIELE

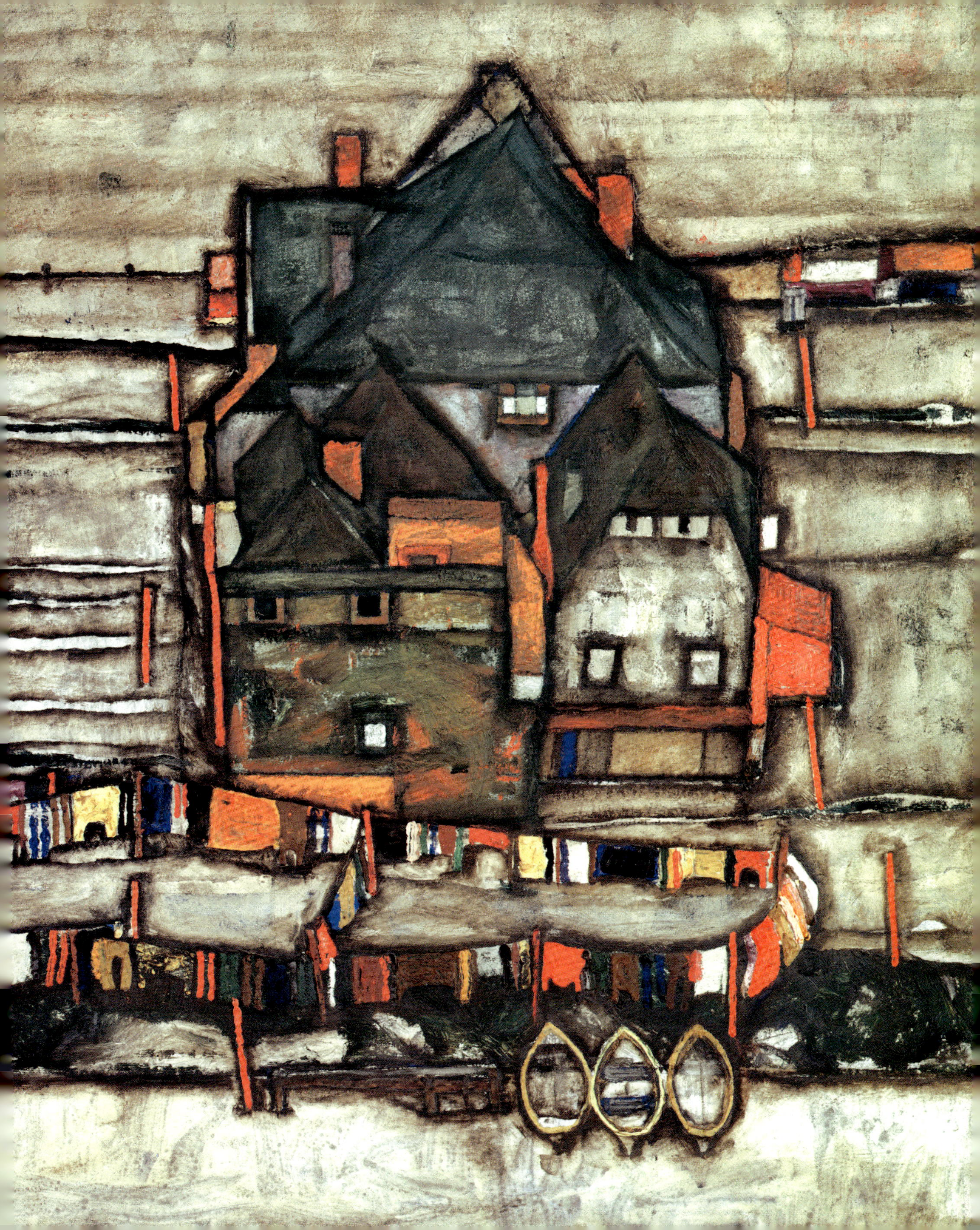

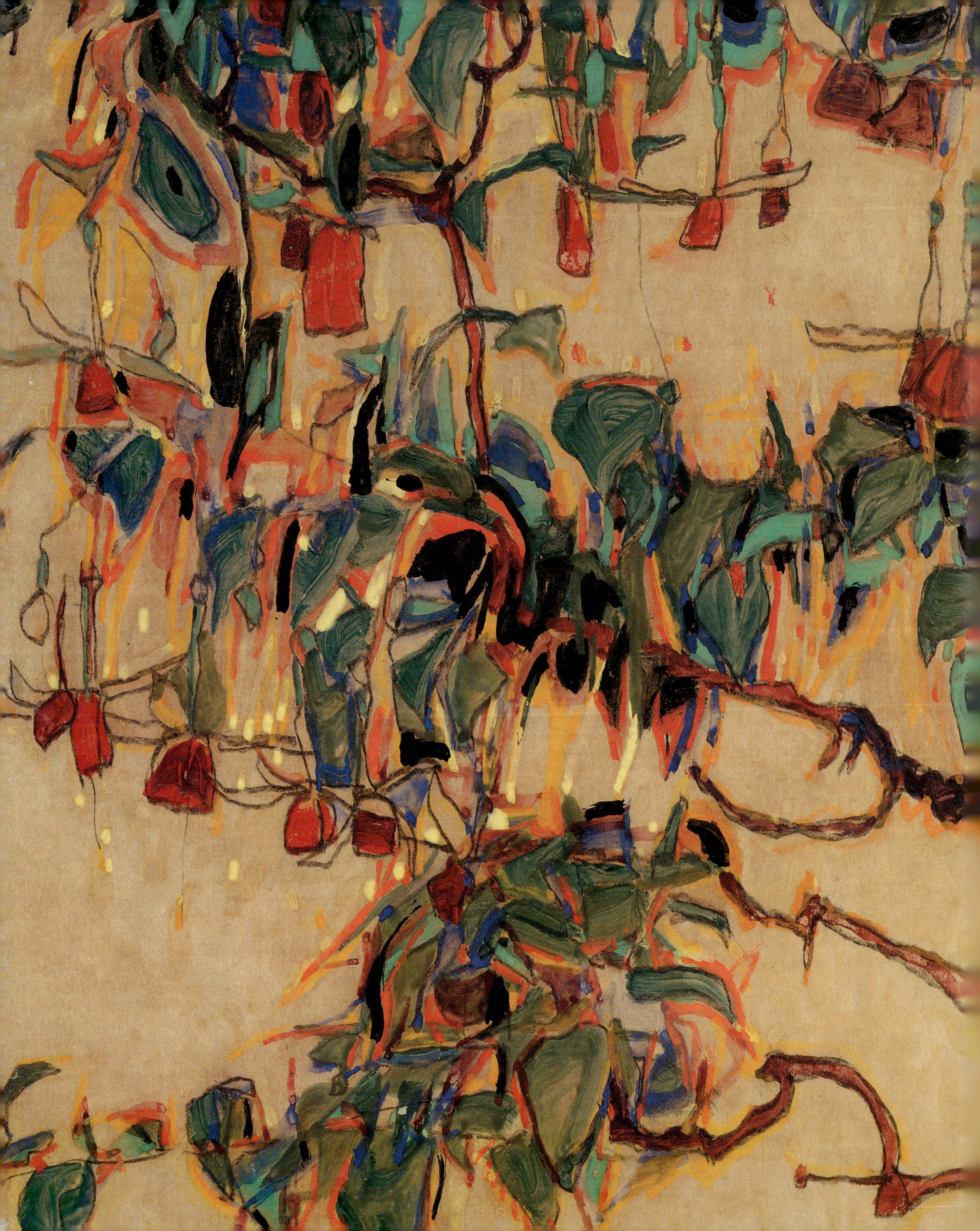

Introduction

Depictions of houses, in an urban and occasionally rural setting, play an important role in Schiele's painting œuvre both in terms of number and significance. From the time he attained to his original, independent style, Schiele began to alter given motifs to an ever greater degree. This process generally consisted in changing existing forms and colors, and in omitting certain parts of a motif. Rearrangements or displacements of motifs into imaginary landscapes also occurred.

These changes can be traced by comparing Schiele's pictorial solutions with the existing original motifs, in so far as these are still localizable. As such comparisons have revealed, his alterations took different forms in each phase of his development. In his naturalistic-impressionistic beginnings Schiele depicted the natural scene basically just as it struck his eye. If any alteration was made, it was mainly in terms of color, in which the influence of the Viennese Secession rapidly made itself felt. From the middle of 1908 onwards, both choice of palette and mode of composition relied largely on currently fashionable approaches. Yet by as early as 1910, Schiele had arrived at his own style, achieved artistic autonomy. Although this was first reflected in his figurative works, it was soon confirmed in his landscape depictions. Like the portraits and compositions with figures, the landscapes were conceived in terms of a heightened expressiveness and enhanced by typifications. A group of houses in Krumau, for example, could become a "Dead City", or a hill with fields a "Thunderstorm Mountain".

At this point not some prevalent fashion in art but personal involvement became the determinant factor. Schiele's increasingly painterly approach went hand in hand with a decidedly visionary quality, as reflected in the numbers of ghostly paraphrases of Krumau motifs that now emerged. House groupings were spirited out of their original context, modified, and blended into unfamiliar surroundings that lent them a symbolic meaning.

As another consequence, the format of the paintings grew considerably larger in the years 1913–15. At the same time, as in the figurative depictions, landscape motifs were increasingly reduced to geometric terms. Cubic and pyramidal shapes were emphasized, as were overlappings in space. Yet despite the formal tendency of these compositions, the actual experience on which they were based still remained evident. During the three last years of his life, Schiele's architectural landscapes grew much more schematic in character. Their coloration was more posterlike, blatant, and the previously strong suggestion of spatial depth, especially in the works of 1913–15, gave way to an increasing decorativeness. In part these late works were reprises of earlier compositions, but occasionally sheer inventions not preceded by any involvement with objective situations or based on transformations of these.

Fuchsia Branches ("Sun Tree") 1910 (see p. 63)

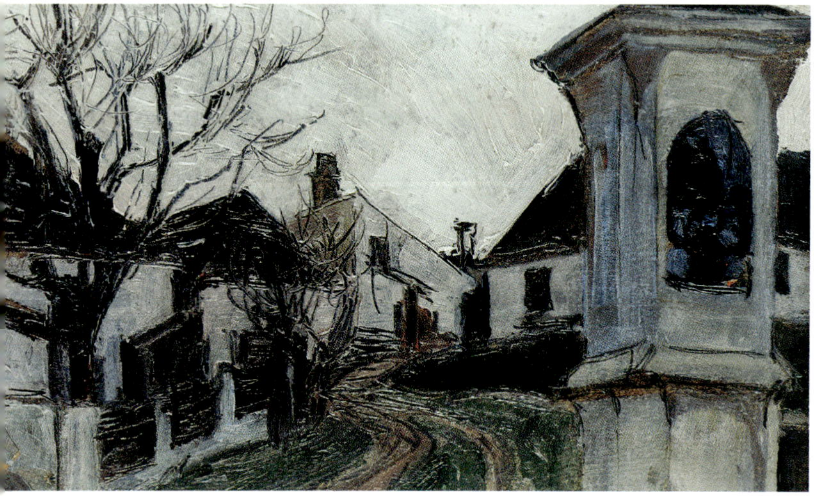

Bare Trees, Houses and Shrine (Klosterneuburg) 1907
(see p. 39)

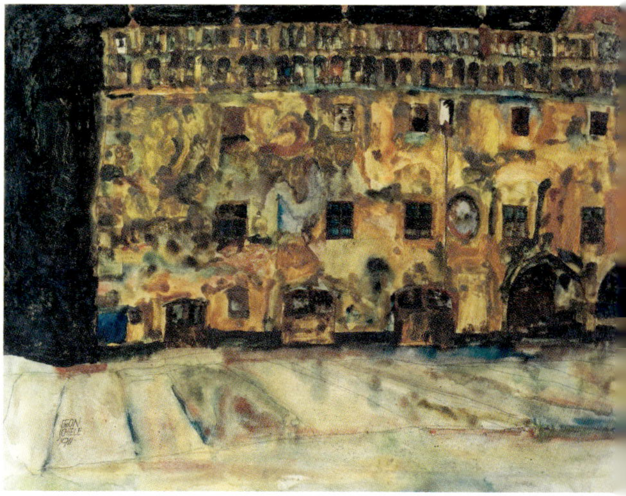

Krumau Town Hall II 1911
(see p. 79)

In principle, the works in the present volume are arranged chronologically. In so far as a painting of a certain motif existed, it, rather than a drawing or compositional study, determined the place of the motif in the sequence. In cases where Schiele later employed the same motif for further paintings, these have all been reproduced together with the earliest version.

The majority of Schiele's usually small-format oil studies of motifs in Klosterneuburg emerged in 1906–08. These were followed before the latter year by three studies from Krumau, Bohemia, his mother's home town. This lovely old place exerted a magical attraction on Schiele, and he moved there in 1911. Trouble with the inhabitants, however, compelled him to leave Krumau after only a few months, although he later continued to make regular short trips there. This explains why Krumau motifs held a predominant place in his mature depictions of houses and townscapes from 1910 onwards.

Böhmisch-Krumau (Český Krumlov) lies in southern Bohemia, on a triple bend of the Moldau. It was from this "krummer Au", or "crooked lea", that its earlier name "Krummau" derived. By the First World War, the second "m" had been dropped, as seen in contemporaneous postmarks citing the German Krumau and the Czech Krumlov.

"Island Town" 1915
(see p. 160)

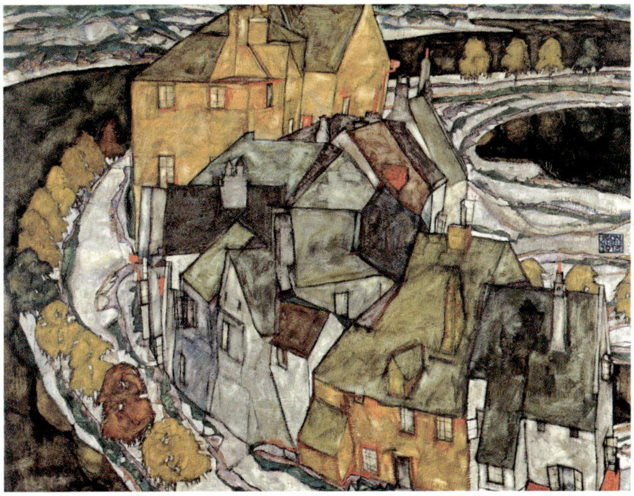

Essentially Krumau consists of two sections: the inner district, located in the middle Moldau loop, established as a town in 1309 by Heinrich von Rosenberg; and Latron (Latrán) in the northern loop, a settlement inside the castle walls that goes back to the thirteenth century. The houses built in the course of time outside the town to the southeast soon developed into a separate district, the "New Town". These buildings were later enclosed by the second fortified wall built around the Latron district.

The name Latron has various possible etymologies. One is from the Latin latro, or thief, which might go back to the legendary smoking out of a robbers' nest on Krumau rock by the Witigons. Other derivations are from "ad latera castelli", or beside the castle; from "in latere arcis", or in the bend; or from the Greek-derived word "latris", or servant. This last interpretation, advanced by Karl Tannich, according to which Latron took its name from the dwellings of the castle lord's servants and laborers, is generally considered the most likely. In 1555 the inner town was amalgamated with Latron. Schiele was fascinated by its old houses and lanes. In 1911 he described in his sketchbook how they "fit together closely like letters" in a word. This idea was wonderfully conveyed in the townscapes he painted at the time, which had already begun to display his own personal style.

Expressive art is essentially characterized by the way in which emotional reaction takes precedence to visual impression. Schiele's mature townscapes provide abundant examples of this, precisely because it is so often possible to compare them with the original motifs. Unlike the Expressionism that emerged in the orbit of Die Brücke and the artists' group Der Blaue Reiter, in which architectural motifs tended to be extremely generalized or abstracted, the Expressionist Schiele adhered to the specific traits of the motifs that inspired him. Although they were altered and heightened in an Expressionist manner, the idiosyncracies of the motifs remained recognizable.

This link with objective perception was one of the most striking features of early Viennese Expressionism. Even though Schiele attempted a portrait of a building in each depiction of an individual house, he represented many of their real details quite literally. (This was not the case in full-fledged German Expressionism, which intentionally strove for an indeterminate "somewhere, nowhere" particularly in depictions of houses. To a greater or lesser extent, of course, a departure from the natural impression underlay all Expressionism.) The differences pointed out here should therefore be understood as qualifications within the overarching whole of a common artistic striving – in the context of which Schiele's rank and extraordinary place stand assured.

"Sketch from Krumau" 1906

Pencil and watercolor on paper, 10.4 x 21.1 cm
Dated and titled 'Krumau' upper right;
inscribed on the reverse 'Skizze aus Krumau'
Private collection

This was the title Schiele inscribed on the reverse of this small, only approx. 10 x 21 cm sheet. On the obverse, he dated it precisely to the day: "30. VIII. 06" (30 August 1906).

The houses on the left are only cursorily sketched, and the group of trees at the bottom merely suggested by a uniform green. In contrast, the houses above it (that is, in reality behind it) are accurately rendered in pencil and watercolor. We can also see how skillfully the sixteen-year-old artist was already capable of depicting windows with reflections and chimneys with cast shadows.

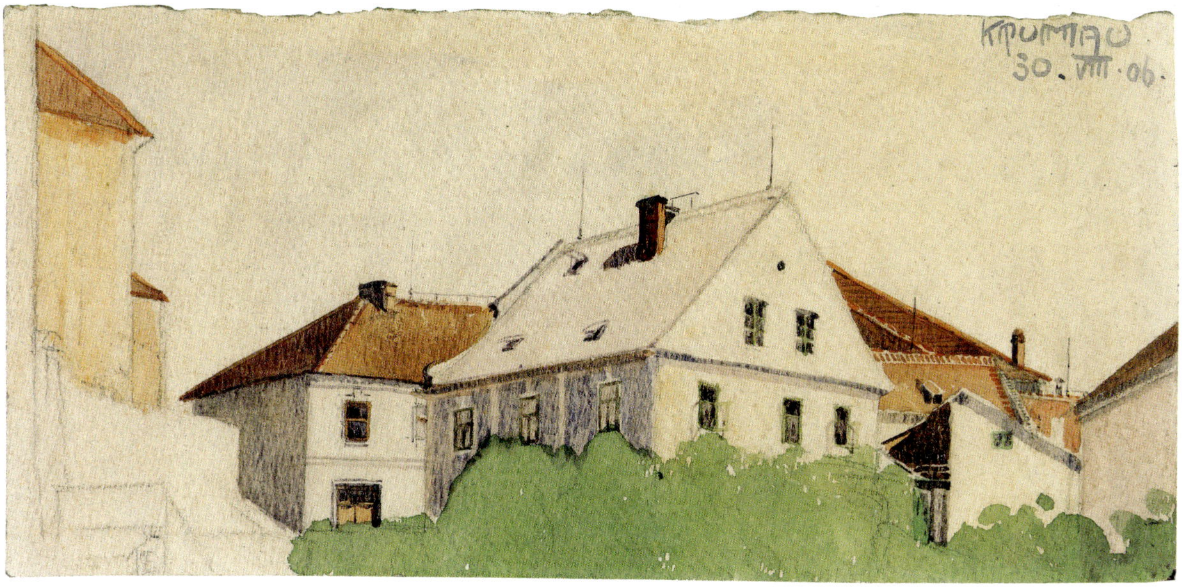
Krumau
30. VIII. 06.

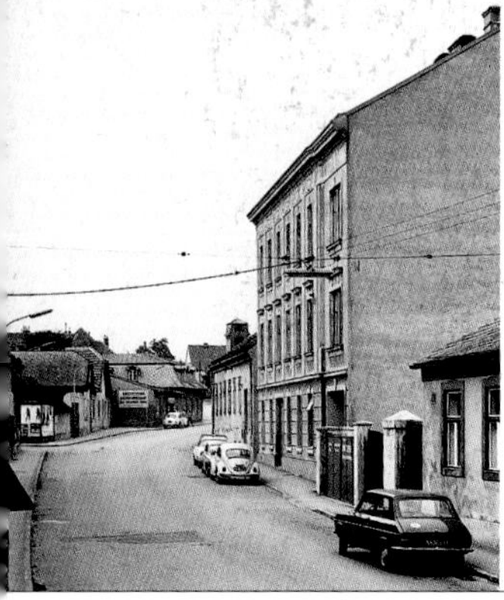

Albrechtstrasse in Klosterneuburg 1906

L 3 K 5
Mixed media on cardboard, 29.8 x 19.6 cm
Signed upper right
Stiftsmuseum Klosterneuburg, inv. no.: GM 552

The street is depicted from a high vantage point. In view of Schiele's development at that period, the brilliant blue sky, the highly contrasting colors of the remaining passages, and the skilfully employed lighting effects speak for a date of execution in late summer 1906. Although the painting still has a bit of the student work about it, the handling of the overall perspective is entirely convincing. Yet even more importantly, Schiele has altered a given motif for compositional reasons, rendering the shadowed house wall at the left front in a gradation much lighter than it would have been in reality, in order to establish a formal counterpoint to the sunlit façade on the right.

Despite the pedantically precise rendering of the wine dealer's sign at the upper right, the charming, luminous colors of the composition evoke a compelling atmosphere.

Schiele has depicted a section of Albrechtstrasse that runs uphill. Judging by the angles of the perspective lines and the vanishing point, and the fact that a small part of the façade of the building at 2 Ziegelofengasse is visible at the upper left, the artist likely painted this view from a window on the first floor of 65 Albrechtstrasse, where he lived at the time.

The two-story house cut off by the left edge is 69 Albrechtstrasse, and the adjacent single-story building is 69B. Farther up, sunlight emerges from a lane, Karl-Rudolf-Werner-Gasse. As this indicates, it was afternoon when Schiele painted this view.

The houses in the foreground are all still in existence. Perhaps the most striking is the three-story building at 62 Albrechtstrasse (whose southeastern firewall then bore the advertisement mentioned above). Its façade and that of the low house beyond (64 Albrechtstrasse) receive the most intense sunlight.

Albrechtstrasse, Klosterneuburg

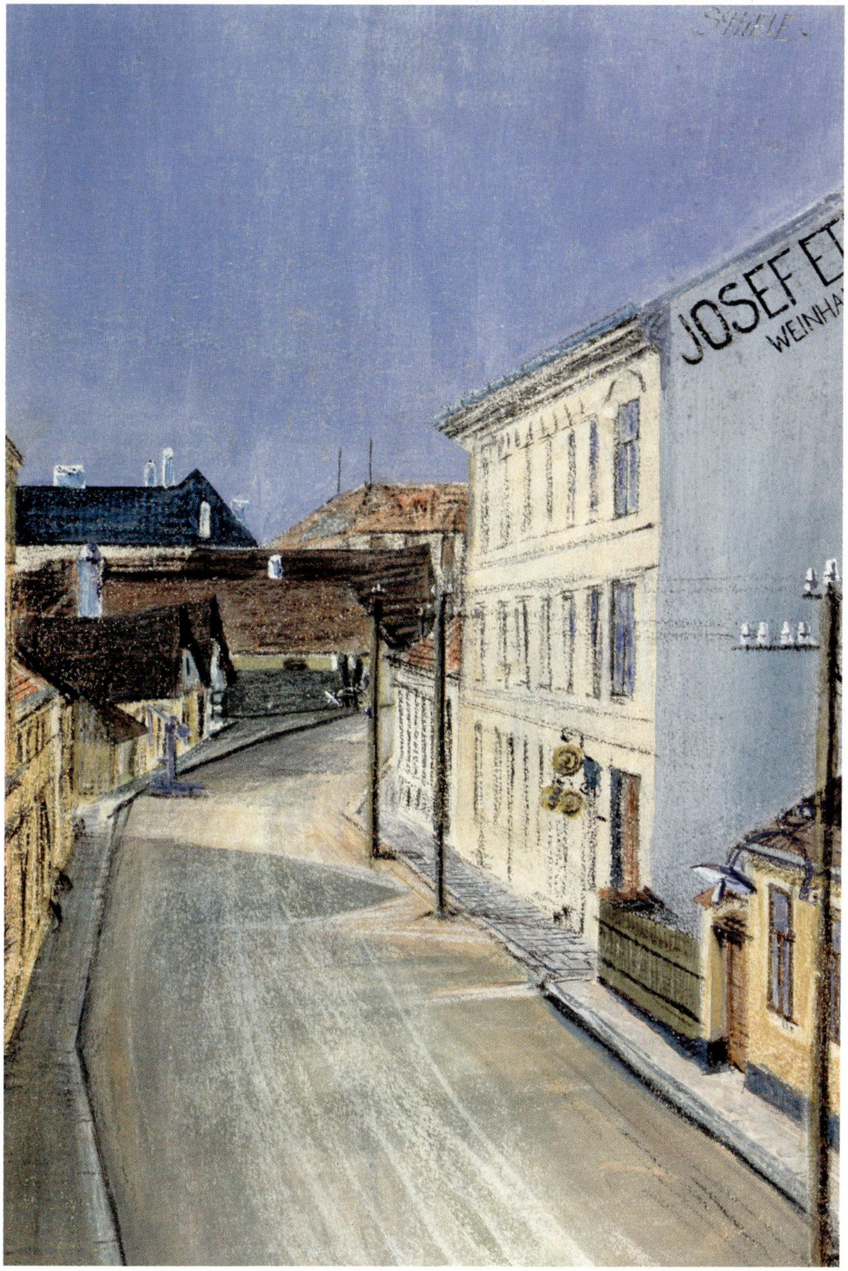
JOSEF

Farmhouses 1907

Pencil, opaque colors and opaque white
on natural paper, 24 x 30.6 cm
Private collection

Schiele dated this painting of farmhouses "4. VII. 07" (4 July 1907). He executed it on greenish paper. Its color, however, is almost nowhere in evidence, since the work was done in opaque gouache rather than transparent watercolor washes.

Here Schiele was probably inspired less by the uniform gray of houses and wall than by the window openings with their light-colored crossbars interrupting the darkness inside, not to mention the contrast between the sunlit gable wall under the mansard roof and the walls lying in shadow. The perspective view of this gable wall is likewise skillfully handled.

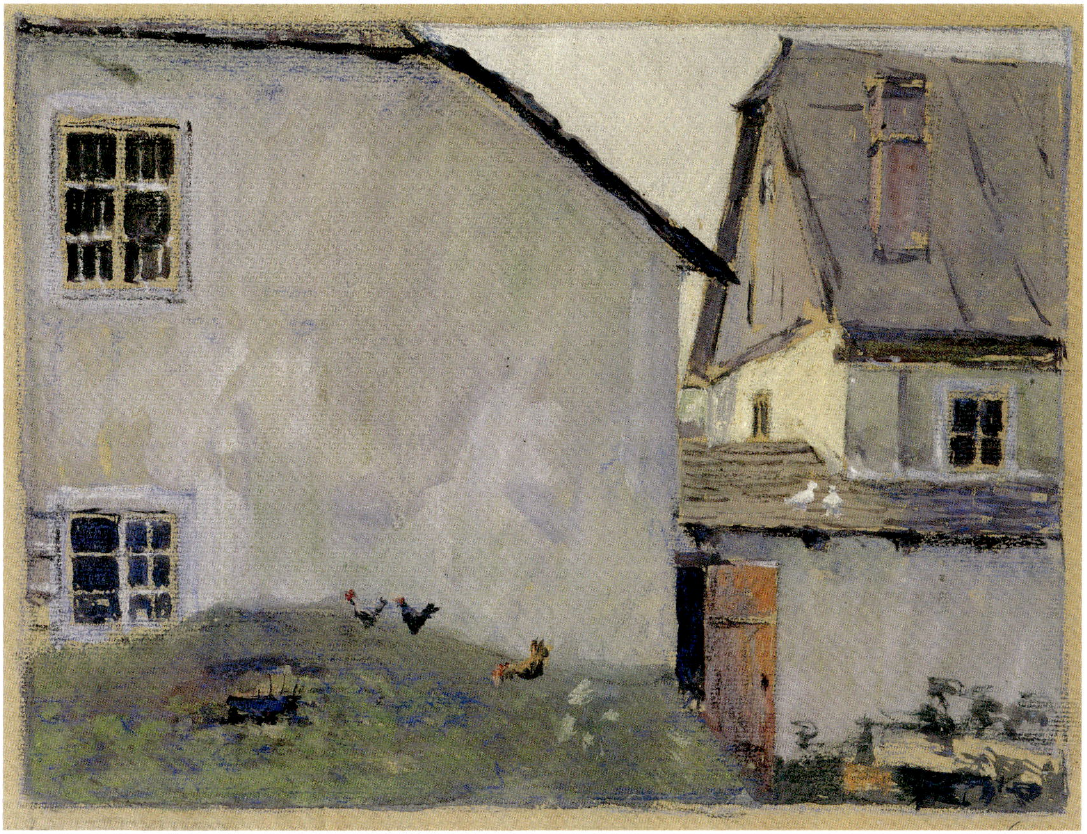

Quarry in the Vienna Woods 1907

L 23 K 41
Oil on canvas, 16.5 x 23.5 cm
Signed and dated lower right
Egon Schiele Museum, Tulln on the Danube

In the present study Schiele has attempted to play off various relatively bright, light colors against one another, as in the contrast between the pink hue of the quarry and the bluish-green of the shrubbery. To emphasize texture, he employed a coarse canvas, some of whose tufts he left unpainted to let the white of the ground show through. In the area of the green meadow, on the other hand, he used a dry brush – as it is known in painter's lingo – to wipe carmine red over such tufts in the canvas to produce a contrast. Schiele presumably executed this delightful study shortly before the beginning of summer 1907.

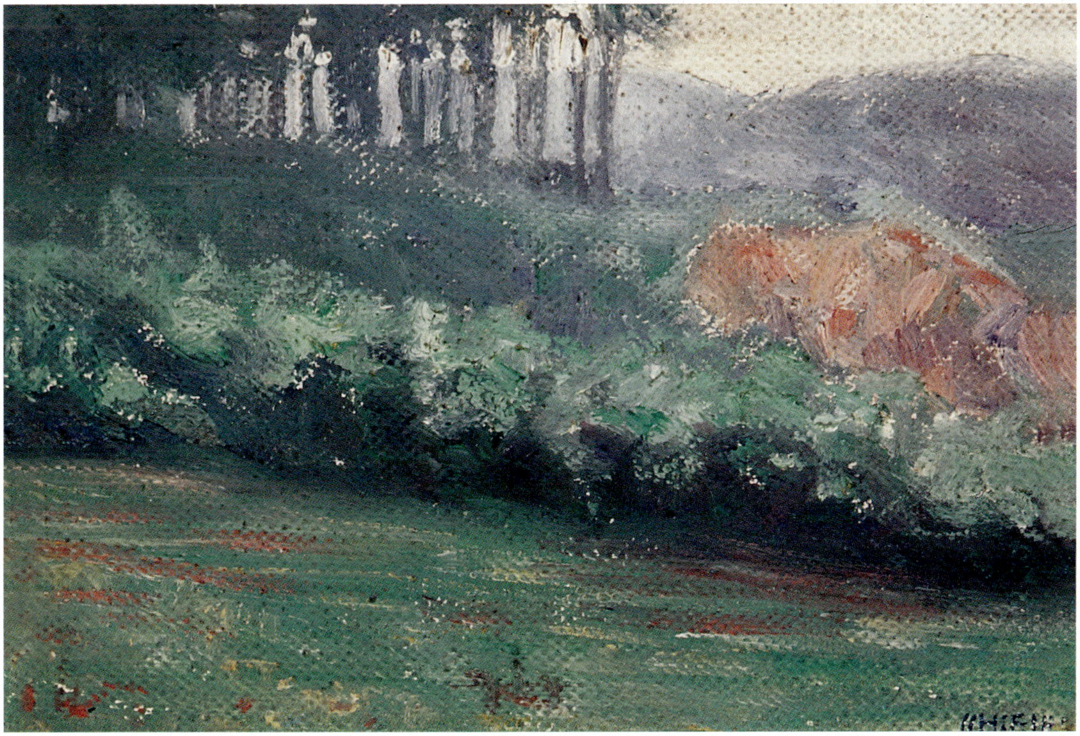

Trees Mirrored in a Pond 1907

L 47 K 48
Oil on cardboard, 30.5 x 19.7 cm
Signed and dated lower right
Private collection

The skillful rendering of the principal section of the picture, the water surface with trees reflected in it, is an astonishing achievement for an artist who was not yet seventeen.

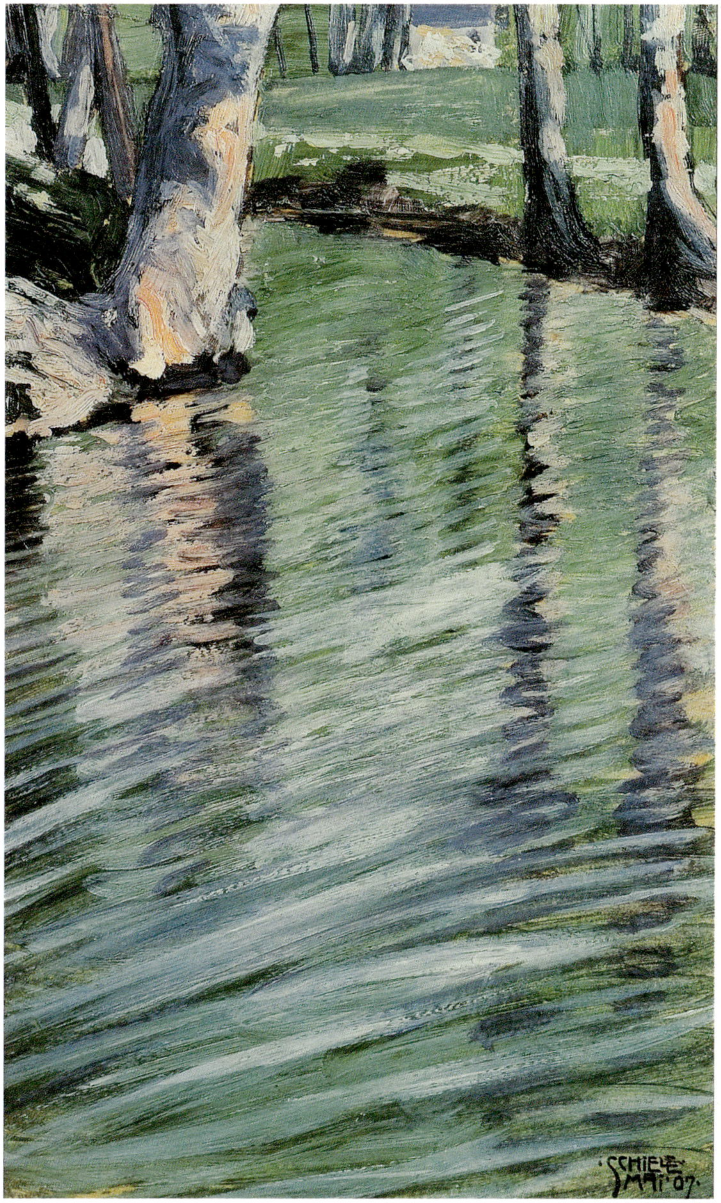
SCHIELE
MAI 07

House with Blooming Mallows ("From Bregenz") 1907

L 45 K 56
Oil on cardboard, 24.8 x 17.8 cm
Signed and dated upper right
Private collection

An insouciant, rapidly executed painting whose brushwork is particularly convincing in the group of mallows. The striking chiaroscuro in the lower area far surpasses the academic character of earlier such attempts. In term of palette, Schiele vacillates a bit here between a "naturalistic Impressionism" and color values influenced by Jugendstil.

The seemingly accidental excerpt favored by the Impressionists was not Schiele's forte. This is reflected especially in the handling of the drawing. For instance, the direction of the two fence slats, together with the related, more or less diagonal lines of the façade perspective, do not engender any real formal tension.

According to an inscription on the reverse of the painting support, Schiele found the motif for this picture in Bregenz.

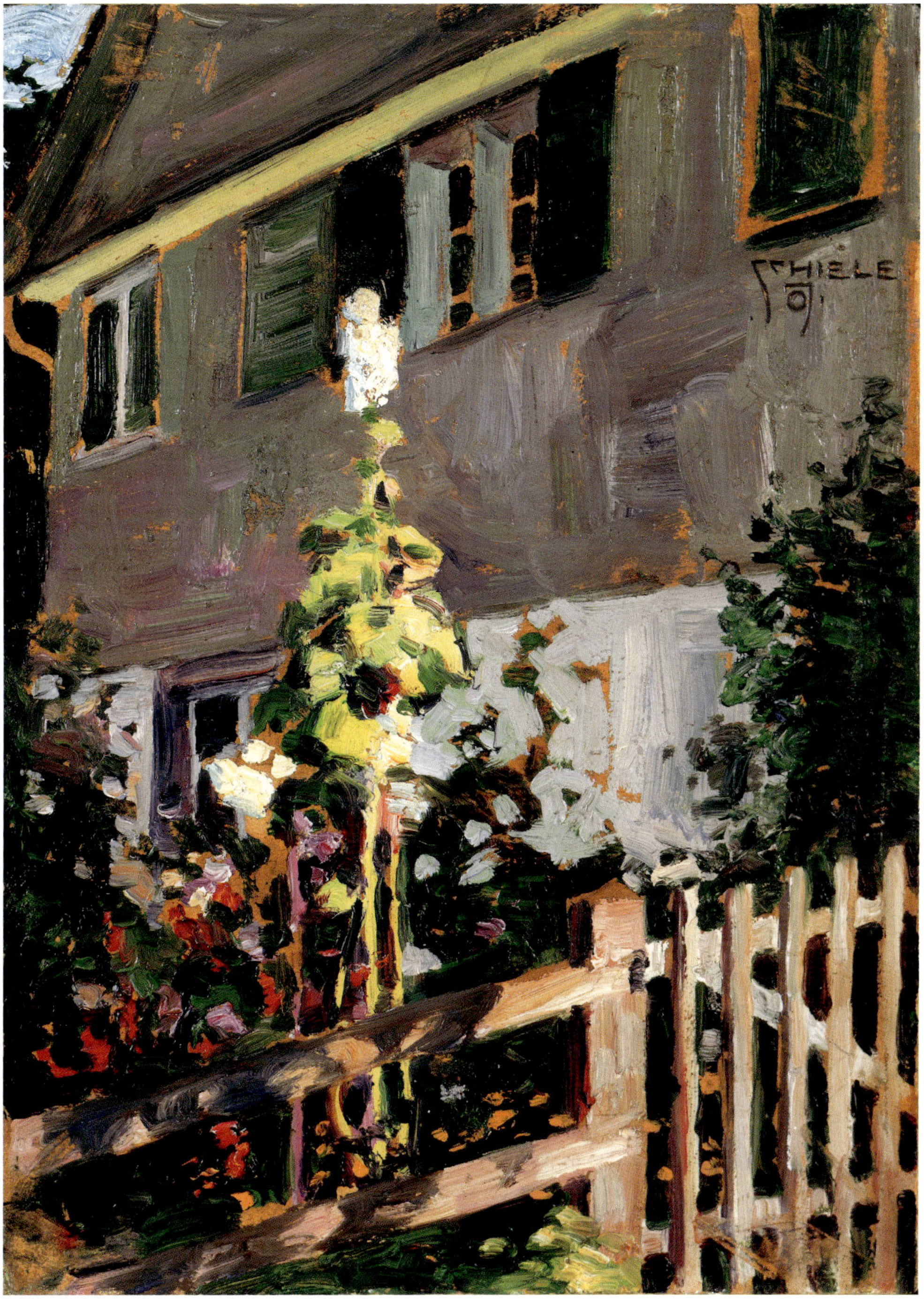
SCHIELE

On the Danube Canal 1907

L 36 K 78
Oil and pencil on cardboard, 16.7 x 27 cm
Unsigned, undated
Private collection

The cardboard support of this painting has been trimmed on all four sides. Possibly the signature and date were on the lower edge, and were therefore lost.

Still, the work is clearly from Schiele's hand, and was likely painted in summer 1907. On the whole it evinces a pleasing, light color scheme, and the distribution of lights and shadows is likewise well handled.

This is one of the earliest examples in which Schiele drew through the still wet paint – in this case, with a comparatively hard pencil and rather amateurishly. It was not until works of late autumn 1907, in which he used a soft graphite pencil to draw into the paint – such as "Woods in Autumn" or "Bare Trees, Houses and Shrine" (L 74/K 86, p. 37; L 75/K 87, p. 39) – that Schiele mastered this technique.

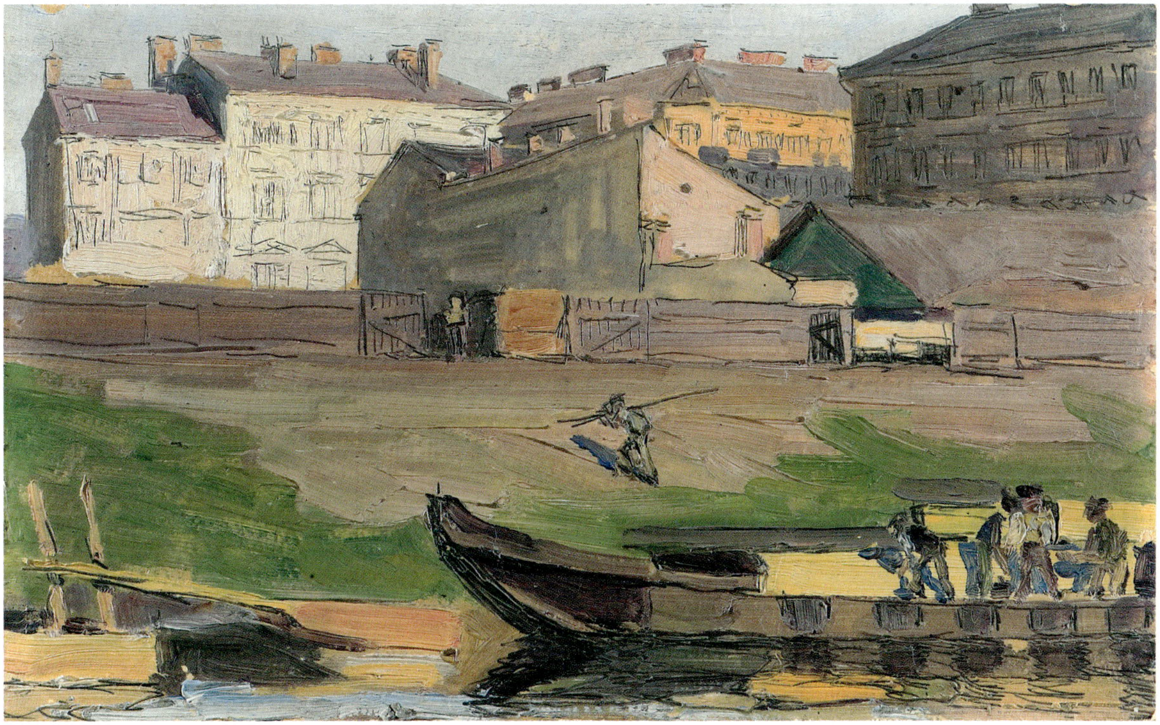

Landscape with Greenish-Blue Sky 1907

L 66 K 72
Oil on cardboard, 17 x 24 cm
Signed and dated lower left
Oberösterreichische Landesmuseen, Linz, inv. no.: Ka 119

An obviously rapidly rendered study of an autumn landscape. This is especially apparent in the somewhat wild and uncontrolled rendering of the stretch of woods bordering the meadow.

Yet on the whole, Schiele managed to produce a lovely concordance of color in the sunny field, the woods mentioned, the mountain in the right background, and the greenish-blue sky with its pink clouds.

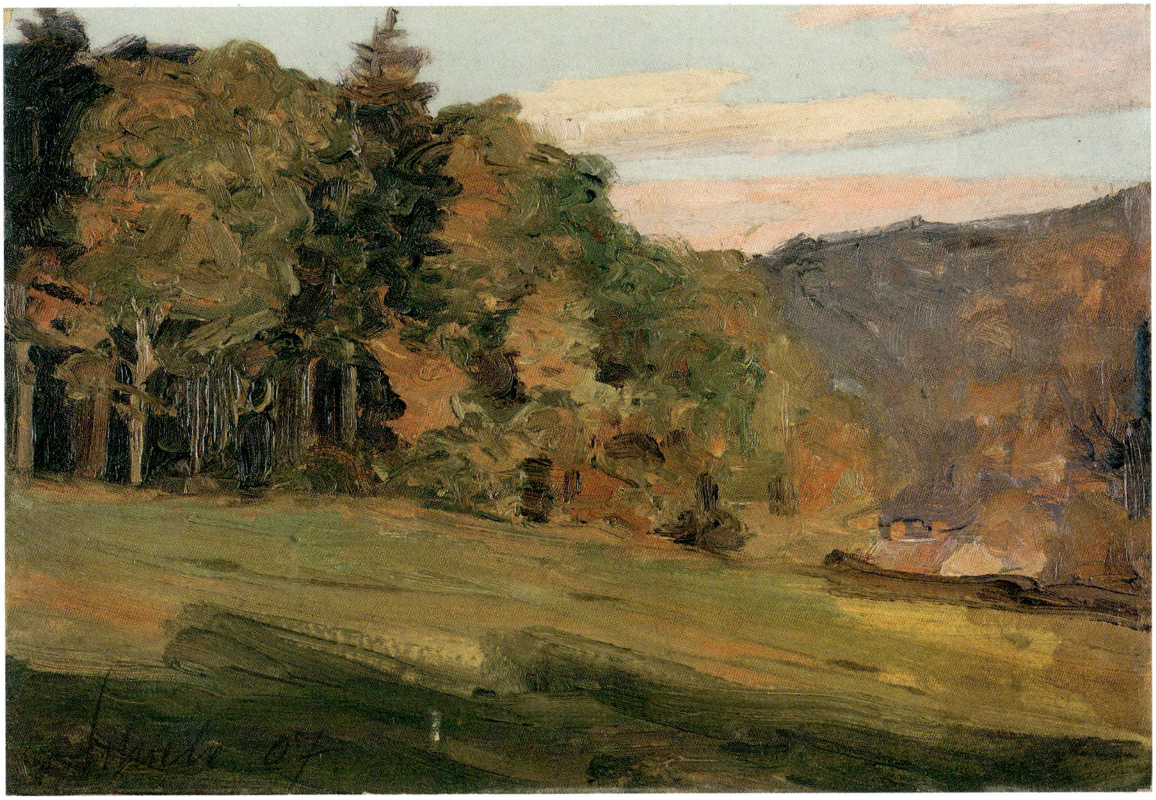

Meadow with Village 1907

L 61 K 66
Oil on cardboard, 19.8 x 34.4 cm
Signed and dated lower right
Österreichische Galerie Belvedere, Vienna, inv. no.: 4326

An early but already very harmonious study. Between the long brushstrokes in the foreground and the sky lies a band of comparatively dark trees with interspersed houses. Their more compactly rendered, lighter façades set an accent in the composition, which on the whole is built on a delightfully delicate contrast between the subdued green of the large meadow in the foreground and the pale lilac and rose in the distance (augmented by a strip of soft light green in the sky).

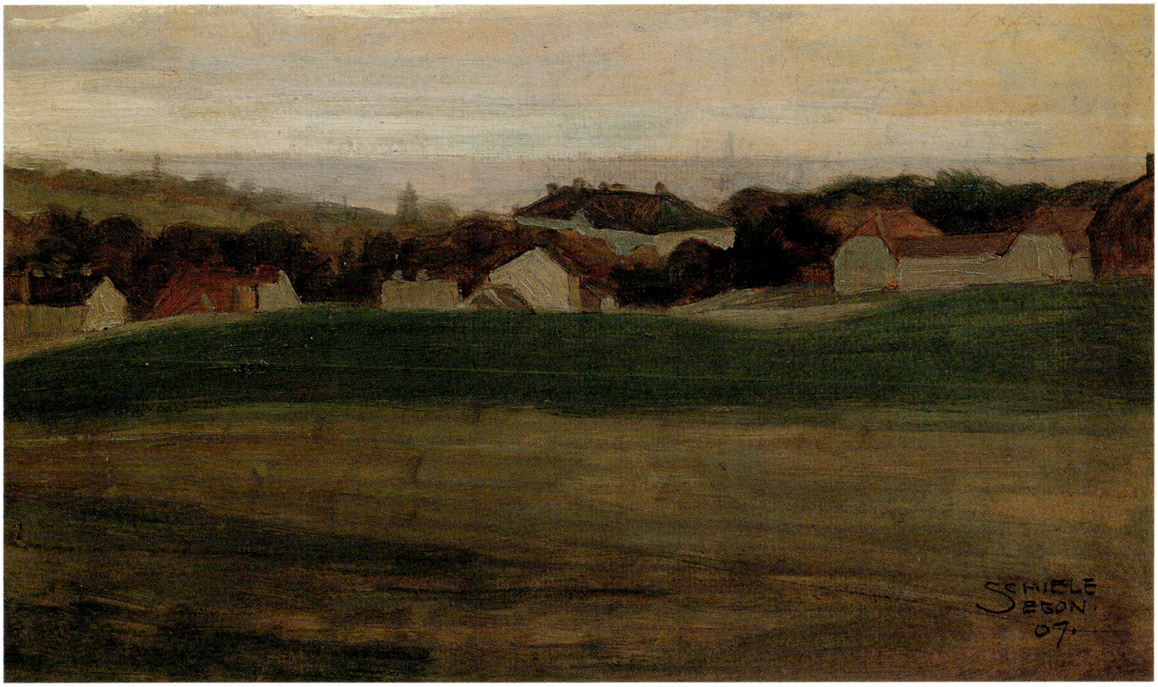
SCHIELE
EGON.
07.

"From Kierling Valley" 1907

L 67 K 75
Oil on cardboard, 18 x 26.5 cm
Inscribed on the reverse 'Aus dem Kierlingertal'
Private collection

This was the title inscribed by the young artist on the reverse of the cardboard support of this fine study. Representative of a series of landscapes done in autumn 1907, it shows the same agitated paint application as the landscape studies of the early summer, such as "House with Blooming Mallows" (L 45/K 56, p. 23). Also, Schiele made frequent and effective use of the contrast between light and shadow at this period.

Now the pictorial events are lent cohesion by rapid brushwork throughout. In terms of palette, Schiele has convincingly evoked an autumn mood by means of reddish-brown values and various nuances of green. By comparison, the unity of many other pictures of the period is compromised by a variegated color scheme that seems not entirely under control (as in "Farmyard with Vine Hedges, Klosterneuburg" [L 64/K 70]).

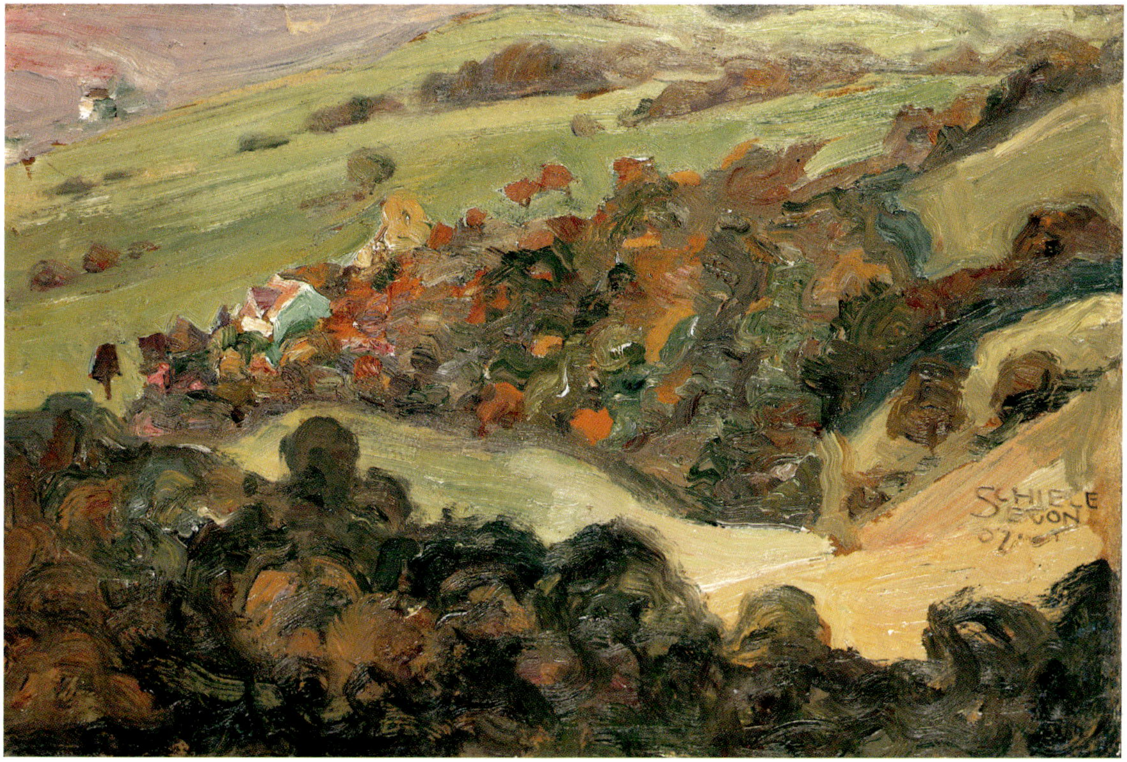
SCHIELE
EGON

Village at the Foot of a Hill 1907

L 60 K 65
Oil on cardboard, 25.5 x 18 cm
Signed and dated lower right
Leopold Museum, Vienna, inv. no.: LM 471

A view from a meadow of houses and trees in autumn colors in a dale, with fields and meadows extending up a hill behind, with a mountain rising in the background. The natural appearance of the scene should not mislead us into overlooking the fine, almost imperceptible changes Schiele made in the actual motif.

The young artist consciously contrasted the diagonal course of the gently undulating upper border of the meadow in the foreground to the opposing diagonal formed by two bush-lined paths on the slope. In addition, this slope, despite a certain effect of depth, appears tipped up into the picture plane, and the mountain behind it is cut off by the picture edge – two features already very much in the manner of Secessionist composition.

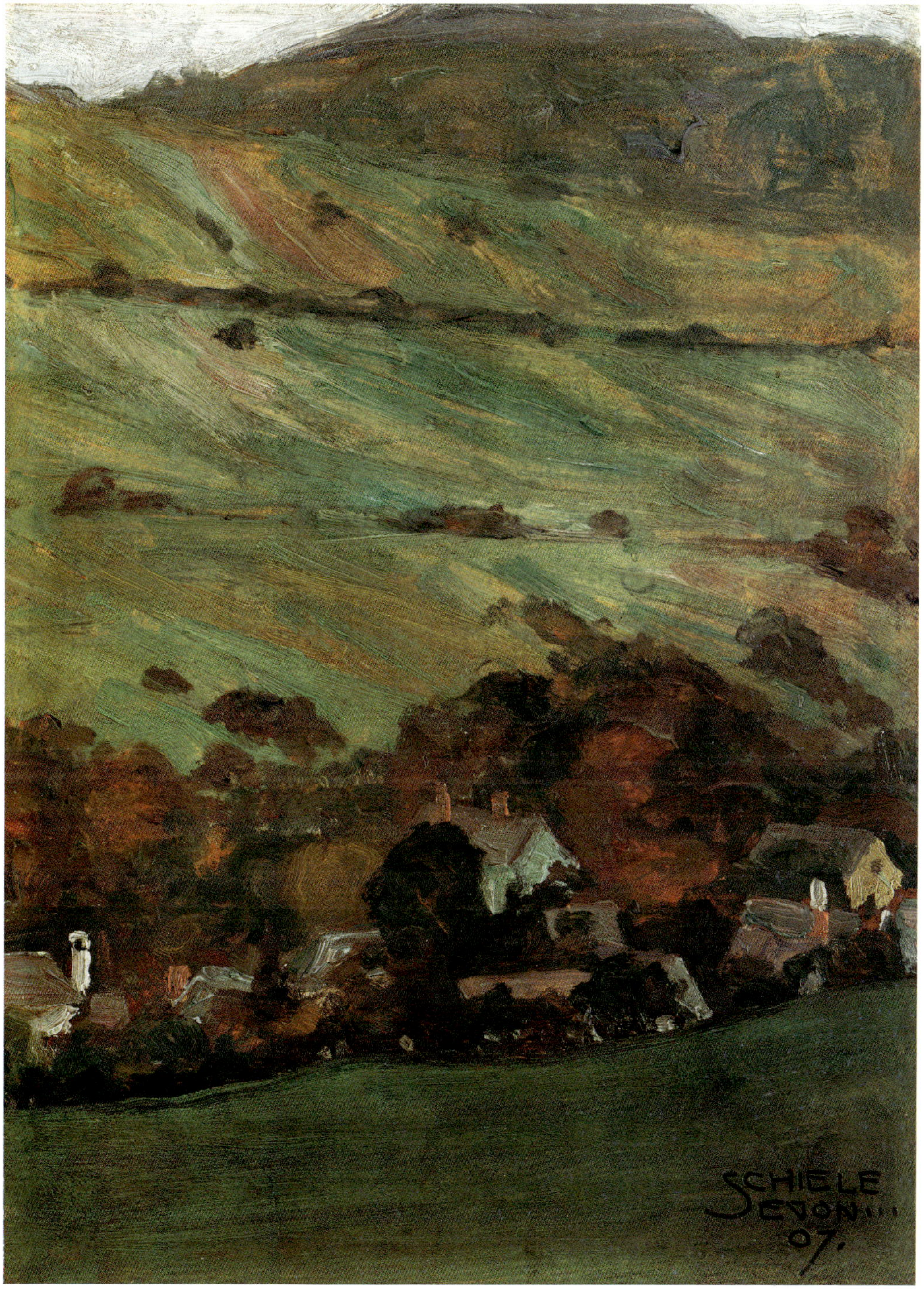
SCHIELE
EGON
07.

Before the Feast of St. Leopold in Klosterneuburg 1907

L 69 K 82
Oil and pencil on wood, 27.8 x 21.1 cm
Signed and dated lower right
Private collection

The emergence of this picture can be dated quite precisely. In all probability it was painted on 15 November 1907, St. Leopold's Day, in Klosterneuburg. The way the crowd in the middle ground has been sketched reflects Schiele's early mastery. In fact the entire upper third of the painting is very compelling, not least due to its fine coloration.

Advancements of another kind, which anticipate the artist's later development, are found in the oddly angular contours of two figures: the standing woman in a cloak, holding a child by the hand, in the middle area of the picture, and the male figure, clad in the then common knickerbockers, in the foreground. Another advancement is the use of a soft pencil to draw over the oil layer in two areas: the edges of the paving stones in the left foreground, and the limbs of an autumn tree at the upper right. These, like signature and dating, were executed in pencil.

The reverse bears pencil notations, including an inscription that translates "before the feast of St. Leopold in Klosterneuburg", and vertically above it a sketch done about a year later, which Schiele framed and captioned "Paradise Lost".

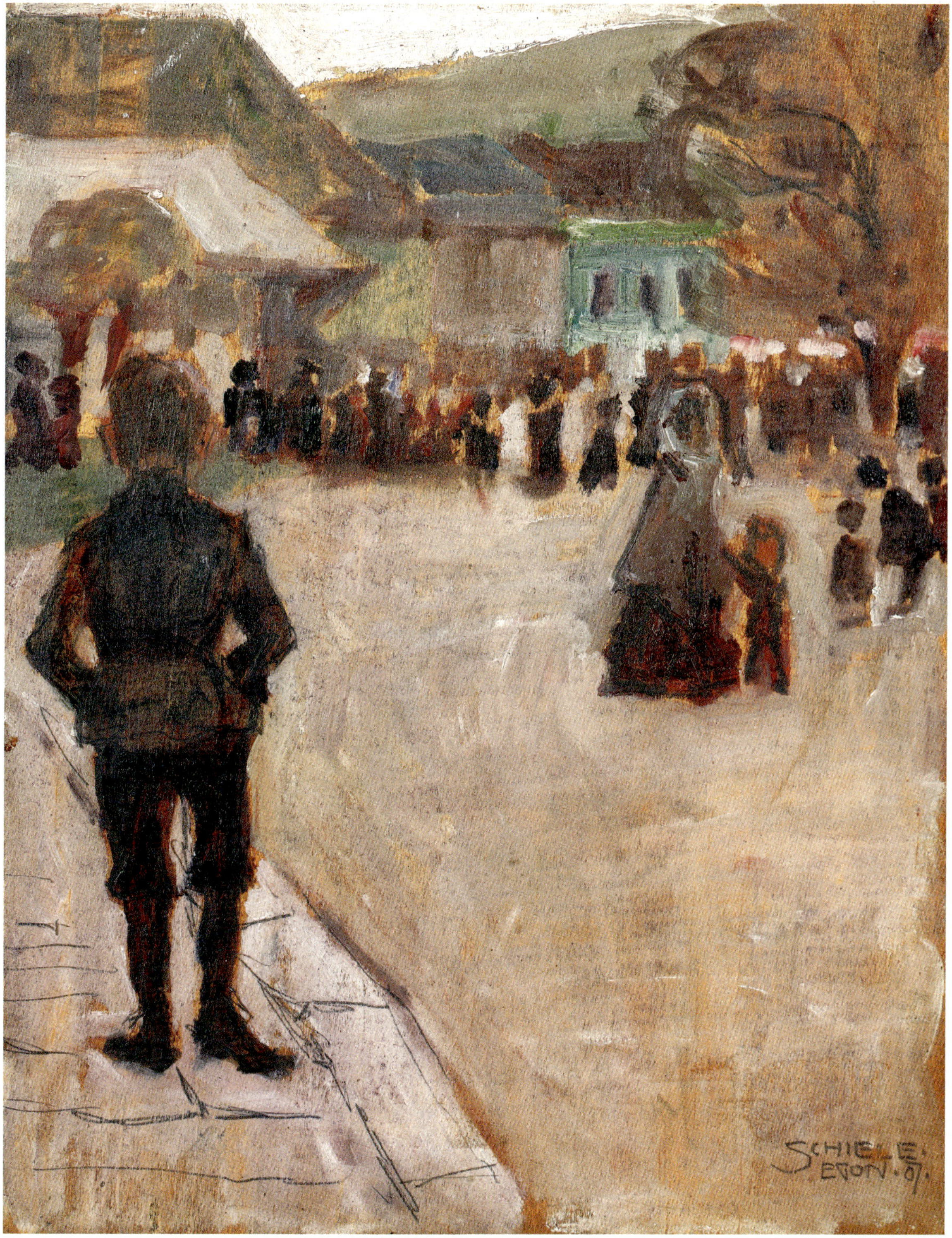
SCHIELE.
EGON.07.

Woods in Autumn 1907

L 74 K 86
Oil and pencil on cardboard, 25 x 17.8 cm
Signed and dated lower right
Leopold Museum, Vienna, inv. no.: LM 472

This study is pervaded by a sense of autumnal melancholy. Although certain of the colors may have been inspired by Jugendstil, their unique combination seems entirely personal. The yellow ground shining through in a number of places was intended to convey the effect of sunlight, yet at the same time these light areas provide relief in an otherwise somewhat gloomy color atmosphere. The problem of including pencil lines in an oil composition, still approached somewhat dilettantishly in the pictures of summer 1907, has here been solved in a very harmonious and skillful way. Although pencil lines are naturally basically graphic in character, here the painterly, chiaroscuro effect of both the pencil strokes and the lighter colors is quite obvious. Schiele exploited the nuances which can be produced by a soft graphite pencil (in both energetic and delicate lines) and integrated these in the painting in a way analogous to "Bare Trees, Houses and Shrine" (L 75/ K 87, p. 39).

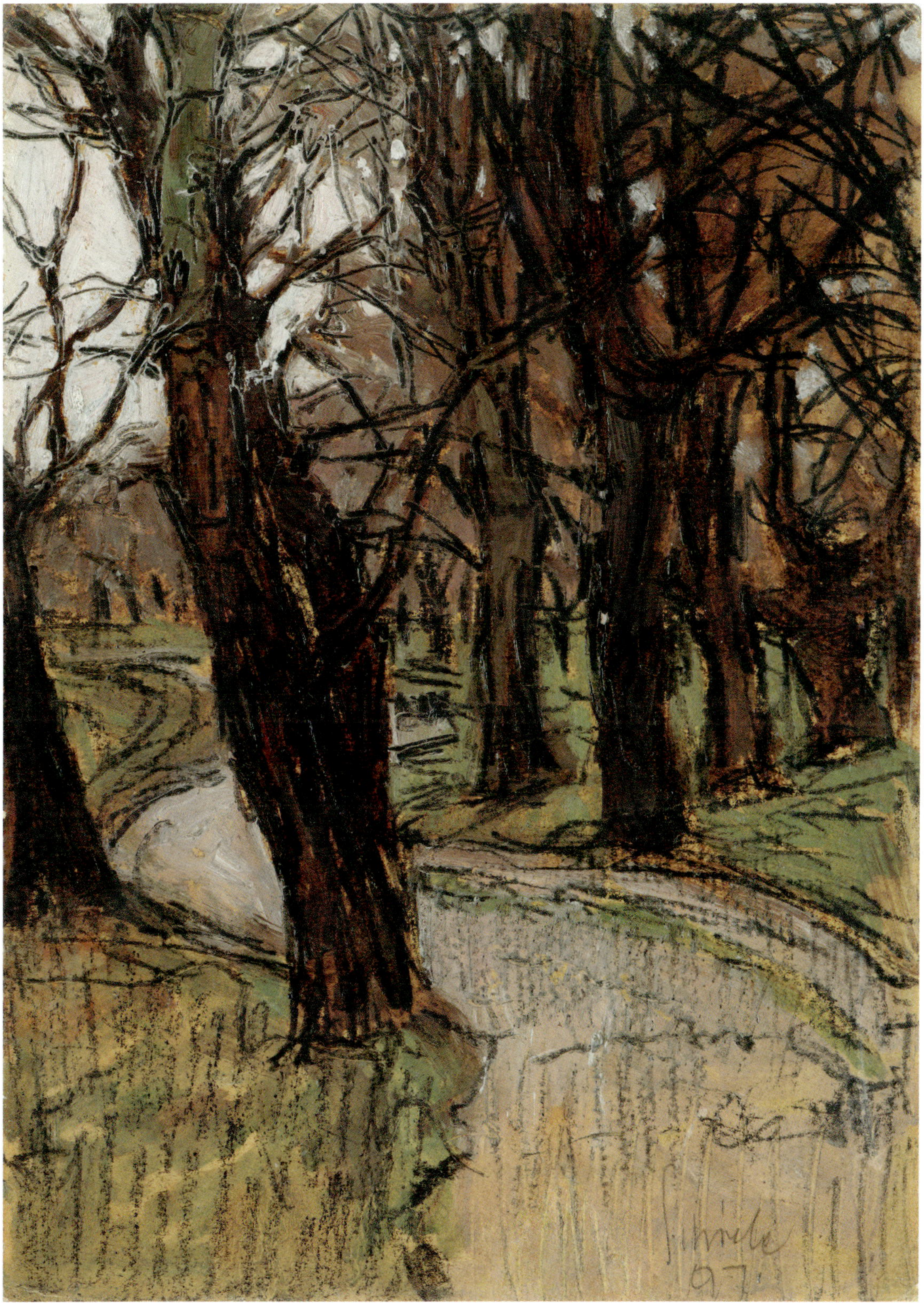
Schiele
07

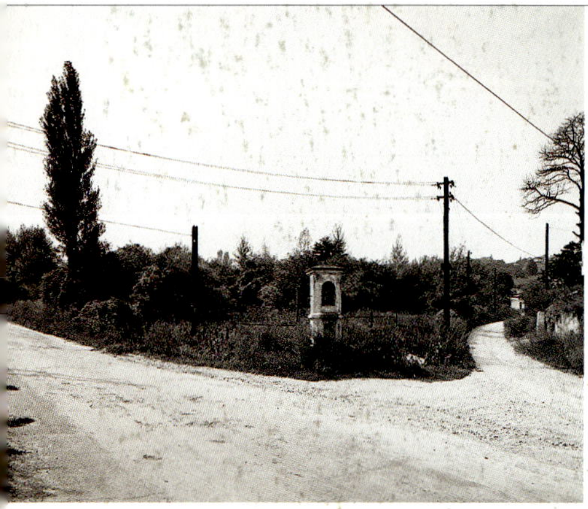

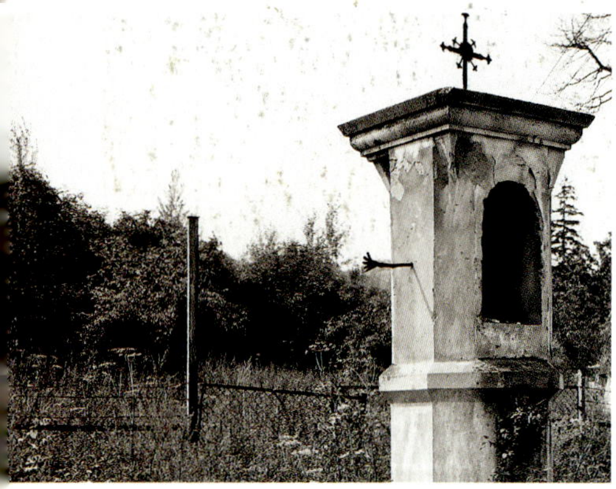

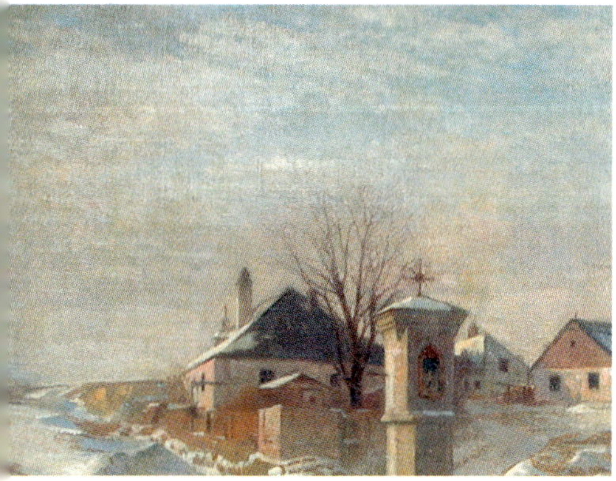

Bare Trees, Houses and Shrine (Klosterneuburg) 1907

L 75 K 87
Oil and pencil on cardboard, 15.5 x 25.5 cm
Unsigned, undated
Leopold Museum, Vienna, inv. no.: LM 473

A painting by the sixteen-year-old Schiele. In this case it is especially interesting to determine the motif from which he proceeded.

It was not easy to find the site, because none of the houses at the intersection of Ziegelofengasse and Käferkreuzgasse in Klosterneuburg still exists. There is only a wayside shrine with an iron hand protruding from its upper third – which furthermore, Schiele omitted! It was only with the aid of a photograph of a painting from about 1910 by Franz Horst (1862–1950) that I was able to discover the location of Schiele's motif.

Unlike the conventional view of Horst's painting, in which the wayside shrine is approximately centered, Schiele has shifted it to the right and depicted it in such an extreme close-up that it is cut off by the picture edge at top and bottom. As mentioned, Schiele, unlike Horst, omitted the iron hand as being compositionally irrelevant. In fact, both wayside shrine and houses have been strongly altered for compositional reasons, with a certainty perhaps surprising for such a young artist.

With the strange colors of the twilit townscape, the contrasting brightness of the agitated sky, and the energetic graphite strokes drawn through the wet paint, Schiele has succeeded in evoking a highly compelling mood.

Intersection Ziegelofengasse/Käferkreuzgasse, Klosterneuburg

Franz Horst
The Iron Hand in Klosterneuburg 1908
Oil on canvas
Stadtmuseum Klosterneuburg

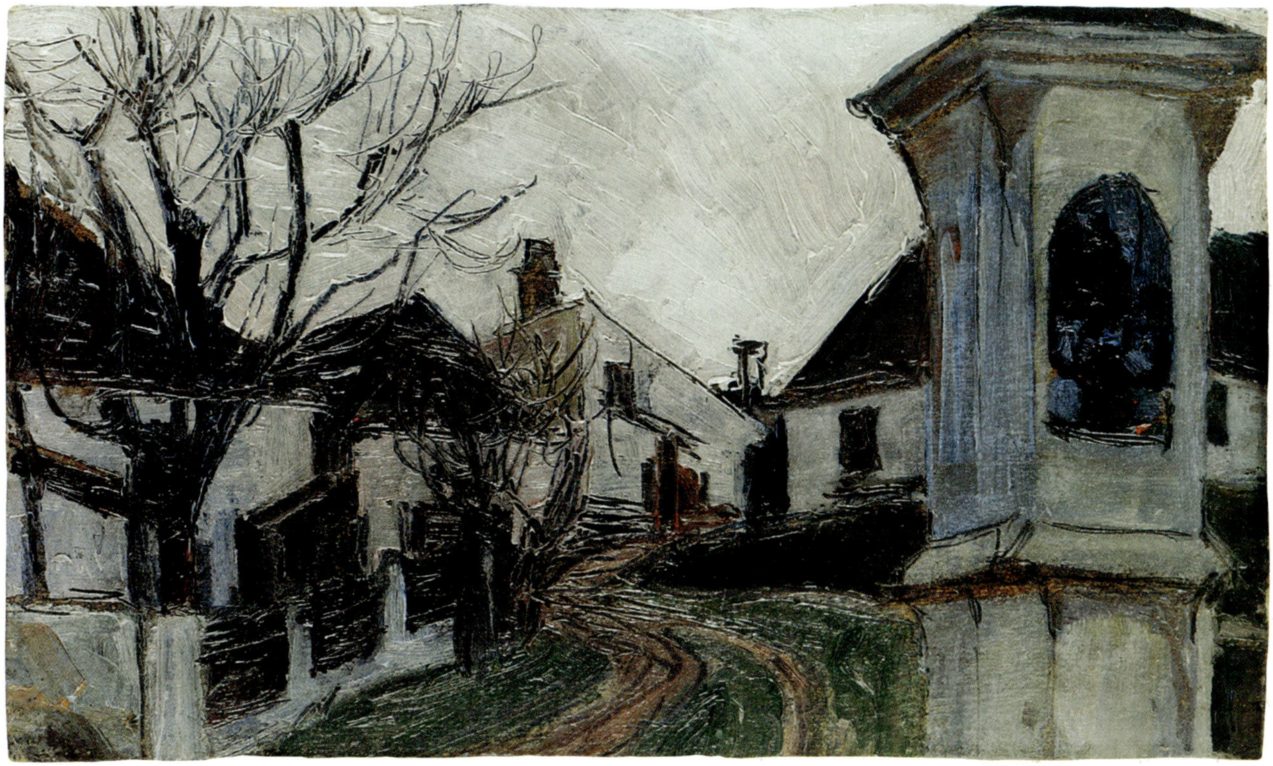

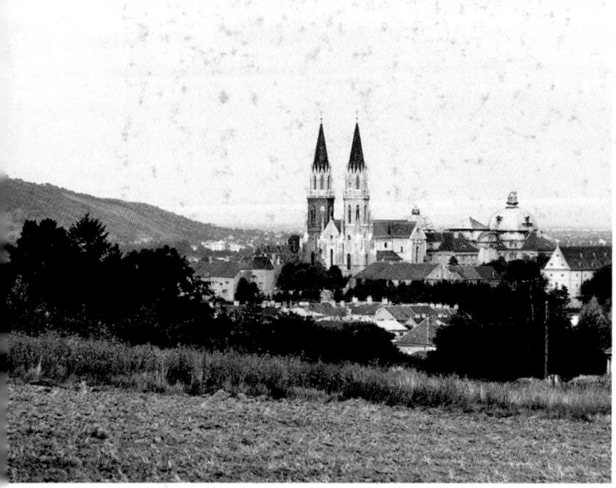

Snow-covered vineyard, in the Background Klosterneuburg in Fog 1907

L 78 K 90
Oil on canvas, 58.5 x 74 cm
Signed and dated upper right
Egon Schiele Museum, Tulln on the Danube

Judging by its advanced technique, this painting, dated 1907, must surely have been executed at the end rather than the beginning of the year.

In the background fog we can recognize Klosterneuburg, especially the two towers and dome of the Canonical Chapter. The vineyard depicted in the foreground has since been replaced by tilled fields.

The vines in the snow – the foremost ones clearly visible, those behind vaguely suggested – and the pale phantom of the townscape in the background give the impression of a dreary winter day. Yet this impression is mitigated by the bare areas of reddish-brown earth in the foreground, which are complemented by the pale blue of the townscape in the background.

Canonical Chapter, Klosterneuburg

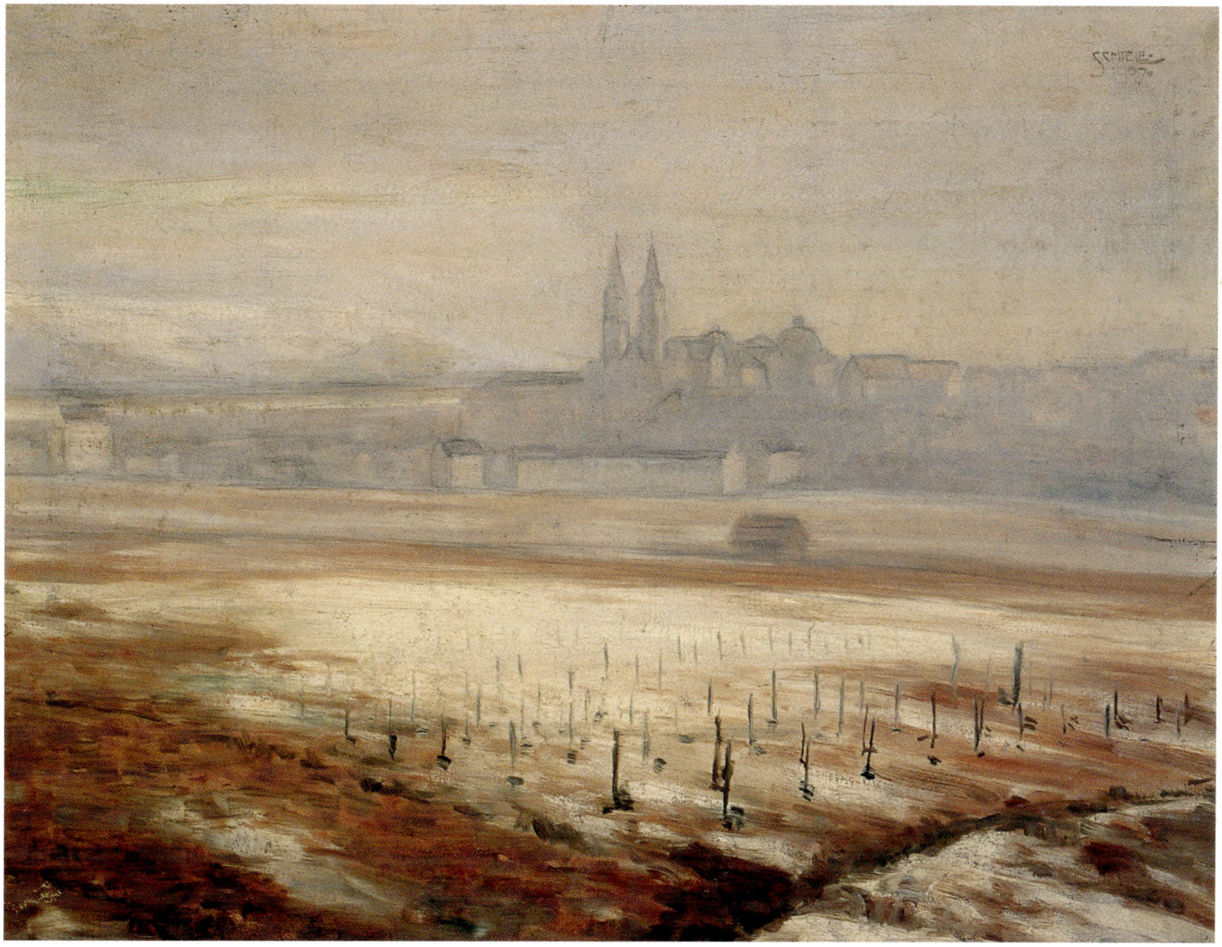

Houses in Winter 1907/08

L 80 K 111
Oil on cardboard, 24 x 17.8 cm
Signed, problably by another hand, lower left
Österreichische Galerie Belvedere, Vienna, inv. no.: 5493

This picture is undated, but bears a signature, "E. Schiele.", which in all probability is not from the artist's hand. Still, it can be securely ascribed to him based on its general effect, technique and painting support. In addition, its first owner was the sculptor Zelezny, a friend of Schiele's. (With regard to the still unidentified motif, however, Zelezny erroneously described it as the view from the window of Schiele's studio on Hietzinger Hauptstrasse. Yet Schiele, as we know, did not move into this studio until October 1912.)

The picture, in which graphic and painterly elements are well integrated, was executed in winter 1907/08.

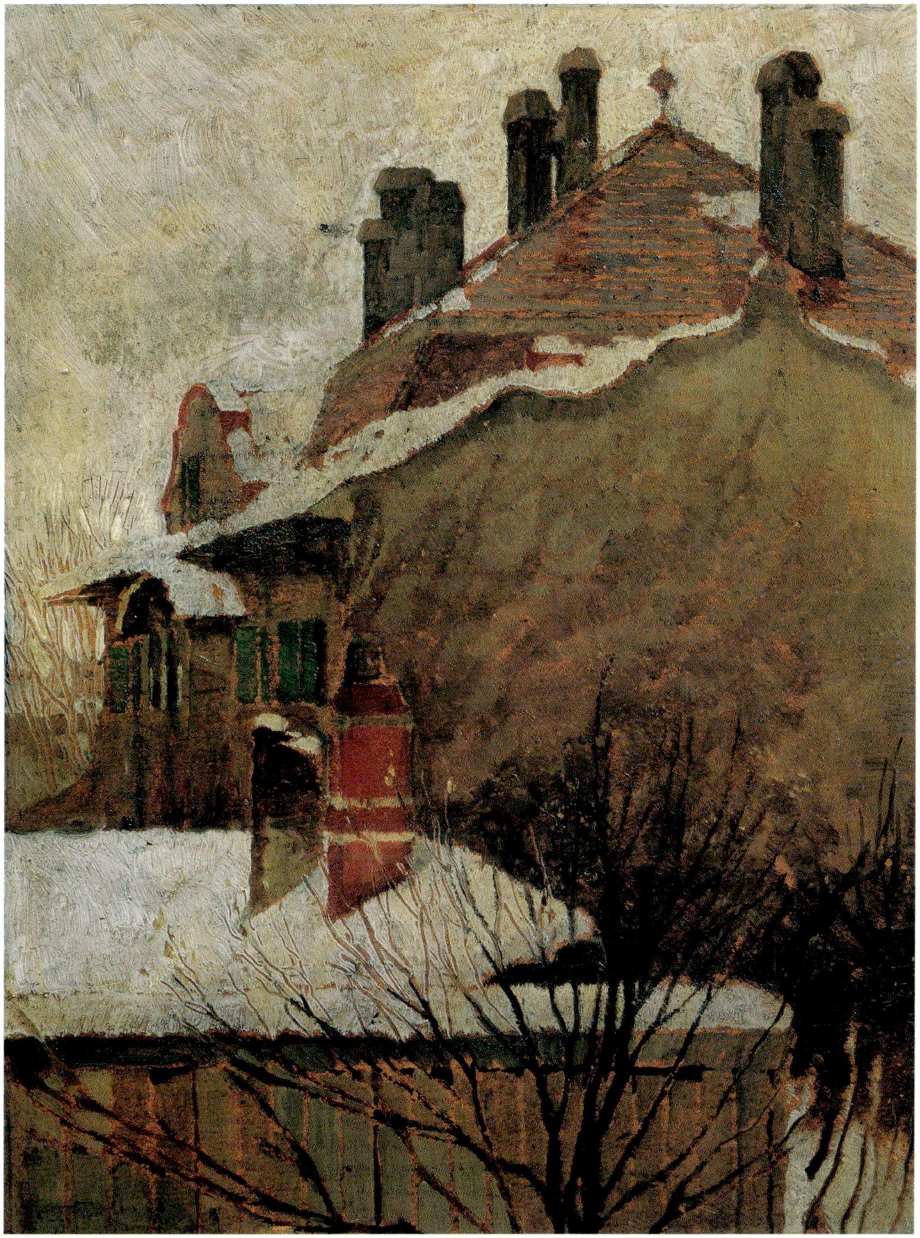

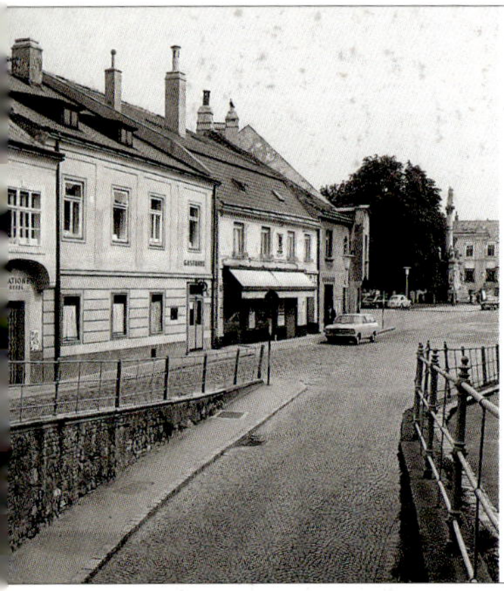

Town hall square (Rathausplatz), Klosterneuburg

Houses on the Town Square (Rathausplatz) in Klosterneuburg 1908

L 101 K 127
Oil on cardboard, 21.2 x 23.7 cm
Unsigned, undated
Reverse: inscribed and entitled by another hand
Leopold Museum, Vienna, inv. no.: LM 4140

Schiele presumably painted this picture from the bridge over the "Hundskehle" that connects Ortnergasse with Albrechtsberger Gasse. Rathausplatz, the town hall square, begins with the houses on the left (10–12 Rathausplatz). To the right appears the uniformly rendered crown of a tree on the square.

Unlike those depicted in "Bare Trees, Houses and Shrine" (L 75/K 87, p. 39) of late 1907, these houses can still be approximately identified today in the town, despite several altered façades and Schiele's simplifications. In contrast to the houses with the wayside shrine, whose compositional scaffolding was primarily graphic, here broad brushstrokes have been used to convey the essence of the scene.

The colors have even more affinity with the Viennese Secessionists' than those of the 1907 painting. Schiele let the initial orange paint layer show through in places, making the coloration more interesting and the overall effect more lively. The Secessionist contrast between the green of the summarily rendered chestnut tree and the light red and blue sky is also noteworthy.

Study of Houses (Klosterneuburg) 1908
L 88 K 128
Oil on cardboard, 26.8 x 25.4 cm
Unsigned, undated
Stiftsmuseum Klosterneuburg, inv. no.: GHM 563

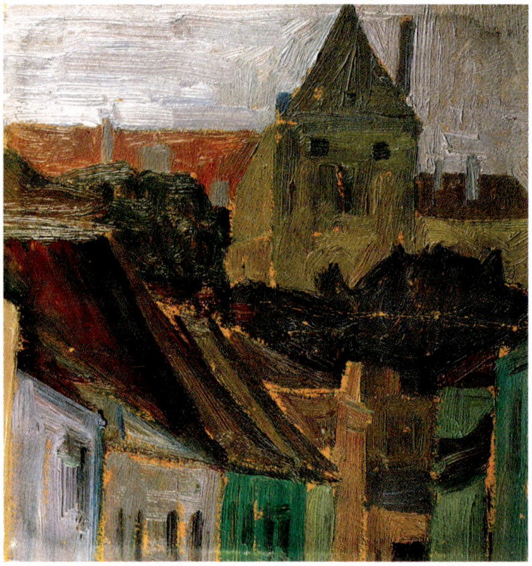

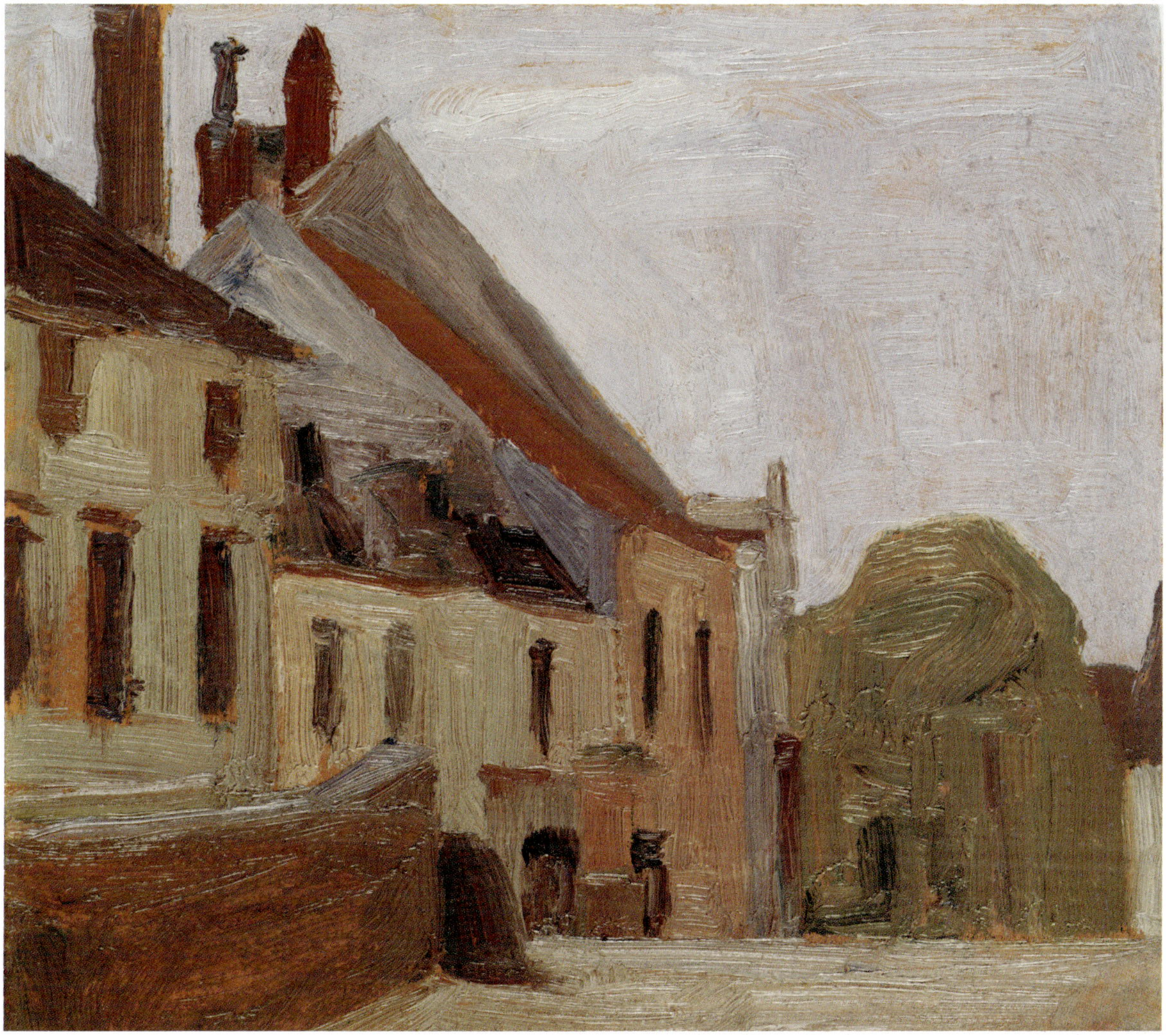

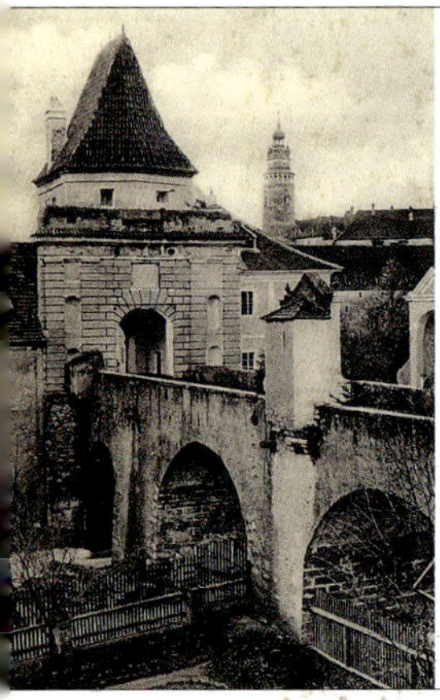

The Budweiser Gate (Krumau) 1908

L 103 K 133
Oil on cardboard, 24.5 x 17 cm
Initialed upper left
Private collection

Schiele depicted this city gate with the stone bridge in front of it from the northwest. Built in the sixteenth century, Budweis Gate is the only city gate still extant in Krumau (the original wooden bridge of 1598 was later replaced by a new one of ashlar).

At this period Schiele executed several small-format paintings like this one in a skilled technique using broad brushstrokes – such as "Study of Roofs, Krumau" (L 106/K 134) and "Houses on the Town Square in Klosterneuburg" (L 101/K 127, p. 45).

The Budweiser Gate in Krumau
Postcard from 1916

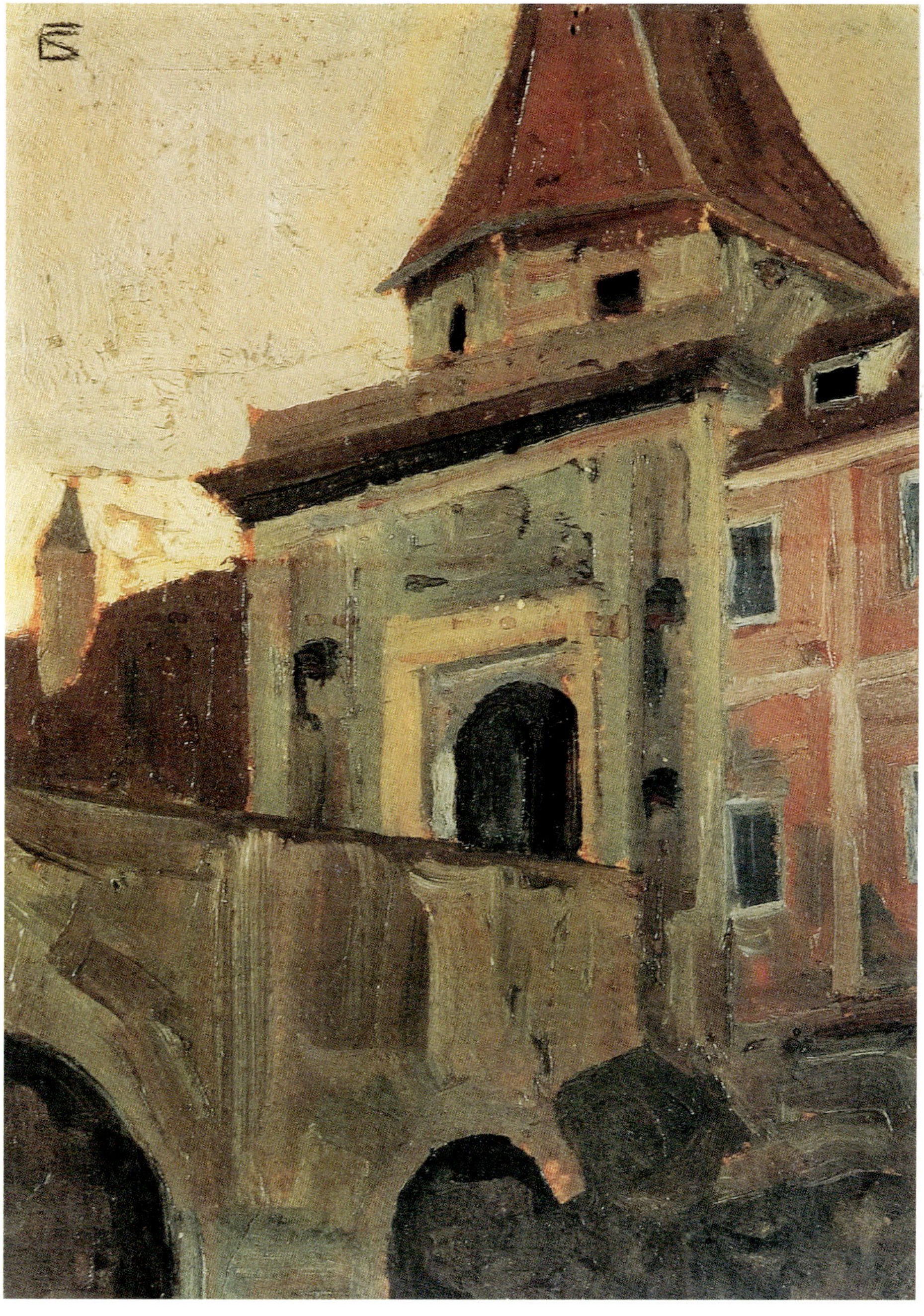

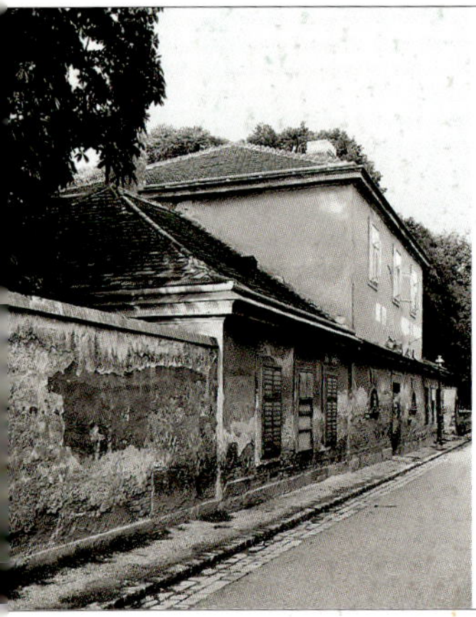

Cemetery caretaker's house, Oberdöbling (Vienna)

House in Oberdöbling 1908

L 104 K 130
Oil on cardboard, 25 x 17 cm
Signed and dated lower right
Niederösterreichisches Landesmuseum St. Pölten, inv. no.: 1916

The great effect of depth in this painting derives from the stringent perspective in which the motif is viewed. At the same time, the graphic composition of the block of houses conveys a relatively monumental impression.

As far as paint application is concerned, Schiele continued the robust brushwork of autumn 1907, yet used dominant colors that departed from the character of naturalism or Impressionism. Brown and ocher tones were now accompanied by brilliant blue-green and orange, favorite colors of the Jugendstil palette. The result is a lovely, harmonious overall color effect.

The building complex depicted, previously designated "Houses in (or Motif from) Klosterneuburg" in Otto Kallir, *Schiele* (2nd ed.) and in every catalogue, is actually the early-nineteenth-century cemetery caretaker's house at the old Israealite cemetery in Vienna, XIX (disused since 1880). It lies on a footpath from Semperstrasse to the interurban train stop on Nussdorfer Strasse, has no building description in the property register, and has been referred to by its inhabitants simply as "64 a Semperstrasse".

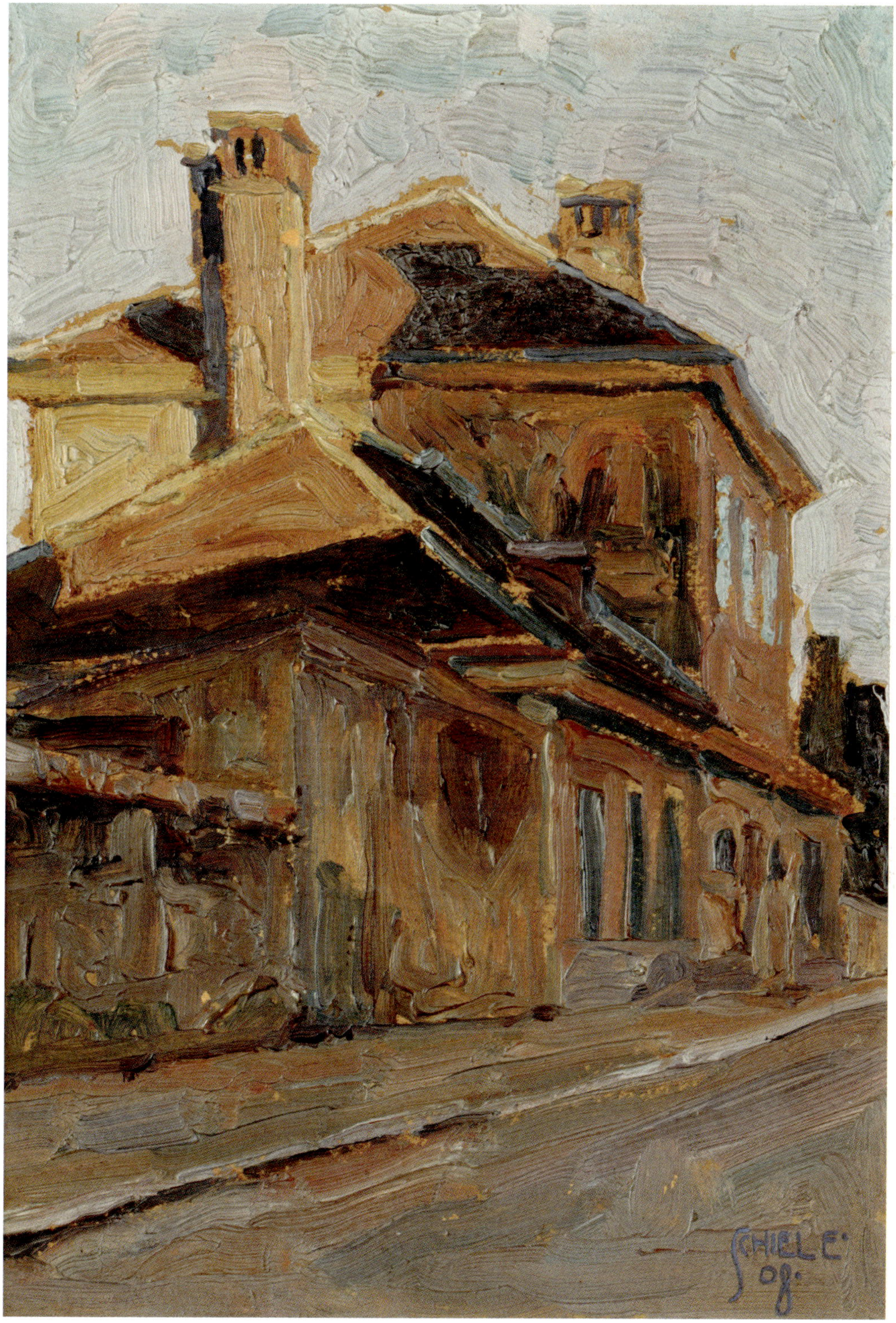
SCHIELE
08

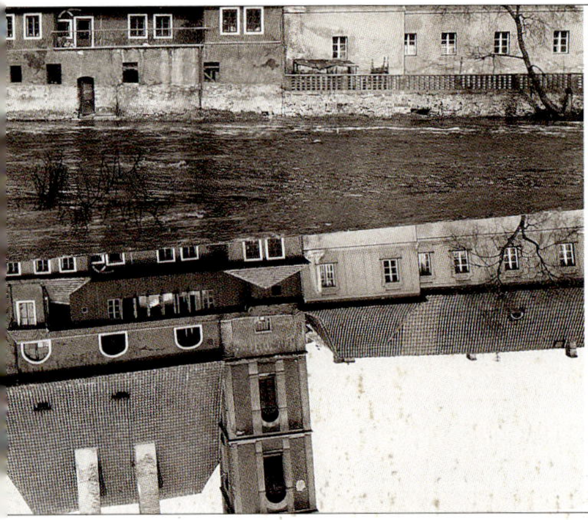

Former St. Jodocus' Church, Krumau

St. Jodocus' Church Reflected in the Water 1908

K 131
Oil on paper, 26.7 x 25.5 cm
Signed and dated upper left
Tiroler Landesmuseum Ferdinandeum, Innsbruck, inv. no.: 3450

The present picture is the first case in Schiele's œuvre in which he rotated a work through 180 degrees and signed and dated it in this position.

Although there are a great number of works on paper that were executed as horizontal formats and then transformed into vertical formats by the signature, only in a few cases did Schiele rotate a work through a full 180 degrees, that is, turn it upside down and sign it in this state. To name only two examples:

1. A depiction of a nude boy, 1913, reproduced in Jane Kallir under no. 1277. One's first impression is that the boy is standing in an entirely unnatural crouching position, yet his feet lack real contact with the floor. But when we rotate the sheet through 180 degrees, everything falls into place: We see a boy, depicted from a position slightly behind him, crouching on the floor with his feet apparently resting on a wall. This wall has been left out, as indeed Schiele omitted everything not belonging to the figure proper in almost all the works from his typical developmental phases.
2. Under no. 1939, Jane Kallir reproduces the drawing of a nude woman who is clearly lying on the floor, with her head and loosened hair occupying the lower part of the sheet. After drawing the nude, Schiele rotated the depiction through 180 degrees and, with his signature, turned it into a "Falling Nude". (In the Strache portfolio, 1920, a reproduction of this drawing appeared under the not quite correct title of "Kneeling Nude", which Kallir has adopted.)

But to return to the 1908 painting: Here Schiele has depicted the façade of the former St. Jodocus' Church,

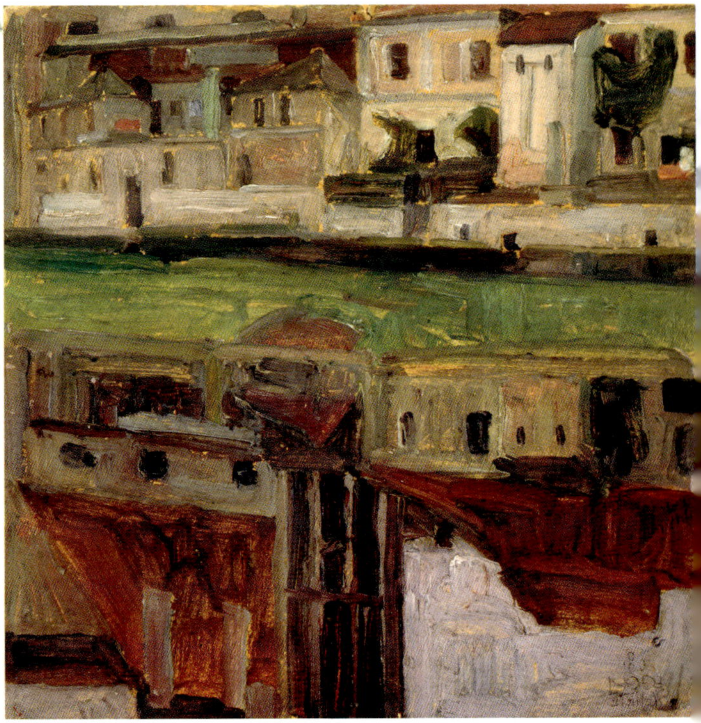

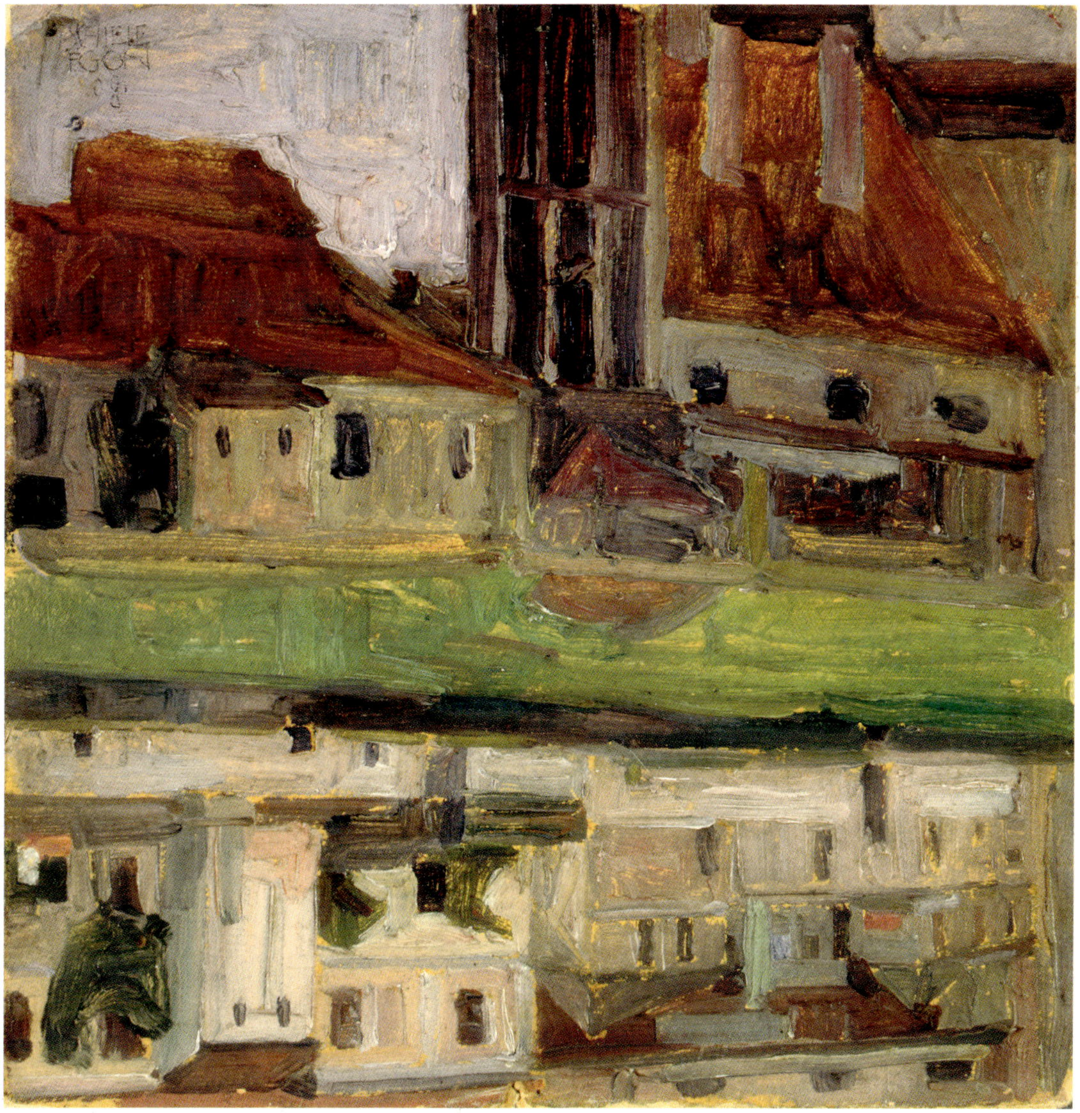

secularized in 1788, which faces onto the Moldau. The reflections in the water include the upper section of the building with roof and part of the tower, which has been considerably altered, probably for aesthetic reasons.

The buildings and especially their reflections are rendered in intriguing color gradations applied with broad brushstrokes. Perhaps it was with the intention of turning this passage of reflections with its more intense hues into the upper section of the picture that Schiele affixed his signature as he did.

In other words, after the painting was finished, the artist rotated it through 180 degrees and signed it. The motif cannot be properly identified until the picture is turned back to the position in which it was executed, as my wife, Dr. Elisabeth Leopold, was the first to note. This would clearly disprove the view, previously advanced in the literature, that the motif originated from the town of Stein on the Danube.

Meadow with Flowers and Trees 1910

L 117 K 178
Pencil, watercolor and opaque colors with spray technique on paper, 29 x 40 cm
Unsigned, undated
Private collection

The characteristic drawing style of these tree crowns indicates, first, that this work was authored by Schiele and, second, that it originated in the first third of the year 1910.

In addition, the reverse of the sheet bears the monogram "S", clearly from the artist's own hand, of the type he occasionally used in 1910 and 1911. Apparently he thought it inappropriate to sign the sheet on the obverse, due to the dense pattern of paint dabs there. (Also present on the reverse is the signature of the work's first owner, Mela Schiele, the artist's older sister, who in turn gave it to Egon Peschka, the younger son of her sister Gertrude. That he now owned the work was confirmed on the sheet by Egon's brother Anton. Moreover, the reverse bears an estimation of the drawing's value made in 1961 by Otto Benesch, then director of the Albertina and responsible for amassing its Schiele collection.)

The young artist may well have had an eye on recent directions in art when he executed this image, yet it is neverthless a very personal statement. It does, however, contain a few stylistic inconsistencies. The tree tops with their watercolor washes and idiosyncratic contours seem inconsistent with the strongly colored, strangely pointillistic treatment of the other areas of the picture. Yet this contrast was likely intended on Schiele's part. The unmixed, pure color of the dabs in the meadow and the no longer so "loud" red madder of the middle ground already introduce a spatial differentiation. This is reinforced by the delicate blues of the sky, which cause it, as in reality, to recede into the distance. And the so differently executed parts of the picture have been given a certain coherence by the employment of the spray method not only in the meadow but in passages of the sky.

All in all, the not yet quite twenty-year-old artist succeeded in producing a very vivacious work in terms of color. It holds an entirely singular place in his œuvre. Subsequently Schiele chose to take an entirely different path.

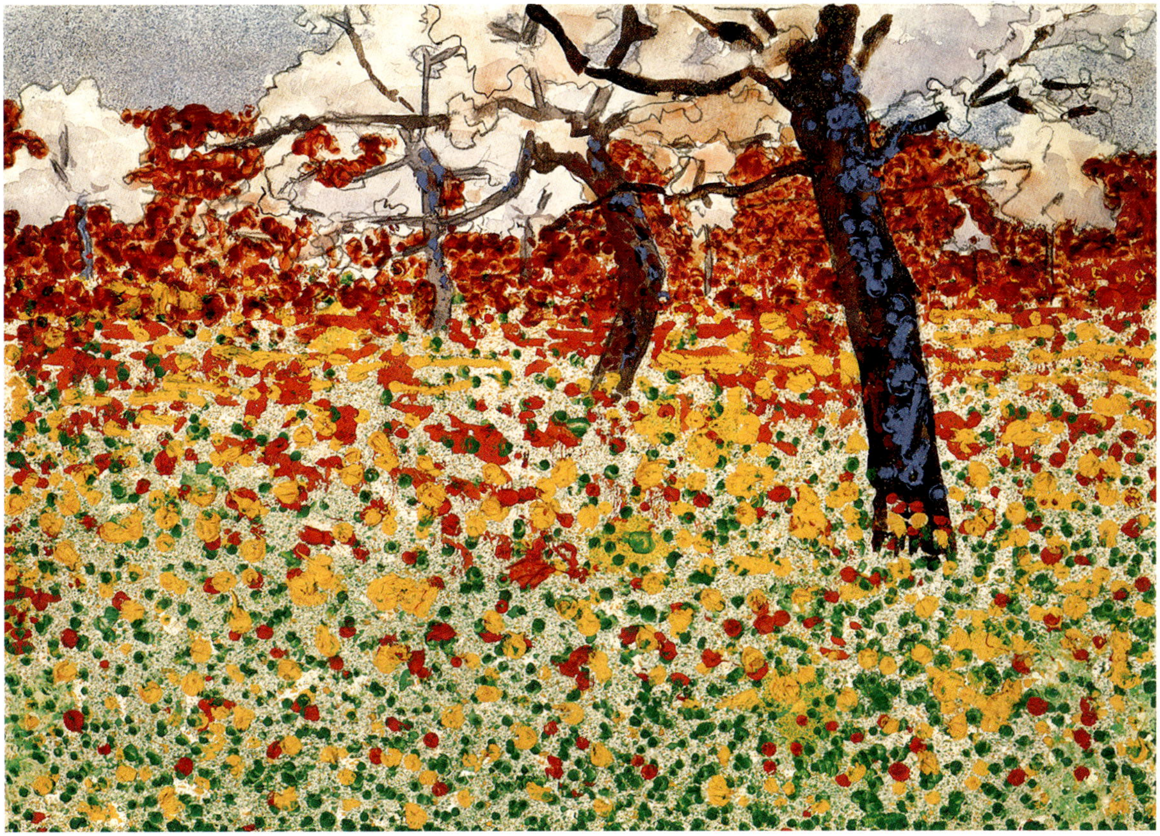

"Sunflower" II 1910

L 139 K 159
Pencil and oil on canvas, 150 x 29.8 cm
Initialed upper right
Wien Museum, Vienna, inv. no.: 117523

This is a subject which Schiele would address several times, for the last time in 1914. Although he painted sunflowers at a very early date, this is the first rendering to display his personal style, even though its composition partially echoes Klimt's "Sunflower" of 1906/07 (Dobai 146). Whereas Klimt treated the plant's root in an entirely planar way, Schiele's rendering of this passage evokes great depth. Moreover, Schiele has abandoned the dark background of leaves extending far beyond the flower on both sides, against which its lighter hues stand out. In Schiele's picture the background is very light and entirely homogeneous, and the sunflower is rendered in darker tones. But above all, Schiele has restricted the picture format to the width of the flower, emphasing its vertical growth and the contrasting wilting leaves. This was not seen either in Klimt's "Sunflower" or in Schiele's study of 1909, illustrated below, in which decorative, Jugendstil or Art Nouveau composition still predominated.

Even though the combination of bright orange and violet in the center of Schiele's "Sunflower" still owes much to Jugendstil, the drawing of the petals projecting out of the center at the upper left already reflects the style employed in the 1910 "Chrysanthemums" (L 142/K 180). Even when Schiele's rapid development at that period is taken into account, the probability that "Sunflower" was likewise not executed until 1910 (more precisely, during the first third of the year) is increased when we consider the seemingly skeletalized, bizarre contours of the sunflower leaves and compare these with details of the contours in Schiele's four large-format nudes on canvas (L 140/K 168, L 141/K 169, L 144/K 171, L 145/K 172) and the portaits of Zakovsek, Kosmack and Roessler (L 148/K 160, L 152/K 165, L 153/K 163) – all dating to 1910. "Sunflower," "Chrysanthemums" and the depiction of "Poldi Lodzinsky" (L 143/K 162) are early manifestations of Schiele's own, highly personal Expressionism in the painting medium. With this flower picture and the sunflower with its drooping, wilting leaves, the artist had already created in this period an allegory of waxing and waning.

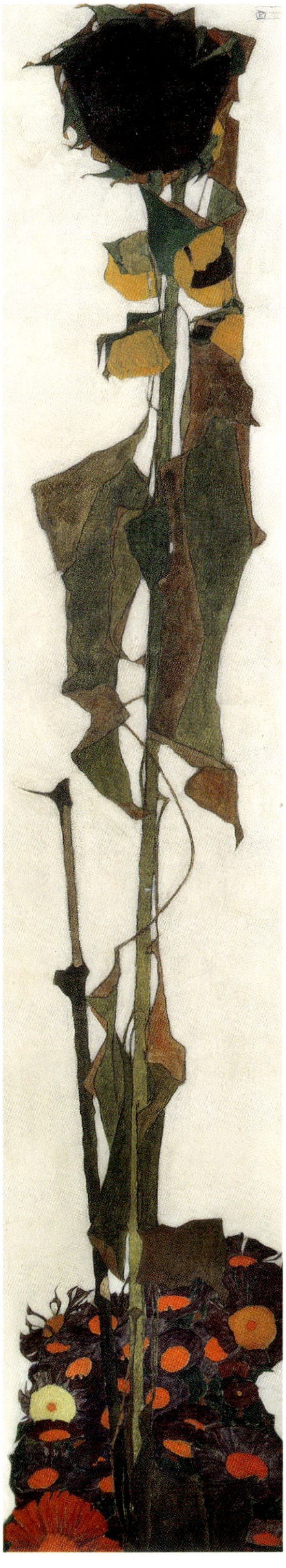

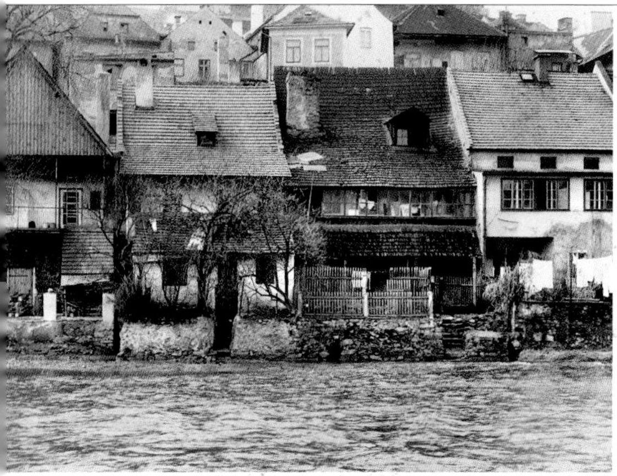

Houses on the Moldau, Krumau

Houses on the Moldau (Krumau) 1910

L 155 K 181
Black crayon, watercolor, opaque colors and opaque white on paper, 31.2 x 45 cm
Unsigned, undated; Austrian export stamp on reverse
Private collection

The present motif represents old houses along Parkgraben (Parkán) on the Moldau. (These are buildings nos. 111 to 114, reading from right to left on the sheet.)

In an old photograph we see that the hip roofs of nos. 113 and 114, which Schiele drew and painted, were later replaced by simple, modern roofs which would not likely have inspired him to depict them. On the other hand, the dwarf hip roof of no. 114, and especially the somewhat warped bottom edge of the roof next door and the balcony façade gleaming in the sun, provided an interesting motif for the artist.

Evidently he has attempted to reinforce the almost romantic impression by depicting the river in quite unnaturalistic red and blue tones. Yet this passage seems somewhat at odds with the otherwise rather realistic depiction, nor are the scattered red and blue accents on the buildings sufficient to produce a truly unified coloristic impression.

On the other hand, the old and dilapidated character of the houses is conveyed with great expressive force.

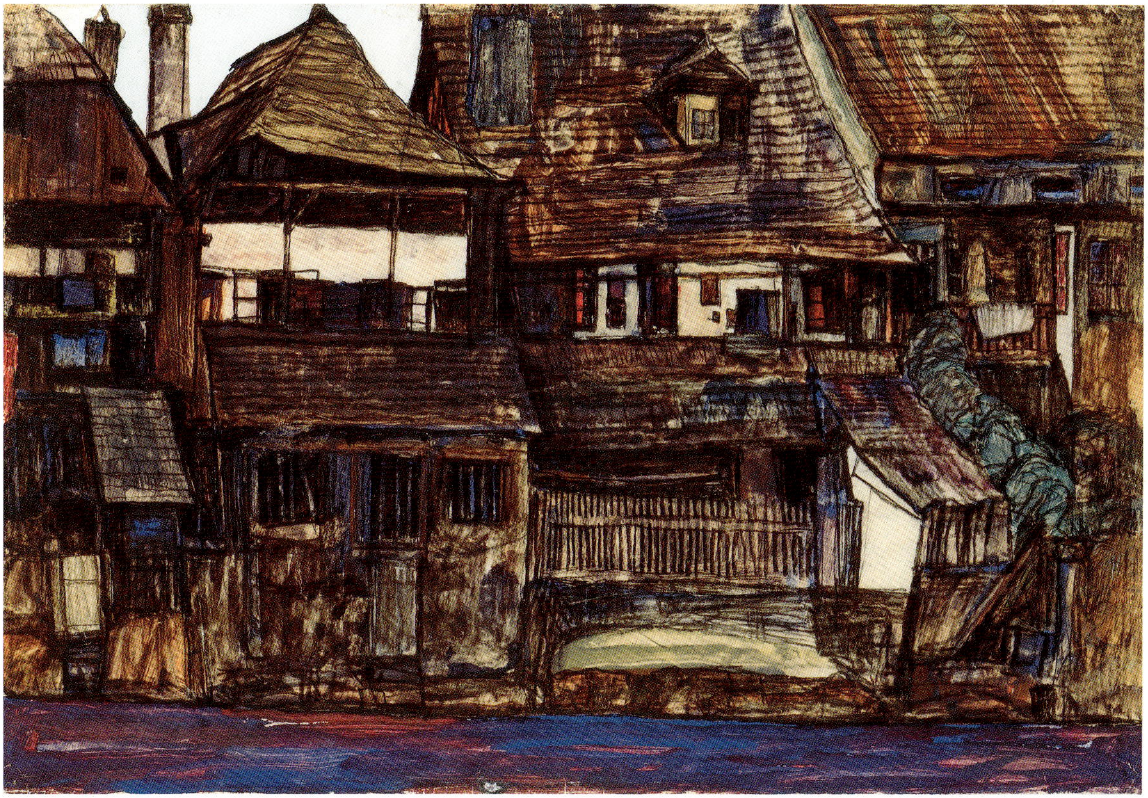

House with Smokehouse 1910

Pencil on paper, 14.2 x 22.5 cm
Signed and dated lower right
Leopold Museum, Vienna, inv. no.: LM 3988

A quite ordinary motif: A house with a smokehouse and a few leafless trees behind it. Yet the longer one looks at this drawing, the more one is taken by its great sensibility.

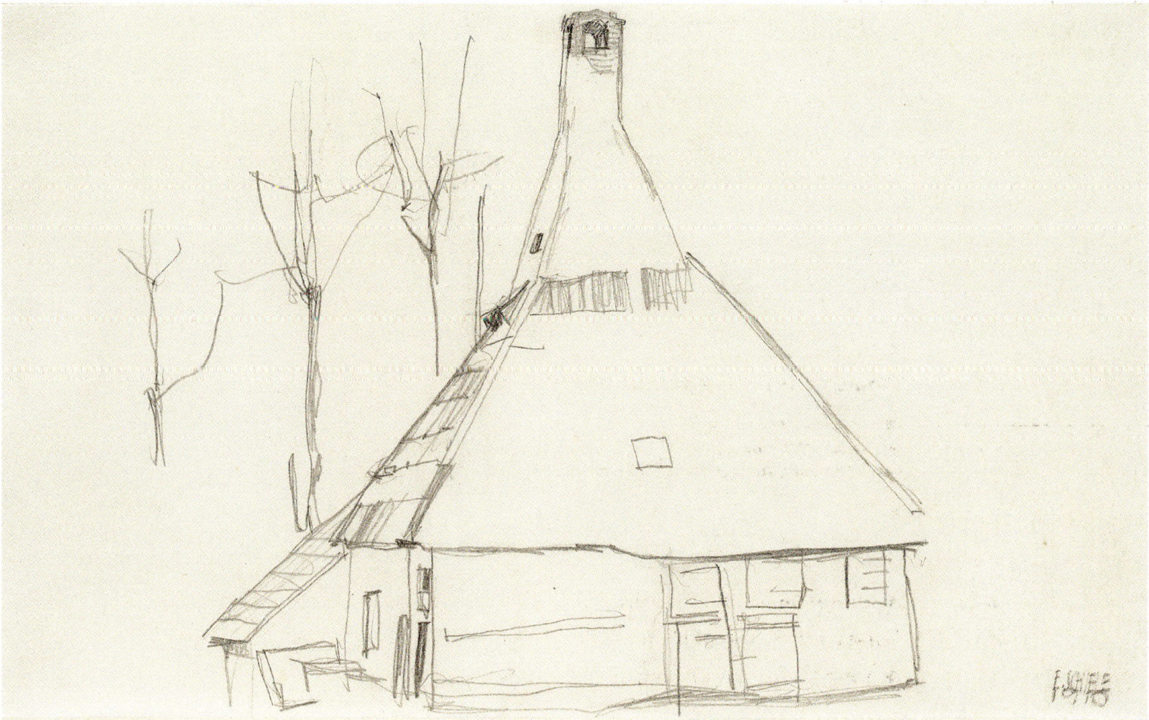

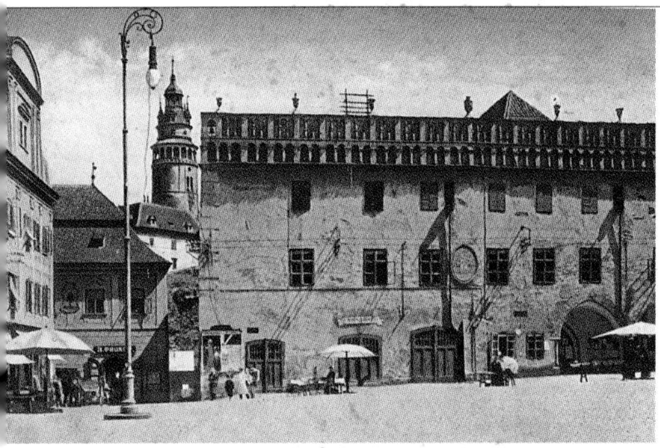

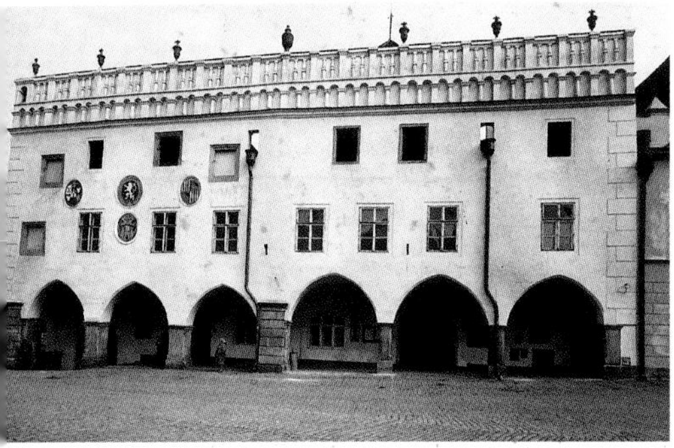

The Krumau Town Hall I (partial view) 1910

L 156 K 182
Black crayon, watercolor and opaque colors on paper, 31.7 x 44.8 cm
Unsigned, undated
Private collection

As far as the motif is concerned, the town hall of Krumau on the Moldau consists of four Gothic buildings which were acquired by the community in 1559 and later connected by means of a Renaissance gallery floor. The lovely original arcaded entrances on the ground floor, except for the two at the eastern end, were built over. It was not until 1924/25 – years after Schiele's death – that two archways were reopened to Rathausgasse (Radnicní ulice), followed by the remainder in 1945.

Schiele drew and painted this building for the first time in autumn 1910, using black chalk and gouache on paper (yet depicting little more than the left-hand half of the façade).

Both in this 1910 work as well as in two 1911 paintings on wood, the view of the façade is from the square known as Ringplatz, and it appears in the state mentioned above.

This partial view of the town hall is dominated by somber colors interrupted only by a few more brilliant accents in blue-green. The façade appears encompassed by a flickering illumination that is swallowed up by a black obscurity. Every detail of the lane to the left of the façade, Rathausgasse, was purposely suppressed. Schiele employed a similar approach in the two wood panels of 1911.

The town hall of Krumau with four of the archways built over Postcard from 1917

A later photograph of the town hall with the archways reopened

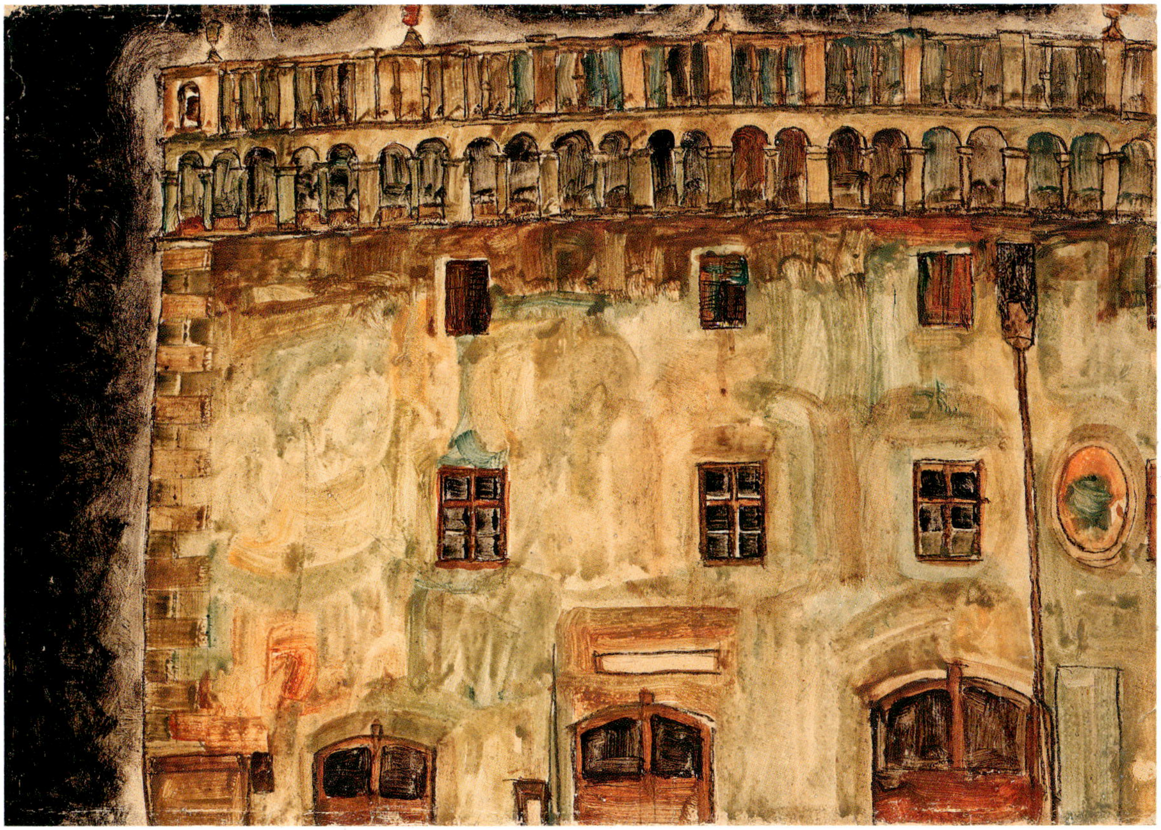

Fuchsia Branches ("Sun Tree") 1910

K 748
Black crayon and gouache on paper, 39.5 x 31.5 cm
Signed and dated lower right; entitled 'Sonnenbaum'on the reverse
Owner's monogram Koloman Moser
Leopold Museum, Vienna, inv. no.: LM 3663

The present work is one of Schiele's most imaginative creations in color. This is reflected in the title he inscribed on the reverse: "Sun Tree".

By comparison to other works on paper and the painting of "Chrysanthemums", the palette is extremely diverse. Although the composition is held together by a graphic scaffolding, it is overwhelmed by an abundance of spontaneously rendered details and the vital swirl of colors. The broken green tones are dominated by many more brilliant values, yet Schiele managed to bring the compositional color into a marvellous unity.

The sheet must have been executed at a point in time very close to that of "Field Landscape" (L 159/K 184, p. 65). This is indicated not only by the identical use of viscous gouache in both works, with which Schiele enriched the brushwork with heavy textures in many places, but also by the appearance of numerous, quite similar color gradations – for instance the light blue-green used to set accents.

The fuchsia branches, leaves and blossoms appear quite naturalistic despite the fact that Schiele gave his imagination entirely free rein here.

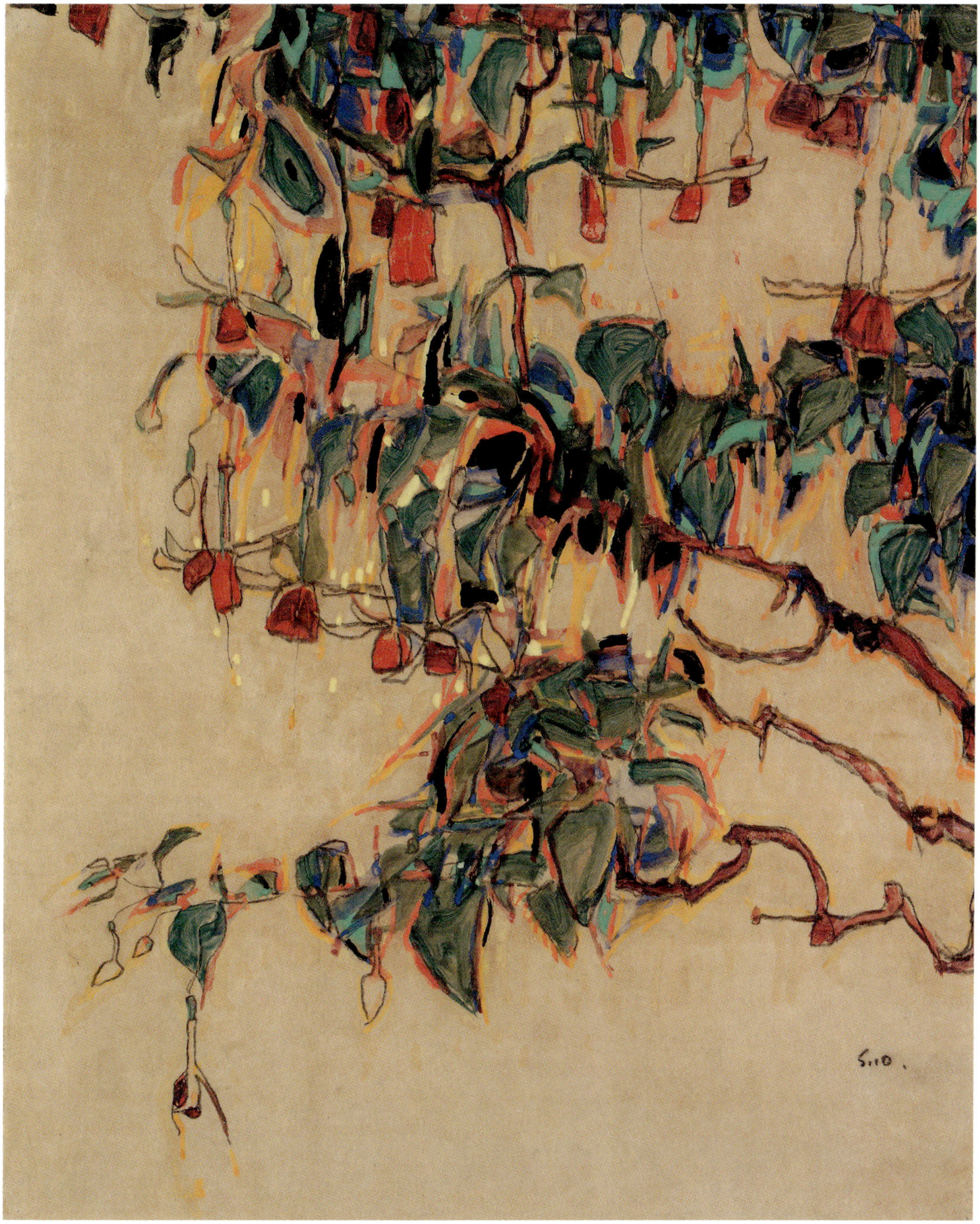

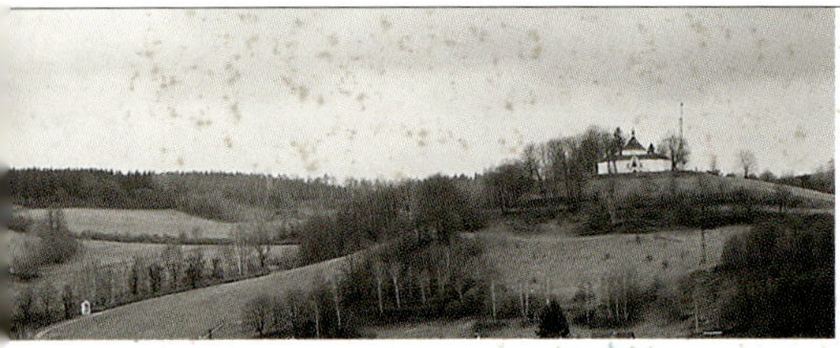

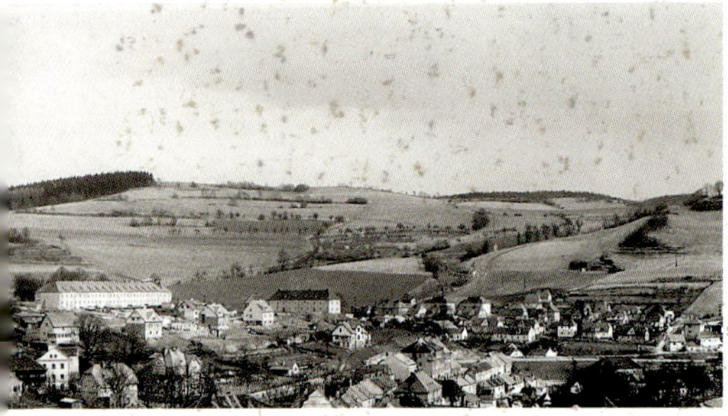

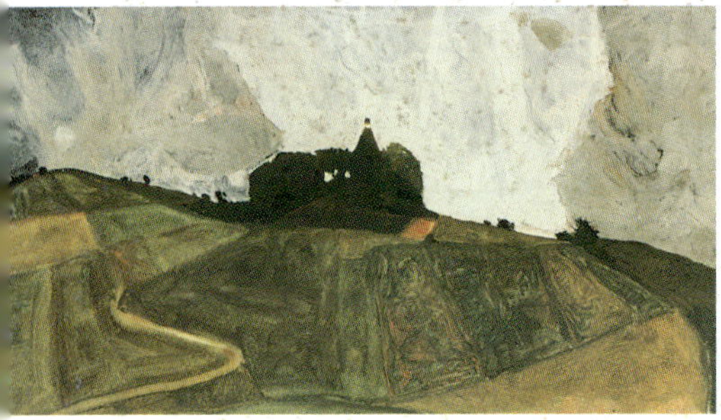

Field Landscape 1910

L 159 K 184
Black crayon, watercolor and
opaque colors on paper, 31.1 x 44.5 cm
Unsigned, undated
Albertina, Vienna, inv. no.: 26.668

The motif of fields inspired Schiele to dynamically divide the sheet into bands and zones which extend to include the sky. The fields projecting into the picture from the lower left abut on the diagonal central axis of the composition. This is formed by a slight depression in the landscape and leads to the upper right, to the chapel cut off by the picture edge. The dark clouds gathered behind the chapel part to leave a sort of bright aura around it.

Judging by a letter of Schiele's, about six weeks after completing this picture he executed one he called "Gewitterberg" (Thunderstorm Mountain), in which the chapel became the center of interest (L 162/K 185). Yet this depiction by no means achieved the aesthetic effect of the previous work on paper, the present "Field Landscape".

Some of the color gradations used to represent these fields are entirely unnaturalistic. Large areas are rendered in a brownish-pink and smaller ones in a harsh light green. The linear articulation of the fields is underscored by rows of bushes and trees, largely in black. Yet despite the in part arbitrary hues, the overall impression created is a highly realistic one. It is a fascinating depiction both in graphic and painterly terms.

Two views of the Kreuzberg, Krumau

Thunderstorm Mountain
L 162 K 185
Oil on canvas
(mounted on composition board)
35.2 x 65.7 cm
Unsigned, undated

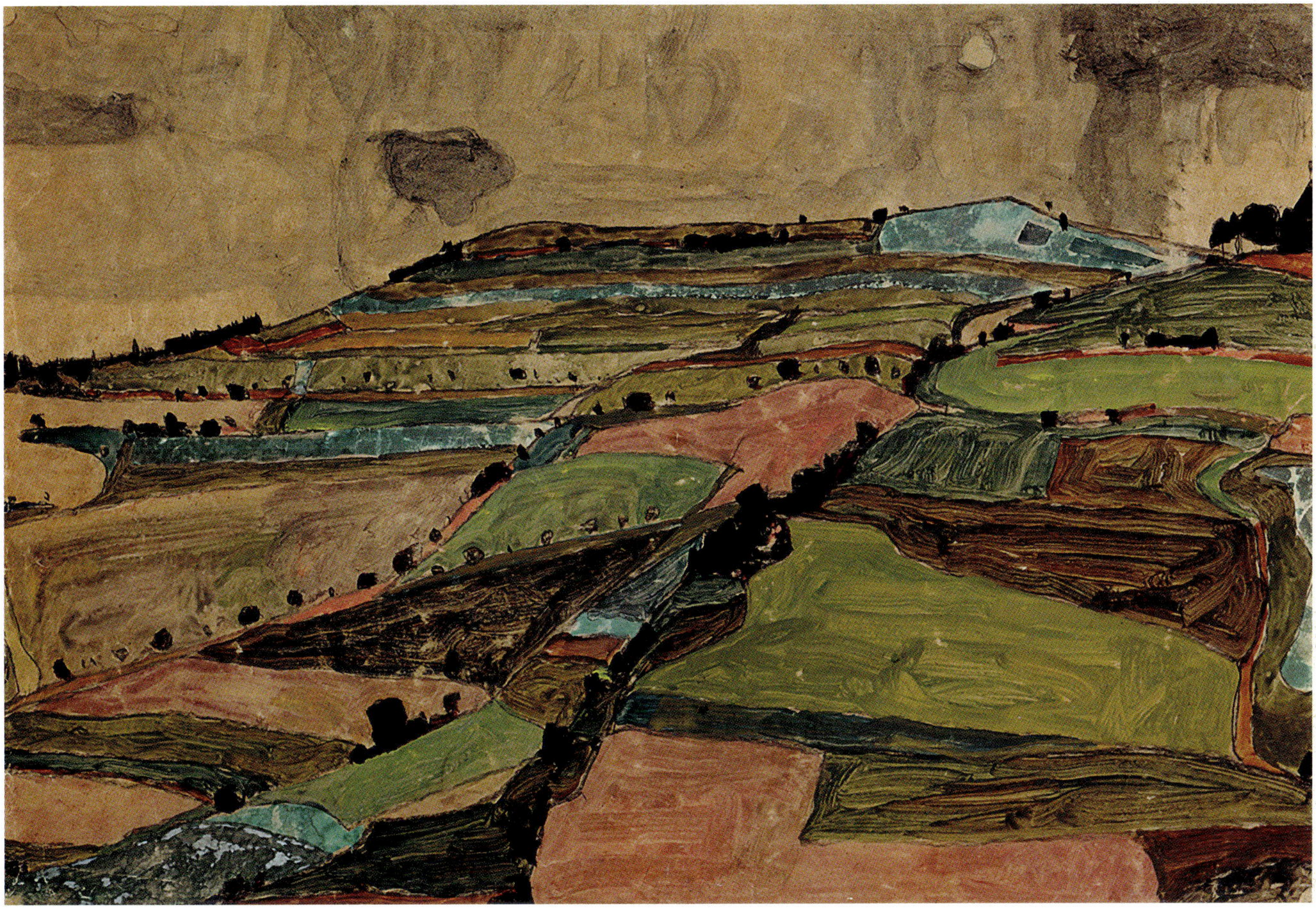

The somewhat decorative treatment of the cloudy sky and the light, rounded configurations that appear in it, here above the highest point of the mountain, are characteristic of Schiele's treatment of sky in works dating from late autumn 1910 to the early months of 1911 (L 159/K 184, L 162/K 185, L 163/K 187, p. 67, L 164/K 188, L 165/K 175, L 168/K 207). The strange "aura" around the chapel in "Field Landscape" and "Thunderstorm Mountain" likewise reappears in a very similar form in the landscape background of the self-portrait with "The Dead City" (L 165/K 175), which Schiele himself described as "World Wistfulness".

South and southeast of Krumau extend heights which include the Kreuzberg (Krízova hora), on which the chapel is situated. This low, gradually rising chain of hills appears much steeper in Schiele's "Field Landscape", the height of the peaks having been considerably exaggerated and depicted as a striking silhouette. At the same time Schiele infused the topography, still recognizable today, with a vital, dynamic effect.

Mountain by the River 1910

L 163 K 187
Oil on cardboard, 30 x 44 cm,
Initialed and dated upper left
Private collection

One of the most peculiar and interesting depictions of this period. The strange treatment of the sky with its comparatively sharply outlined, light and dark configurations in various colors is taken to an extreme, much as in the picture Schiele designated "Red Earth" (L 164/K 188).

The mountain bordering directly on the river is sharply silhouetted against the sky, the red underpainting shining in places through the contours. Whether Schiele derived this striking contour from an actual mountain or perhaps had the shape of a female breast in mind, must remain open. The latter would by no means be improbable in the erotic-minded Schiele's case.

The artist also let flashes of the underlying red paint layer appear in the borderline between mountain and river, and in the single, somewhat lighter triangular green area. The dark gradations in passages of the mountain and river, painted largely in glaze, are also found in similar form in works executed at the beginning of the following year, as in the darker passages of "The Poet" and in the paraphrase of his "Garden House" (L 174/K 208), as well as in the background of "Self-Seer" (II – 1911, L 173/K 193).

These were followed chronologically, in spring 1911, by works of an entirely different character: cityscapes based on Krumau motifs, painted on wood in flowing colors. But after moving to Neulengbach, Schiele returned to a handling of the dark passages similar to that mentioned above, "Landscape with Ravens" (L 191/K 216, p. 87). Yet in this marvellous ravens landscape and its magisterially rendered sky contrasting with the terrain, Schiele found a painterly solution that was by far more convincing.

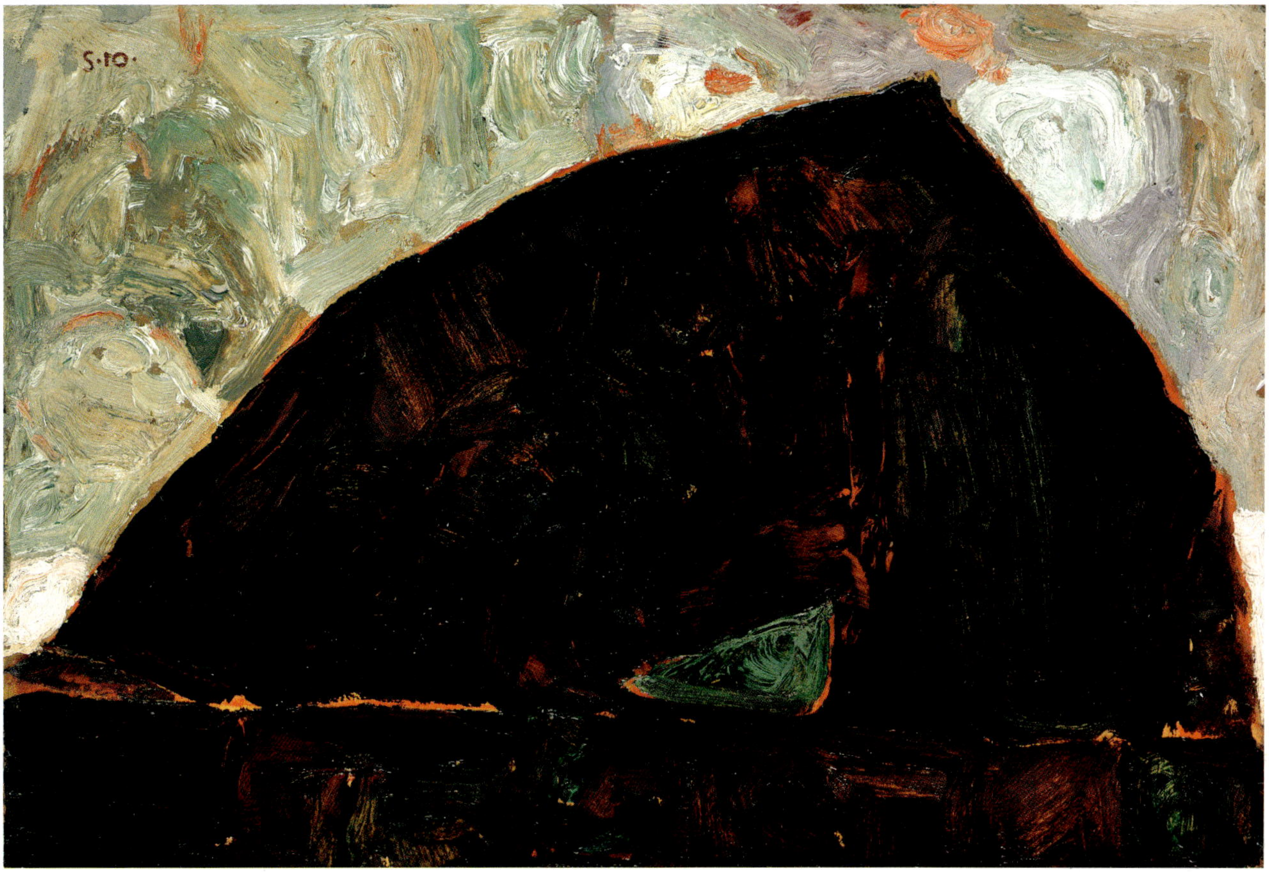
S.10.

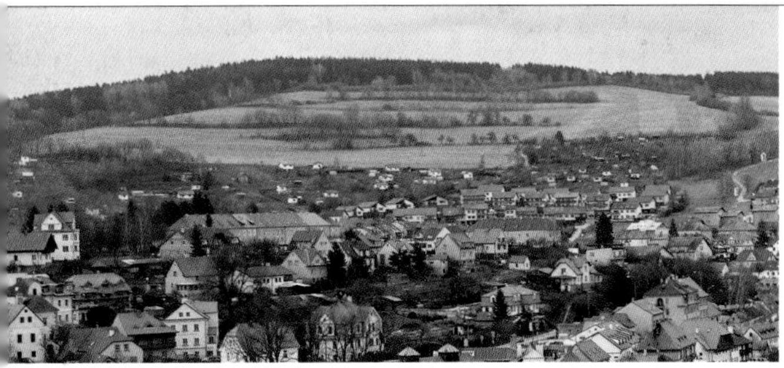

Area around the Kreuzberg, Krumau

Landscape in Front of Kreuzberg, Krumau 1911

K 984
Pencil on paper, 30.8 x 44.3 cm
Signed and dated lower left
Leopold Museum, Vienna, inv. no.: LM 1412

An eminence of the Kreuzberg, near Krumau. The actual foreground has been left empty, causing the houses to recede. These are spatially clearly distinguished from the Stations of the Cross behind and above them, an effect augmented by the surrounding hatchings.

Schiele has concentrated on the essence of the motif and, despite the apparent sketchiness, produced a coherent composition. The drawing, in soft pencil applied with considerable pressure, is masterful.

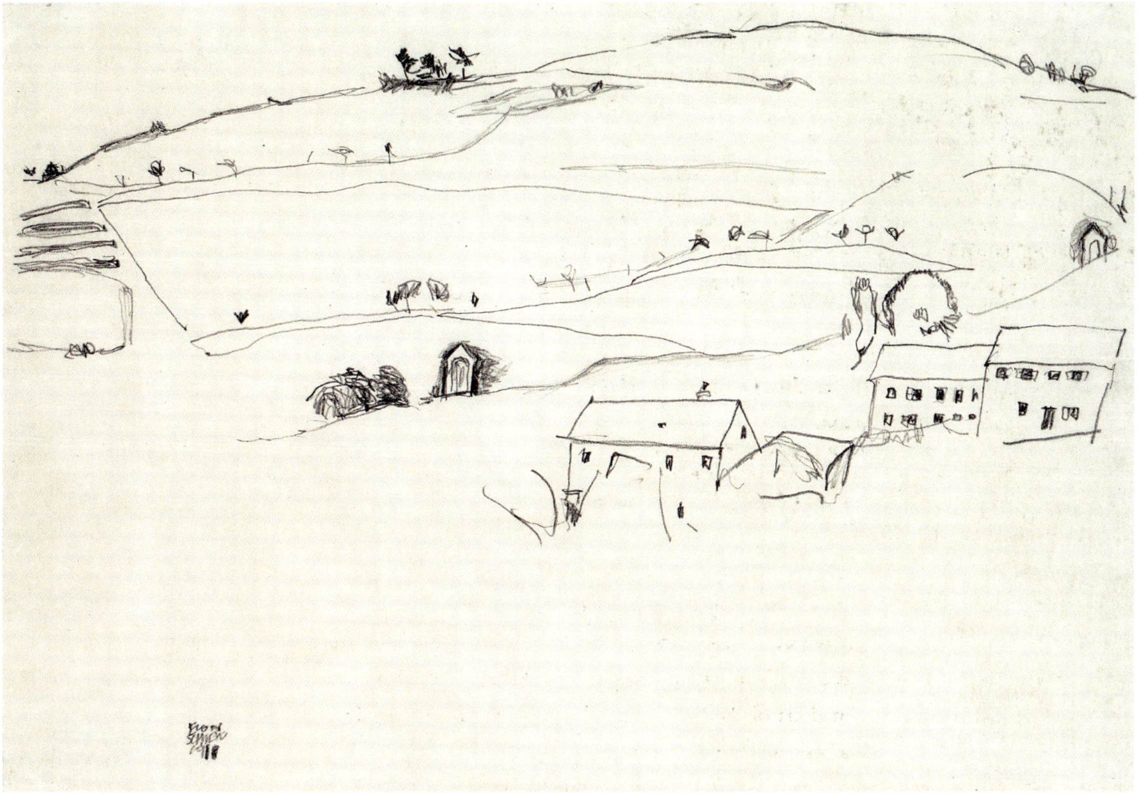

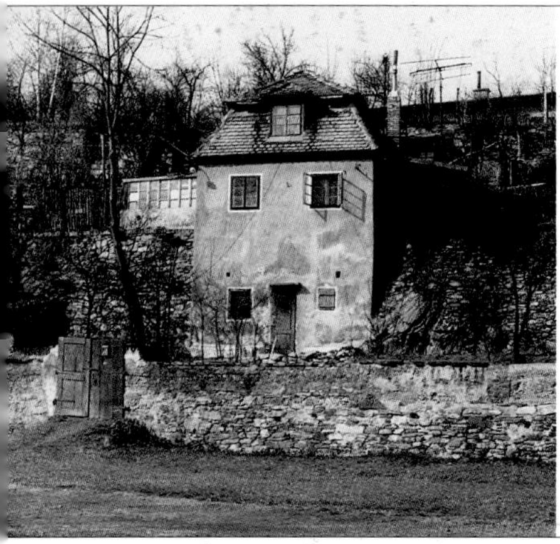

Schiele's studio and apartment in Krumau

House and Wall in Hilly Landscape 1911

L 174 K 208
Oil on canvas, 52 x 43.7 cm
Initialed and dated upper left
Leopold Museum, Vienna, inv. no.: LM 476

On the left bank of the Moldau, where the terrain falls steeply to the river in a series of stone terraces, stands a ruined building with a mansard roof. This roof dates back to a complete conversion of 1913, when it replaced the saddle roof of the Biedermeier-period building, which served its original owner as a summer house. In 1911 it became Schiele's "garden house", to which he also referred as his "little terrace house".

Despite its then already run-down state he intended to furnish it and live and work there on a long-term basis. Not long after he moved in, however, the locals began to harrass him about his cohabitation with Wally and the life-studies of nude young girls he made in the garden. In consequence, Schiele had to leave Krumau after only three months.

This house inspired Schiele to a highly idiosyncratic but artistically significant work. It was the final picture in the stylistic phase in which he sometimes reduced given realities to highly abstract terms and often employed heavy impasto. This is much in evidence in works dating to the first months of 1911, "Prophets", "Poets" and "Self-Seer" II–1911 (L 271/K 191, L 172/K 192, L 173/K 193). Both in terms of painting technique and palette, the second "Self-Seer" shows great affinities with the present picture, which was probably done soon after Schiele's arrival in Krumau, in early May 1911. Yet here the given motifs were even more strongly altered and apparently combined at random with imaginative additions.

Naturally the towerlike superstructure on the right was not in reality out of plumb. Its obliqueness is formally counterbalanced by the opposing diagonals of the furrow in the adjacent terrain and the row of fenceposts farther right. The gateway in the right section of the wall is probably just as much of an invention as the small castellated tower which is intersected by the right edge of the picture. This is rendered in the same ocher tone as two other passages to the left and right of the tower mentioned, with its oblique, eyelike windows and roof recalling a rakish hat. The red fleck next to it is entirely non-objective, but provides a fine color accent in the dark brown terrain with which Schiele replaced the stone terraces, perhaps thinking them not visually interesting enough. As a last instance of freely invented passages one might point to the light-gray areas to the right of the fence.

The second "Self-Seer" evinces similar if somewhat lighter color gradations than the house and wall in the painting under discussion. The contrast to the dark brown terrain lends it an even more painterly effect. Beyond this, despite the composition's high degree of abstraction, the eerie scene conveys an extremely concrete effect.

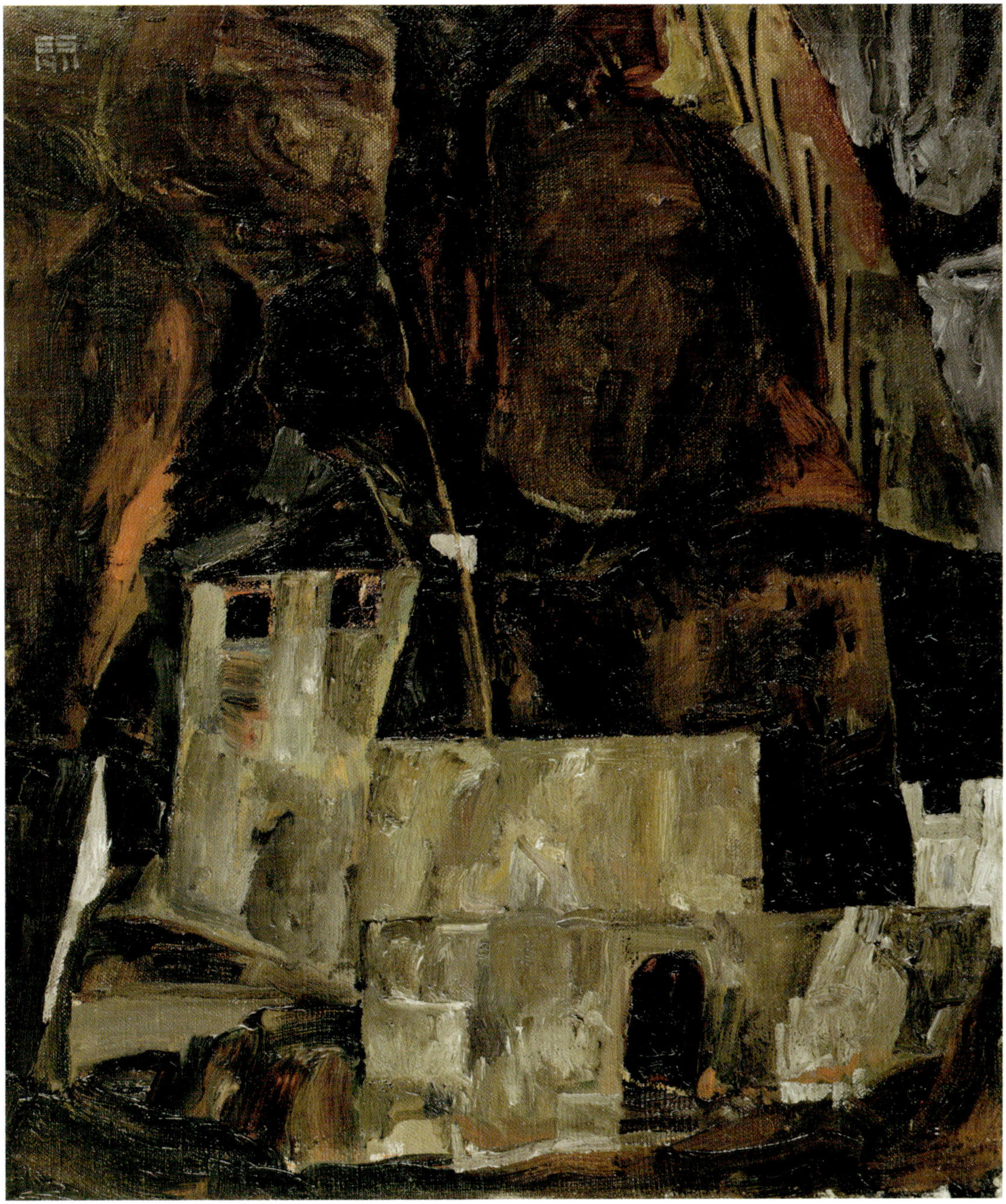

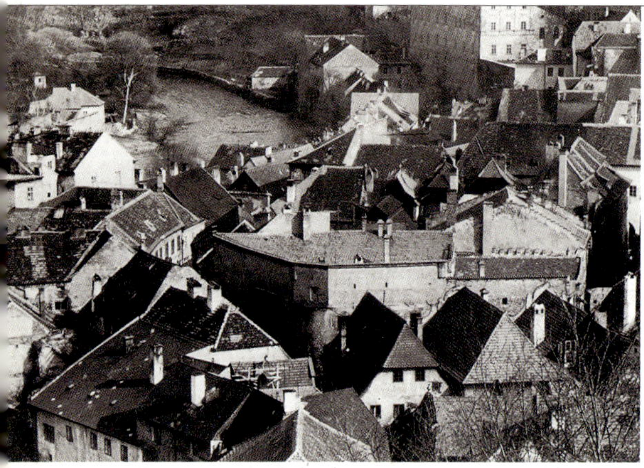

City on the Blue River II 1911

L 180 K 212
Pencil, opaque colors and oil on wood, 37.2 x 29.8 cm
Signed and dated upper right
Private collection

The photograph above shows approximately the viewpoint from which Schiele represented the scene, and the photograph on this page (top center) the side of the tourist hostel on Lange Gasse and its corner on the intersection with Tuchmachergasse. A photo taken in this lane gives an idea of the hostel's imposing appearance. Built by connecting a number of old houses, it extends from Herrengasse over Tuchmachergasse to Lange Gasse. At this point, Schiele foreshortened the lower tract of the building, but not the next house on Herrengasse in the direction of the town hall, with its two stepped gables cut off by the picture edge (whose steps he drew in, in contrast to "Krumau at Night" (L 177/K 209, p. 77).

The angular network of dark roofs east of the tourist hostel (leading upward from it in the picture) consists of houses on Lange Gasse, Fleischgasse (Masná ulice) and the park moat. At its end (at about top center in the picture) lie two houses on the Moldau, which are visible in the photo as well. The blank wall of one of them, facing the viewer, is rendered in an orange-ocher. To the right, Schiele replied to this hue with the harsh grass-green of a horizontal oval square, which no more actually exists than do the dwellings behind it. In fact, a steep cliff rises at that point on which the tall edifice of the former Jesuit seminar stands (which now contains the Museum of Local History and the County Archive).

Even more radically than in other paintings of the period, Schiele has left out numerous rows of houses – all located south of Tuchmachergasse and north of Lange Gasse – in order to let a watercourse symbolizing the Moldau flow around the mighty building complex of today's tourist hostel (32 Lange Gasse). In addition, the artist foreshortened the lower tract of this building, lending it an even more massive appearance. The walls are rendered in various gradations of light yellow that contrast with the dark blue of the Moldau, which Schiele spirited here from its actual site.

Krumau, as seen from Castle Hill

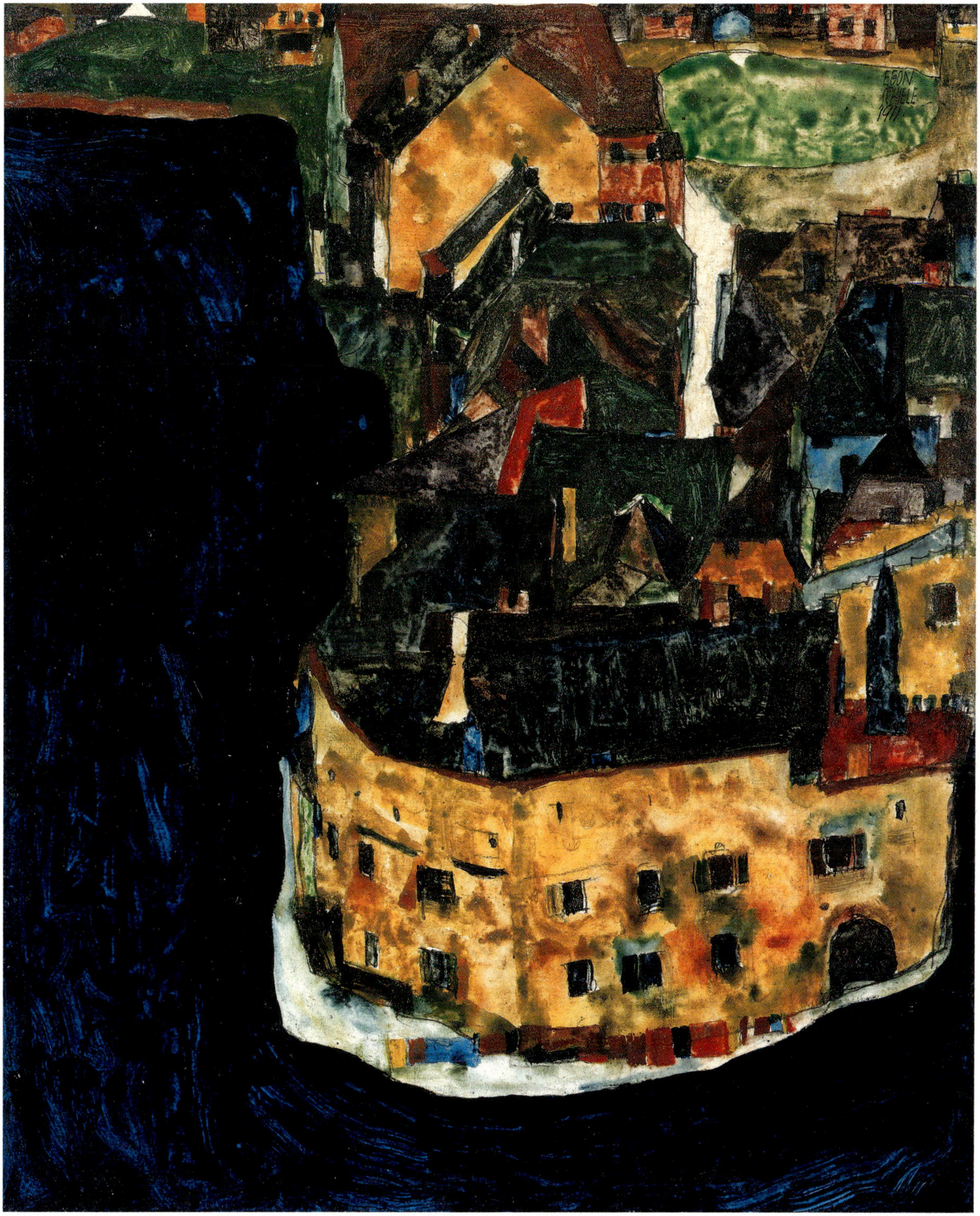
EGON
SCHIELE
1911

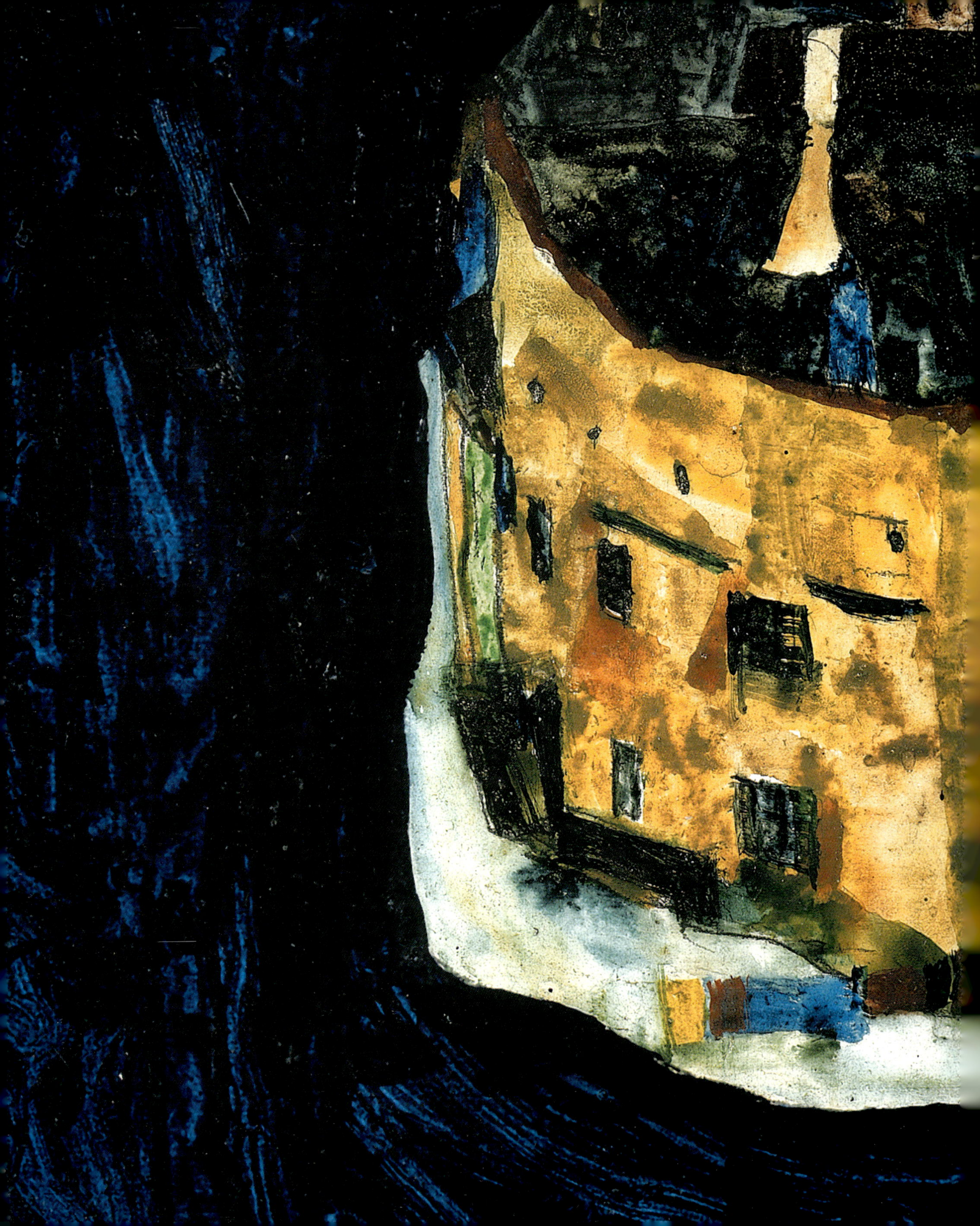

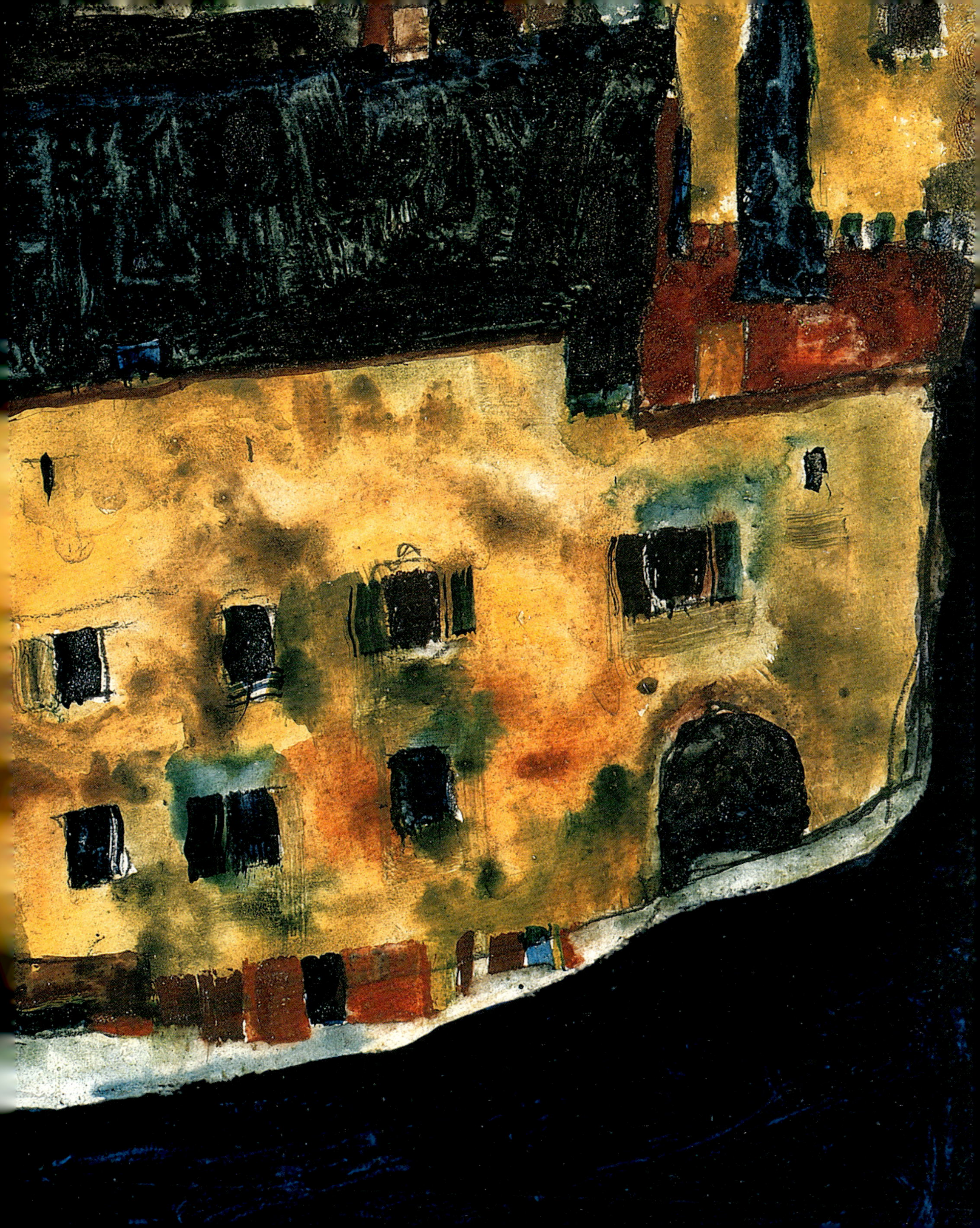

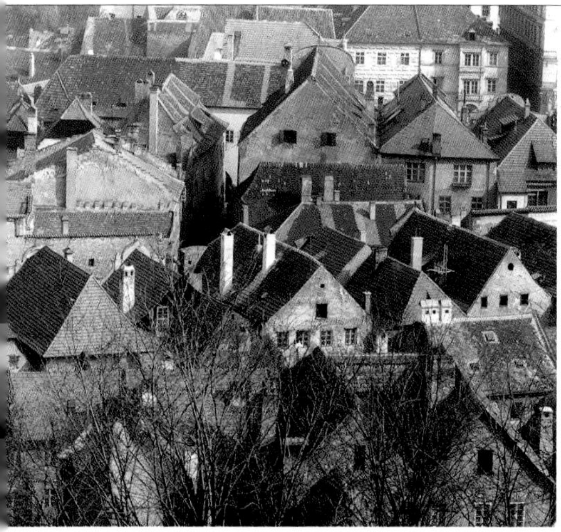

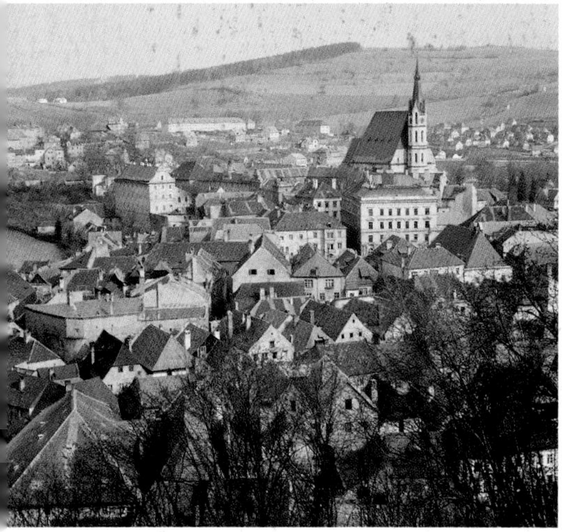

Krumau, as seen from Castle Hill

Krumau at Night (also known as "Dead City" II) 1911

L 177 K 209
Pencil, opaque colors and oil on wood, 37 x 29 cm
Signed and dated center right
Private collection

The work reproduced here is the second one which Schiele entitled "Dead City". The artist Albert Paris Gütersloh once said that the invention of this title could be valued as highly as the creation of the painting itself.

Schiele employed the designation "Dead City" as early as 1910, for the work in black chalk and gouache mixed with Syndetikon, listed under L 157/K 183. (In another picture list he entitled this painting "City on the Blue River", which actually applies better to the work registered under L 180/K 212 [p. 73], where the houses in fact seem surrounded by a dark blue river. Schiele used the title "Dead City" for a third time – along with "City on the Blue River" – for L 182/K 213 [p. 81].)

Although it may seem odd that Schiele chose the title "Dead City" for all three works, it perfectly expresses their essence in every case. In the case of the picture reproduced here, the unreal illumination engenders the impression of an eerie nocturnal scene.

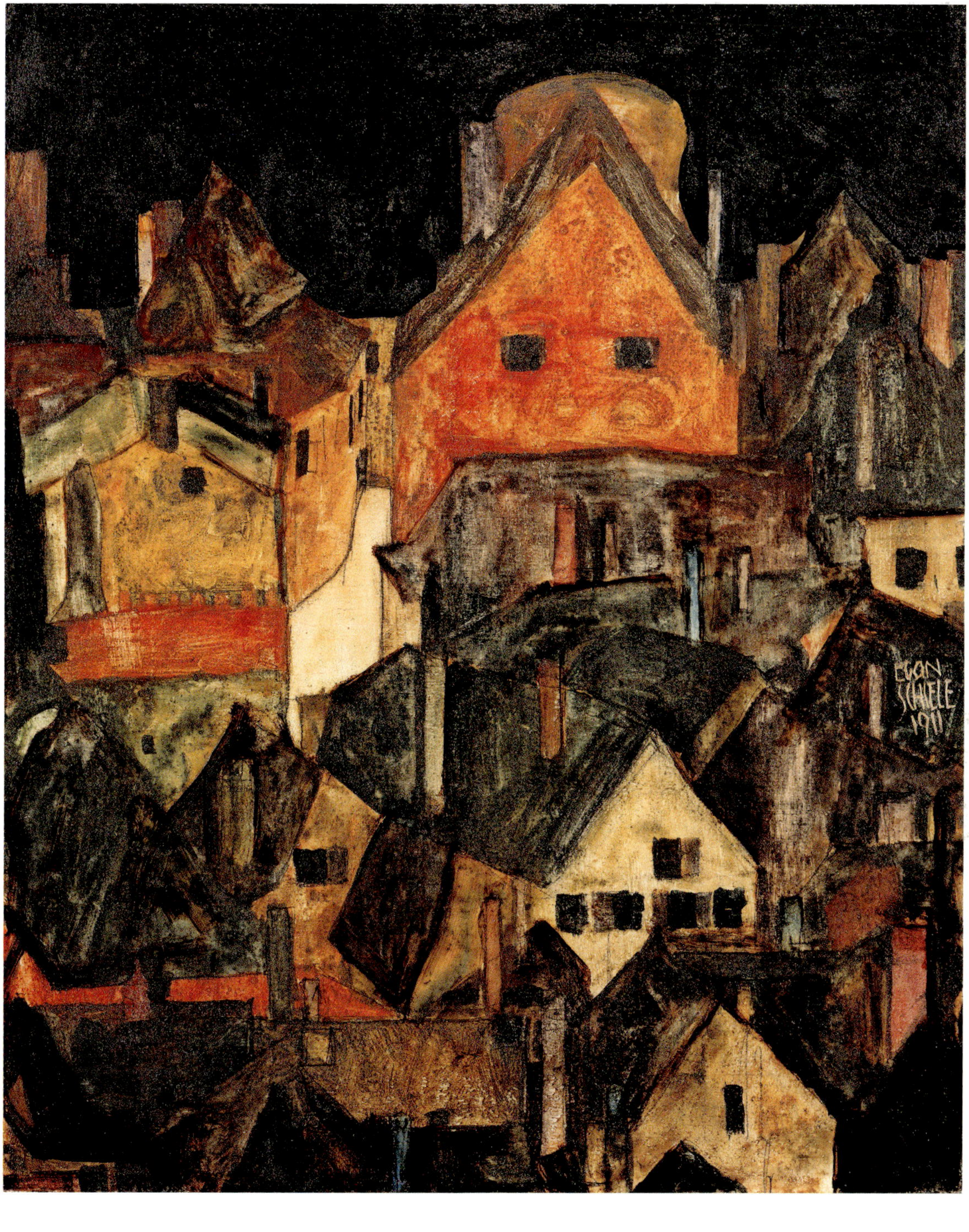
EGON
SCHIELE
1911

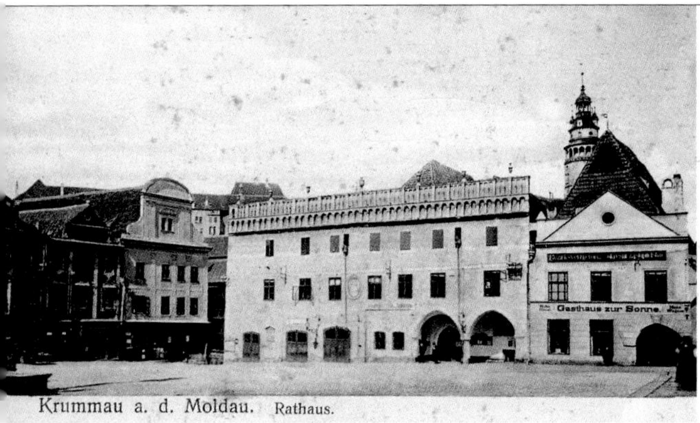

Postcard from Egon Schiele in Krumau
to Arthur Roessler

Krumau Town Hall II 1911

L 178 K 210
Pencil, opaque colors and oil on wood, 29 x 37 cm
Signed and dated lower left
Private collection

As mentioned in connection with the partial view of autumn 1910 (p. 61), Schiele depicted Krumau Town Hall two further times in spring 1911, each time from the vantage point of Ringplatz. In the former case the motif is cut off at the halfway point of the penultimate arcade opening; in the latter (L 183/K 214), the entire façade is depicted. In contrast to the partial view of 1910, both compositions of 1911 include a portion of Ringplatz. Similarly to the 1910 work, the sky and the lane to the left of the façade, Rathausgasse, are plunged in nocturnal darkness, so that nothing can be seen of the cliff on the far bank of the Moldau with its castle outworks and tower.

In this and other cityscapes, Schiele never aimed at producing panoramas or excerpts of the *veduta* variety. Although most of the motifs were taken from medieval Krumau, they were abbreviated and abstracted into new entities, imaginative, visionary cityscapes. Especially in the 1911 pictures, this effect was reinforced by an unprecedented richness of color gradations in gouache and oil, flowing into one another and shimmering like enamel (something Schiele would not manage nearly so well in the oil landscapes with houses of the following year). This becomes quite evident by comparison to the free reprises of "Dead City" II – 1911 (L 177/K 209, p. 77) of 1912, such as "Dead City" (L 205/K 245, p. 95), the larger-format "Dead

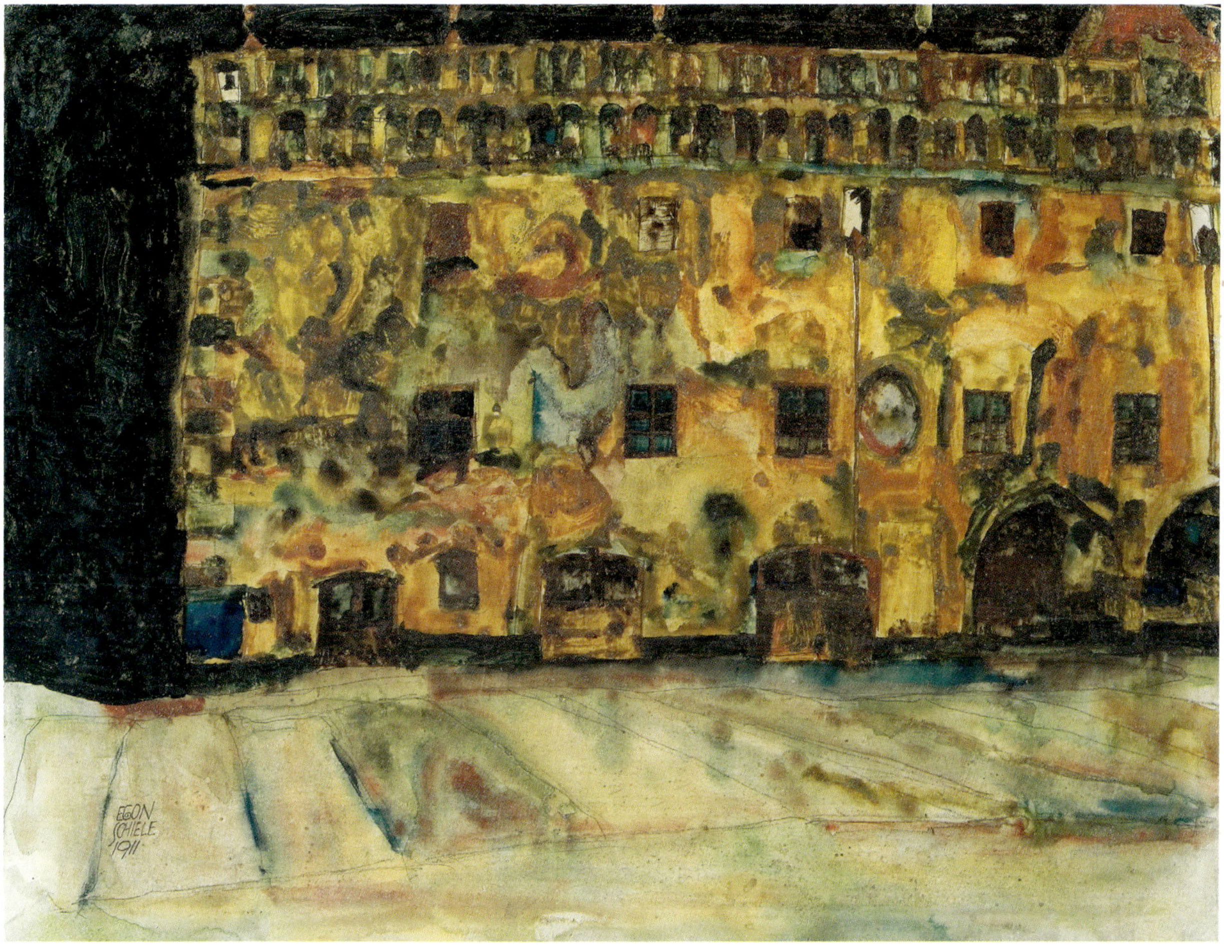

City" (L 222/K 246, p. 111), or a painting like "Meadow, Church and Houses" (L 204/K 243). Schiele's progress in 1912 lay in the figurative works and the landscapes with trees.

Now back to "Krumau Town Hall" of 1911. Here the façade and a section of Ringplatz are rendered in luminous, imaginative colors, and in place of Rathausgasse and the Renaissance top story, a dark area in primarily greenish-blue gradations appears.

Depicted here, in contrast to the partial view of 1910 (L 156/K 182), is the right-hand section of the façade, including half of the last arch. The former third arch (counting from the right), which by then had been replaced by a room with two windows, is shown as being open. And visible in this opening is the gateway, which in reality lies behind the second arch from the right. Further small changes were made as well. For instance, Schiele omitted one each of the three windows on the first and second upper stories.

However, such alterations appear minimal in view of the radical transformation of the façade – with all of two crescent moons above it – in the third 1911 painting of the town hall (L 179/K 214). This lost composition is known only from black and white reproductions.

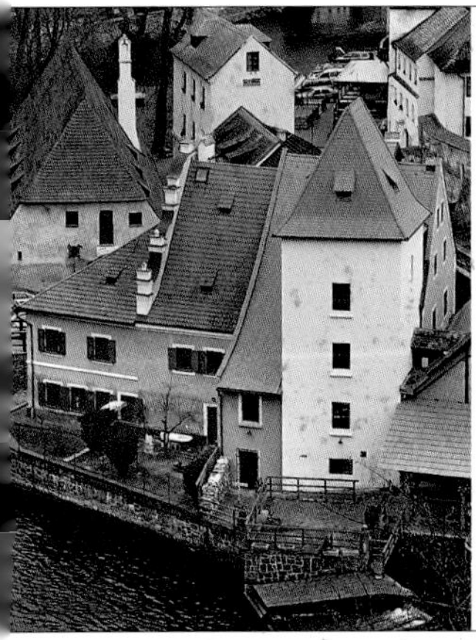

"Dead City" III (also known as "City on the Blue River" III) 1911

L 182 K 213
Pencil, opaque colors and oil on wood, 37.3 x 29.8 cm
Signed and dated upper right
Leopold Museum, Vienna, inv. no.: LM 460

The complex of houses with municipal mill on the bend of the Moldau upriver from Bader Bridge had a special allure for Schiele. Already in 1908 he depicted excerpts of it in colored pencil drawings and small oils (L 106/K 134, L 107/K 135), although these lacked the visionary character of later works based on these motifs. The colored pencil drawing (p. 82), in the then popular palette of the Vienna Secession, shows a part of this group of houses. Initially Schiele depicted it from a high vantage point in a 1910 sketchbook, but here he has included the armory to the left and behind, and excluded the houses adjacent to the – then somewhat lower – towerlike projecting bay on the right. In the succeeding drawing (in black chalk or crayon and gouache mixed with Syndetikon to give it texture), the houses to the right are likewise omitted. Instead, the extremely foreshortened gable wall is surrounded by dark water which extends in the foreground down to a narrow, likewise extremely foreshortened strip of bank. This lends the houses, rendered in subdued colors with dark roofs and light façades with empty windows, an isolated, as if abandoned look. This was the first work to which Schiele gave the title "Dead City". (In a 1911 essay on Schiele, Albert Paris Gütersloh found this title "an idea equal in value to the picture it designates".) The artist would subsequently apply the title to six further compositions of a visionary nature.

The almost ghostly effect of these houses alongside the dark river was increased still further in the 1910 drawing

The municipal mill in Krumau, as seen from Castle Hill

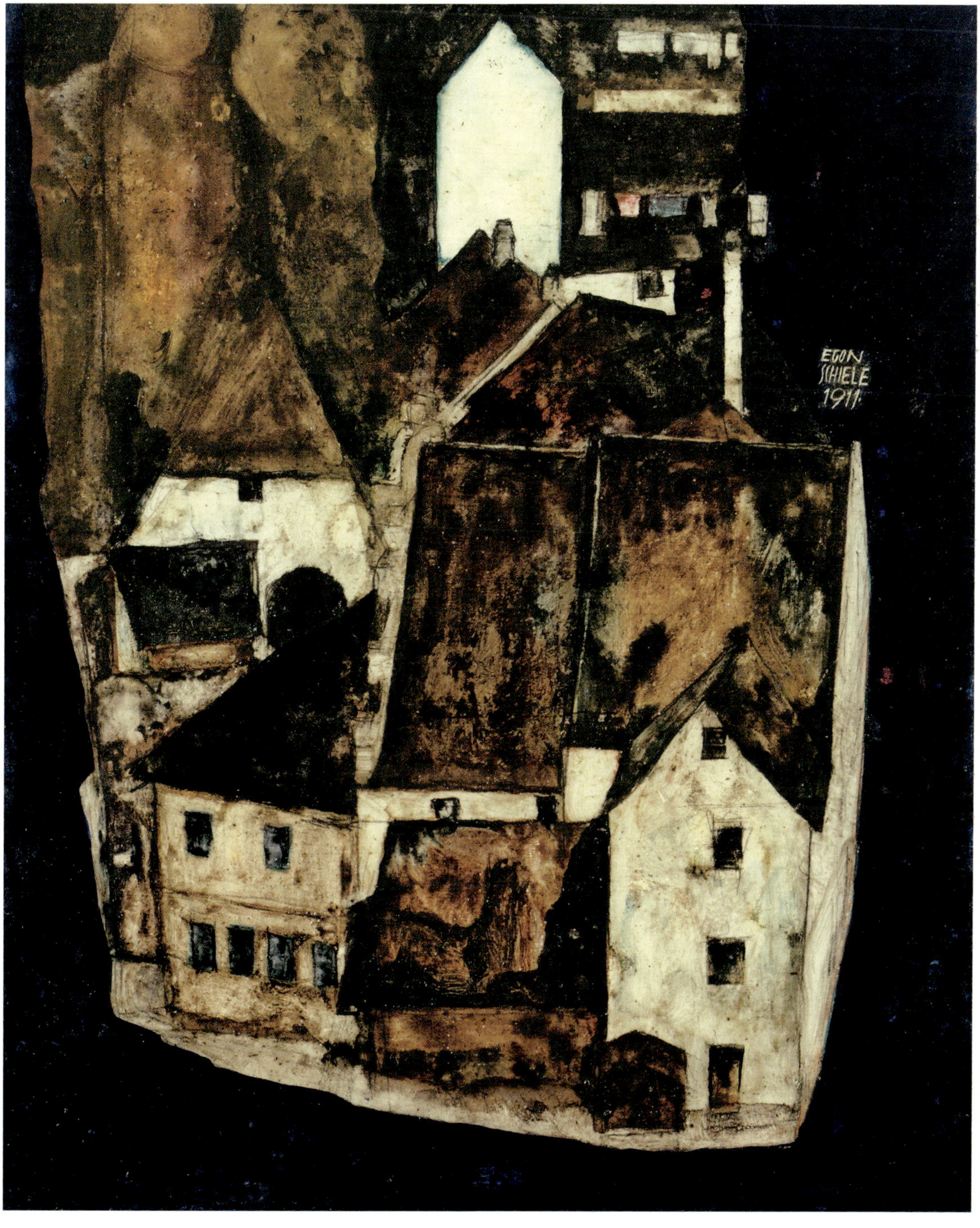
EGON
SCHIELE
1911

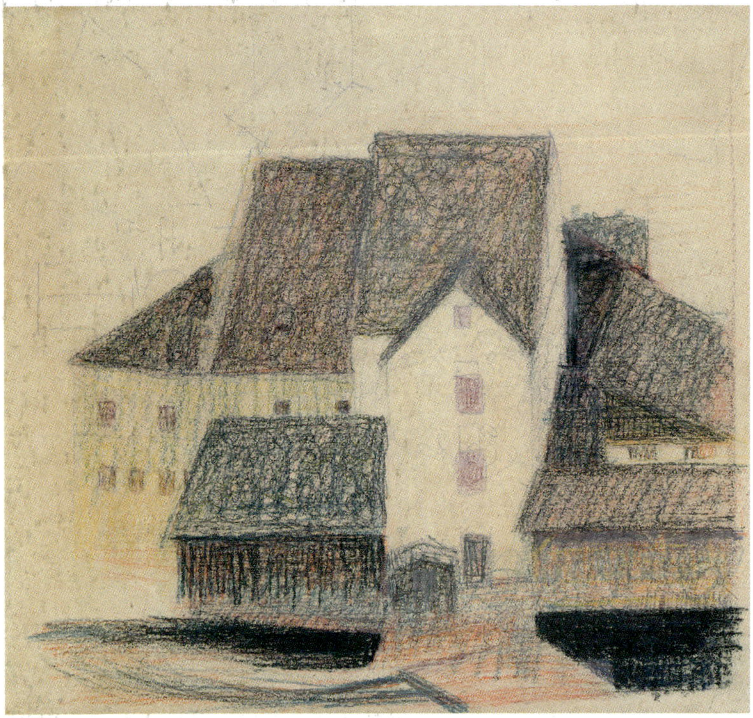

Group of houses around the municipal mill 1907
K 248 a
Colored chalk mixed with Syndetikon on wrapping paper, 29.8 x 31.4 cm
Unsigned, undated
Leopold Museum, Vienna,
inv. no.: LM 3659

by the somewhat lighter hue used for the water, as if a faint light were playing over it. This is clearly evident in early reproductions. Farther up, the water grew entirely dark, providing a strong contrast to the light group of houses. (This interesting effect is sadly no longer to be seen, because Arthur Roessler – as he himself informed me – cut about two centimeters off the sheet at the lower edge, where this faint light was visible. And this for the simple reason that he had a frame that was not quite high enough, in which he framed Schiele's work after its "amputation"!)

Schiele moved to Krumau in early May 1911. And once again he depicted this favorite group of houses, this time from a still higher vantage point at the level of the palace plateau. In a postcard to Arthur Roessler of 15 May, the artist wrote, "The outlined section is the upper edge of the 'Dead City'..."

By comparison to the first version, the group of houses here is brought farther forward and seen from higher up, leading to a foreshortening of the house façades in the foreground. Thanks to this raised vantage point and the now diagonal course of the rows of windows in the left-hand façade, the spatial effect of the foremost houses is considerably increased. This is especially evident in the detail of the lean-to built onto the middle house.

The chiaroscuro in the group of houses is now considerably stronger. The façades seem glaringly illuminated from some imaginary light source, forming a sharp contrast to the dark roofs and especially to the the bluish-black river. This now flows around the houses to the left as well, increasing their sense of isolation. The dark apertures of the windows and the single gate contribute to an appearance of abandonment. This may well have been what prompted

"Dead City" I
(also known as *"City on the Blue River" I*) 1910
L 157 K 183
Black crayon, watercolor and opaque colors on wrapping paper
41.2 x 30.8 cm
Signed and dated lower right
Private collection

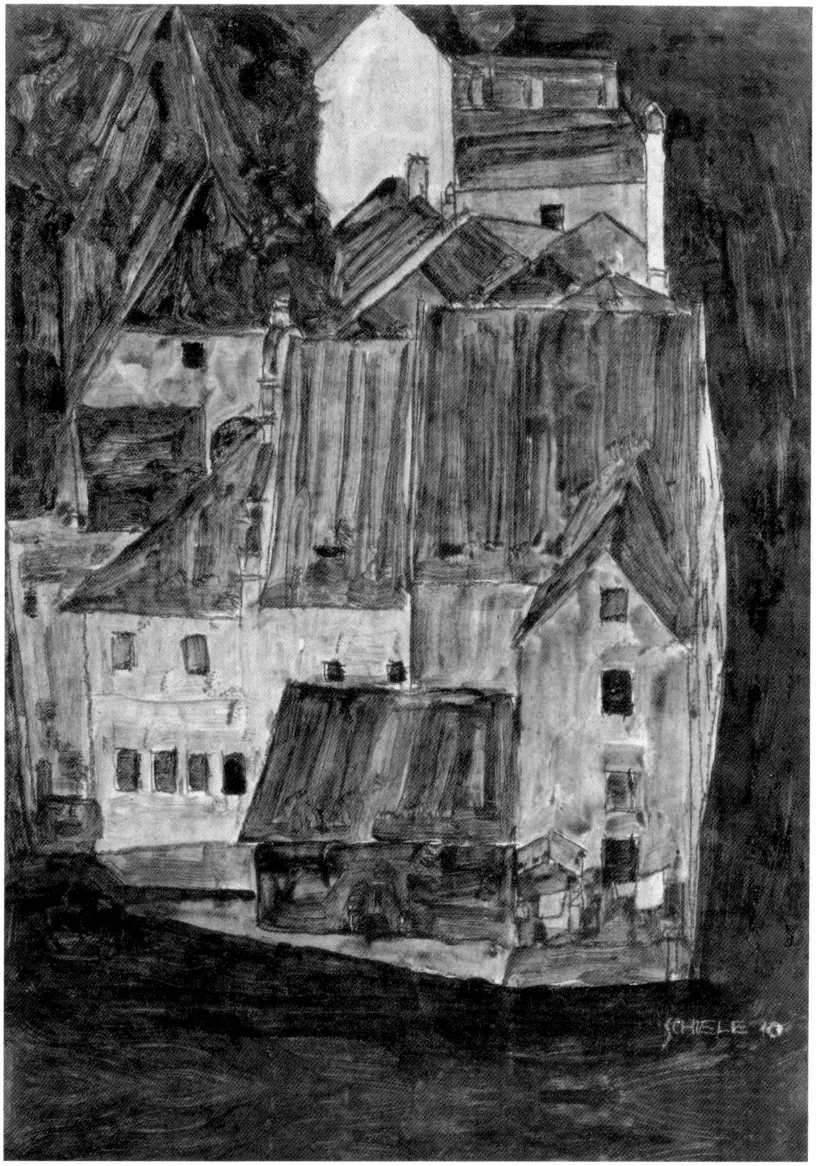

Schiele to apply the title "Dead City" to this work as well. The composition contains only a few more brilliant color values, such as the narrow blue-green outline around the tall gable wall towards the top and the carmine red fleck of a piece of laundry next to it. The sonorous colors of the roofs with their mysteriously shimmering light reflections give the impression that the paint is in perpetual motion.

At the end of August, Schiele wrote to Arthur Roessler that until that point he had kept this picture in particular to himself, and that he thought it was the "most earnest in color". At any rate, with it the young artist had succeeded in producing one of his most compelling phantasmagorical visions.

Autumn Trees I 1911

L 189 K 218
Oil on canvas, 79.5 x 80 cm
Signed and dated lower right
Sammlung Dichand, Vienna

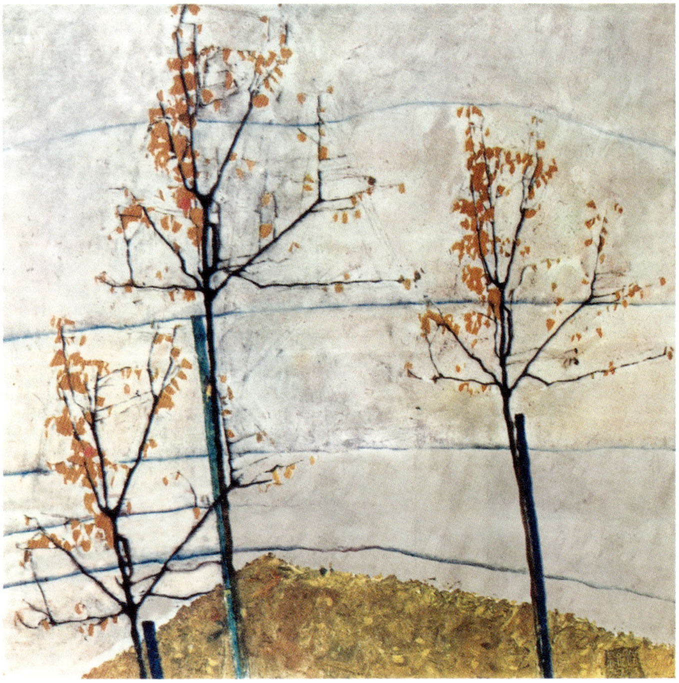

Three trees jut into the sky at an oblique angle to the left. The triangle of ground tends in the same direction. Nevertheless, the potentially unbalancing effect of the diagonal described by tree trunks and posts is counteracted by the rightward-projecting tree limbs and the "etherial lines" in the sky. These blue and pink lines follow a course similar to that of the contours in drawings from the same stylistic period. This undulation is also found, to a lesser degree, in the black branches standing in stark contrast to the whitish-gray sky. Only a few turned leaves still cling to them; most have fallen. The very similar color used for all the branches and leaves of the three trees is strange, but even stranger is the almost identical drawing of the three crowns. This is surely no coincidence. Perhaps Schiele wished to suggest that differences ultimately cease to be important, that everything is the same in the end.

The many and diverse colors in the picture – the ocher of the leaves and ground, the dark blue and blue-green of the tree props, the blue and delicate carmine red lines running through the sky, and the blackish and pink glazes used to characterize the sky in a quite unnaturalistic way – do not clash with one another. Although it is hard to believe, they actually engender a magical color harmony, which raises the evocation of demise and decay to a new level of meaning.

The old reproduction (p. 85) conveys a sense, if no more, of the features described. I was able to view the original several times at its former owner's residence in the 1950s. Sadly, however, the picture is now no longer in its original state, especially as regards the sky. The erstwhile restorer of the Österreichische Galerie, a certain Herr Kainz, removed almost all of the pinks and most of the marvellously

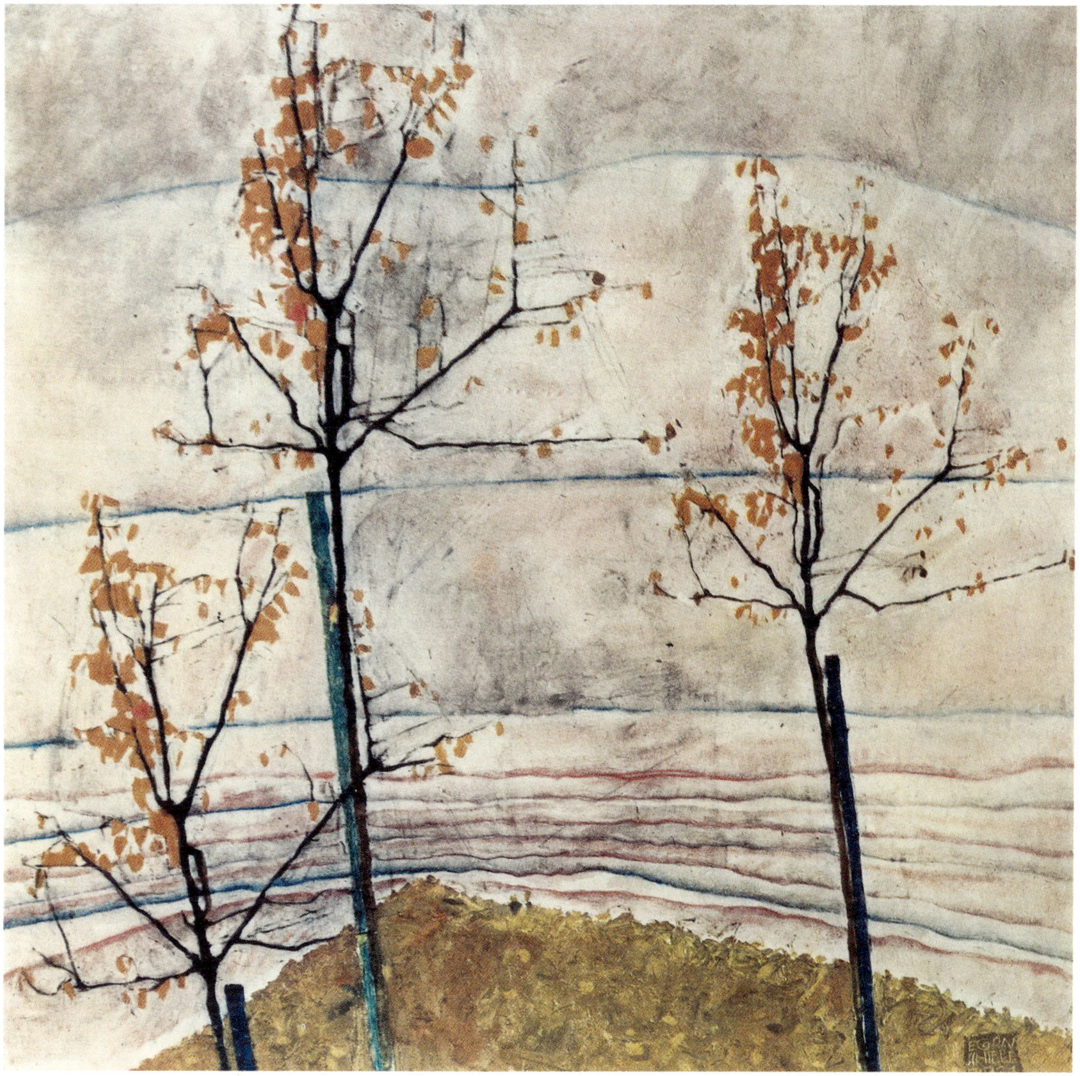

deployed areas of blackish glaze from the sky, which occupies the largest part of the picture – in the entirely erroneous assumption that they were by another hand! In fact, Schiele employed these delicate color values not only to lend the sky unusual charm but to articulate it in terms of space, the separate passages between the colored lines evoking different volumes. Today almost nothing of this effect remains visible. Now, as mentioned, the sky appears whitish-gray, and on the whole flat and empty. Only the surviving, sensitively brushed lines of color attest to the composition's former beauty.

"Landscape with Ravens" 1911

L 191 K 216
Oil on canvas, 95.8 x 89 cm
Signed and dated lower right
Leopold Museum, Vienna, inv. no.: LM 527

A landscape surrounded by a fence – the fence black, the landscape in dark autumnal colors, to which the bright sky provides a sharp contrast. Where the brushwork in the sky opens up, the black of the first paint layer, cut with a white glaze, shines through. At the right edge this black appears unbroken in the form of a band extending from the top to the middle. This band has a formal purpose to play. It has the effect of a wall, a compositional *repoussoir* which makes the fence, its distance already indicated by its reduced scale, appear even farther away.[1]

This black band has another function as well. It is one of several formal counterweights to near symmetry of the composition (the light reddish-brown irregular rectangle below, the small tree, the laundry pole behind it, the cabin on the hill, and the section of the fence cut off by the upper picture edge). Other counterbalancing elements are the unequal distance of the fence at left and right, the fence end slightly shifted to the left at the very top, and the hill in the middle ground, which seems to slope more steeply on the left. This is formally balanced by the opposing diagonal of the upper edge of the light reddish-brown area mentioned, and the fence descending at a gentler angle to the left. These multifarious counterpoints serve to lend dynamics to the rather symmetrical overall configuration.

We see an autumnal landscape in warm hues, a young tree to which only a few leaves and a single fruit still cling, a crooked cabin with an even more precarious framework in front, a bordering black fence, and a cold sky with flying ravens, whose harsh cries one can almost hear. In surroundings like these, the laundry poles metamorphose into *grave crosses.*[2] The high vantage point is further augmented by an area behind the hill that appears to rise up and that culminates, with the fence, in a point: a landscape envisioned as a cathedral. In formal terms, too, this view with every part given equal weight embodies something fundamentally new: the conventional landscape scheme of foreground, middle ground and background has been abandoned.[3] With this painting Schiele also succeeded in conveying a picture of the world. The demise and decay of the autumn season become a parable on transitoriness.

1 This band was omitted in the reproductions both in Otto Kallir's catalogues raisonnés of 1930 and 1966, and in Jane Kallir's catalogue raisonné of 1990 – in the erroneous view that Schiele did not finish the picture. Actually, when affixing the canvas to the stretchers, he purposely reduced the painted area at the right and bottom, but left visible the black band extending from center right to top on account of its pictorial significance. He also very precisely reduced the size of the irregular brownish rectangle at the bottom, to the left of the tree trunk, which actually extended farther down the canvas.

2 This reference is also found in Hans Sedlmayr, *Verlust der Mitte,* Salzburg, 1948 – if coupled with a disparaging judgement that quite misses the point.

3 Oskar Kokoschka's approach to landscape, in contrast, remained conventional from his early to late phases – despite the innovative palette and heavy impasto paint application of the works prior to 1925. The division of his landscapes into foreground, middle ground and background remained beholding to centuries-long tradition and practice.

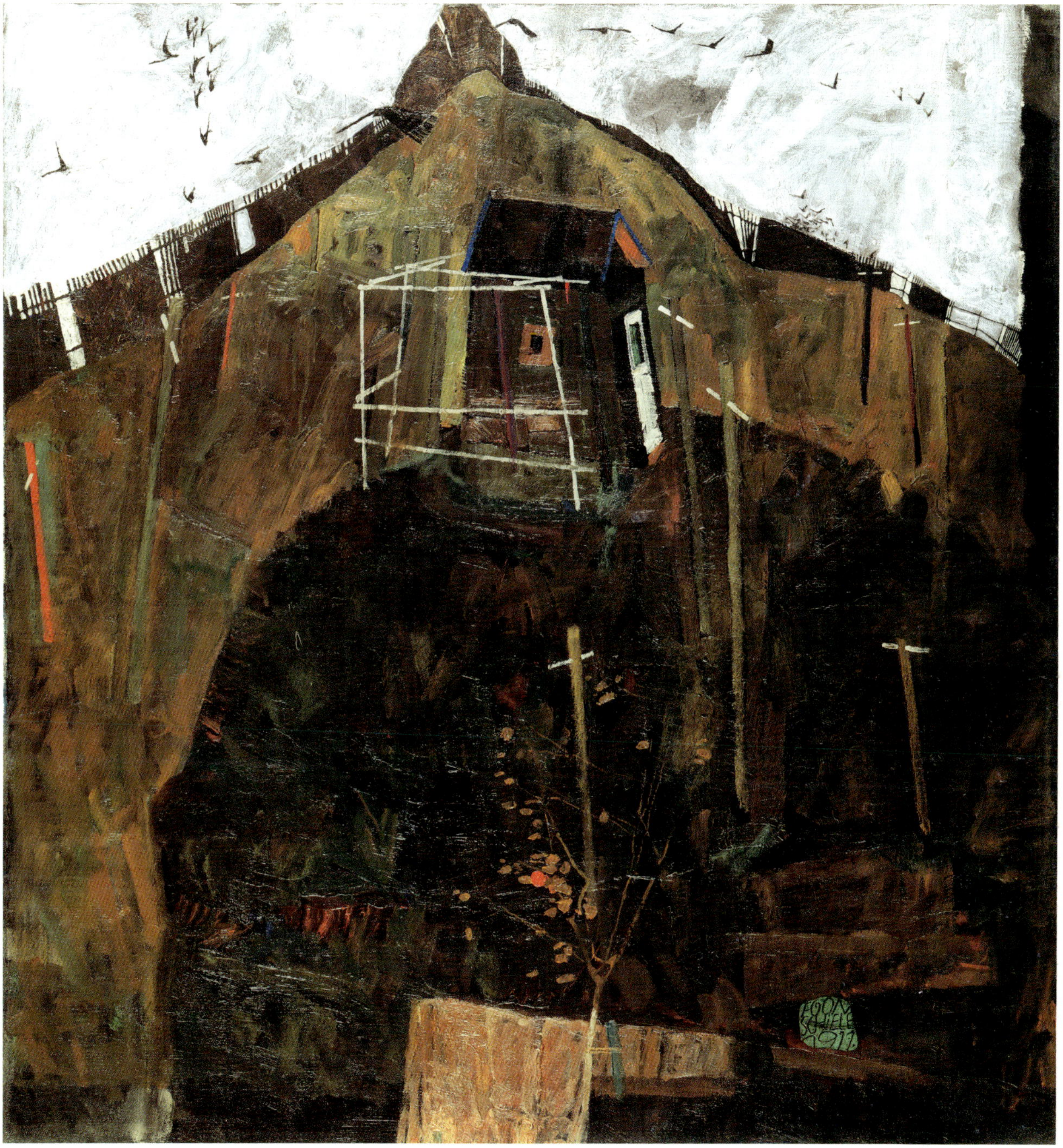
EGON SCHIELE 1911

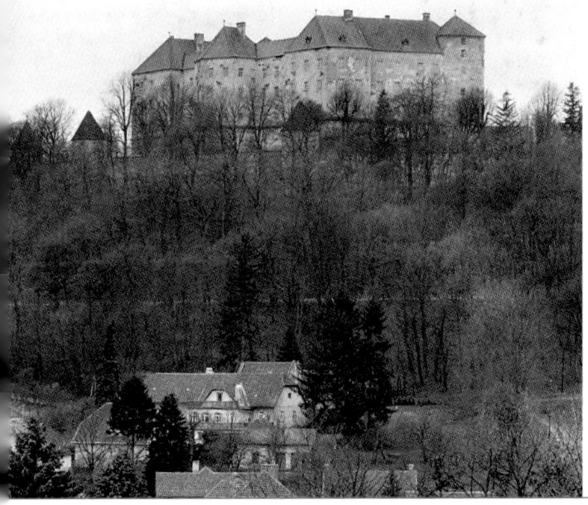

Neulengbach Castle

Neulengbach Castle 1912

K 1200
Sketch in pencil and opaque white on paper, 48.2 x 31.8 cm
Signed and dated lower left
Museum der Moderne – Rupertinum, Salzburg, inv. no.: 1197

Although this is only a sketch, Schiele has lent the depiction of Neulengbach Castle compositional unity by means of oblique lines of clouds above and an undulating ground line below. The small houses sketched in perspective beyond this demarcation and the opposing perspective lines of the castle roof convey the impression that the castle stands higher up the hill – without recourse to a depiction of the actual rising terrain.

Like the depiction of the house with belfry in Knappenberg of the same year (K 1203, p. 105), the present sketch from Neulengbach is one of the few examples in which Schiele depicted motifs from a low vantage point rather, as was much more frequent, from some point high above, looking down.

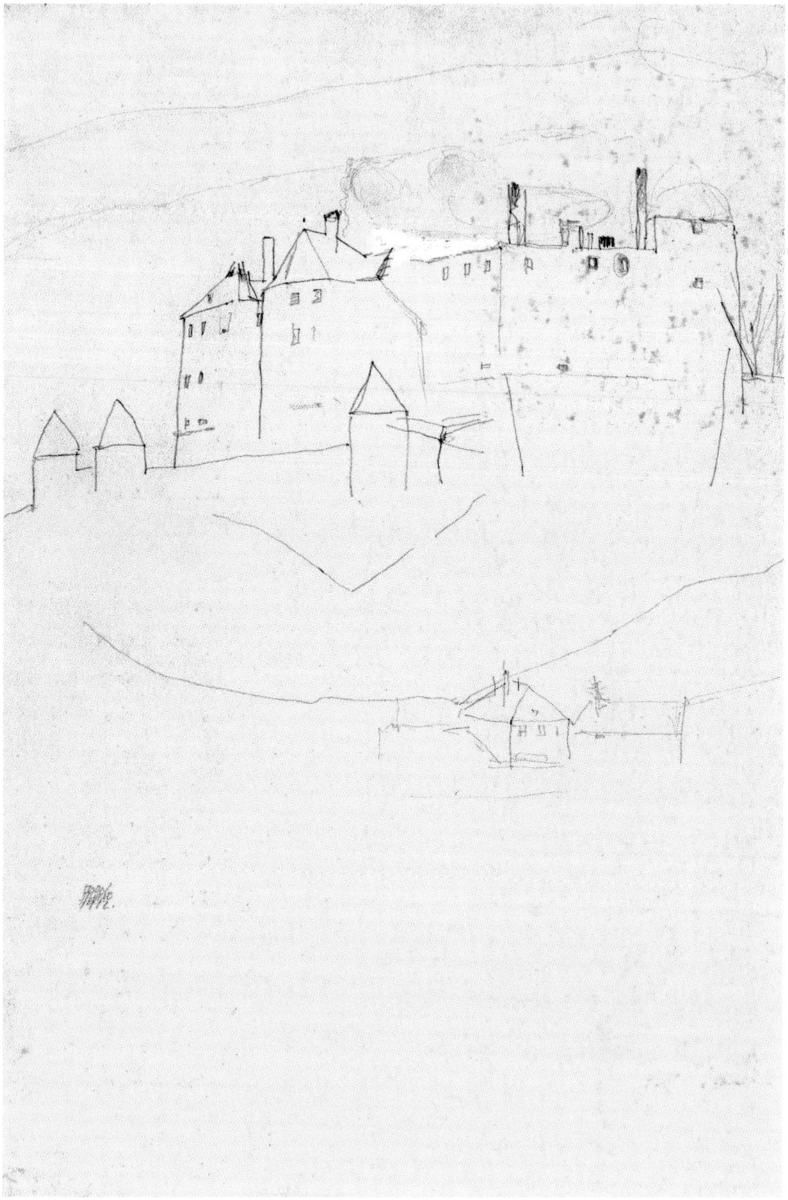

Small Tree in Late Autumn 1911

L 199 K 222
Oil on wood, 42 x 33.5 cm
Signed and dated lower right
Leopold Museum, Vienna, inv. no.: LM 459

A hilltop summarily rendered as a regular arc segment forms a counterpart to the similarly contoured treetop, whose bare branches also show analogous color gradations. On the other hand, its windblown silhouette stands in the strongest possible contrast to the quiet round of the hill.

The tree's crown, the largely blue middle section of its trunk, and the large branch protruding to the right, are isolated from the ground by the limed trunk, further reinforcing the contrast. In terms of color, too, the olive brown cut with reddish-brown in the clumps of dry grass is contrasted to the blue values of the middle trunk. The light pearl-gray sky forms a background for what seems to be the tree's hopeless struggle with the elements. It is being whipped by a storm wind, as indicated by the scudding clouds. The trunk is cruelly bent, and its natural growth has already been brought to a halt at two points. At the upper one, the end of the trunk is thickened; it recalls a human head, and the thin protruding branches seem like wildly gesticulating arms. The main branch extending to the right and below evokes a leg, and the white, limed trunk the second leg.

The tree has become an allegory for human fate. Its configuration is more anthropomorphic than most other depictions of trees in the Expressionism of the time. One inadvertantly gains the impression of a forest spirit, wildly dancing. Yet basically the picture is a dramatic allegory of human loneliness and helplessness in the face of hostile forces: a Dance of Death of a new kind.

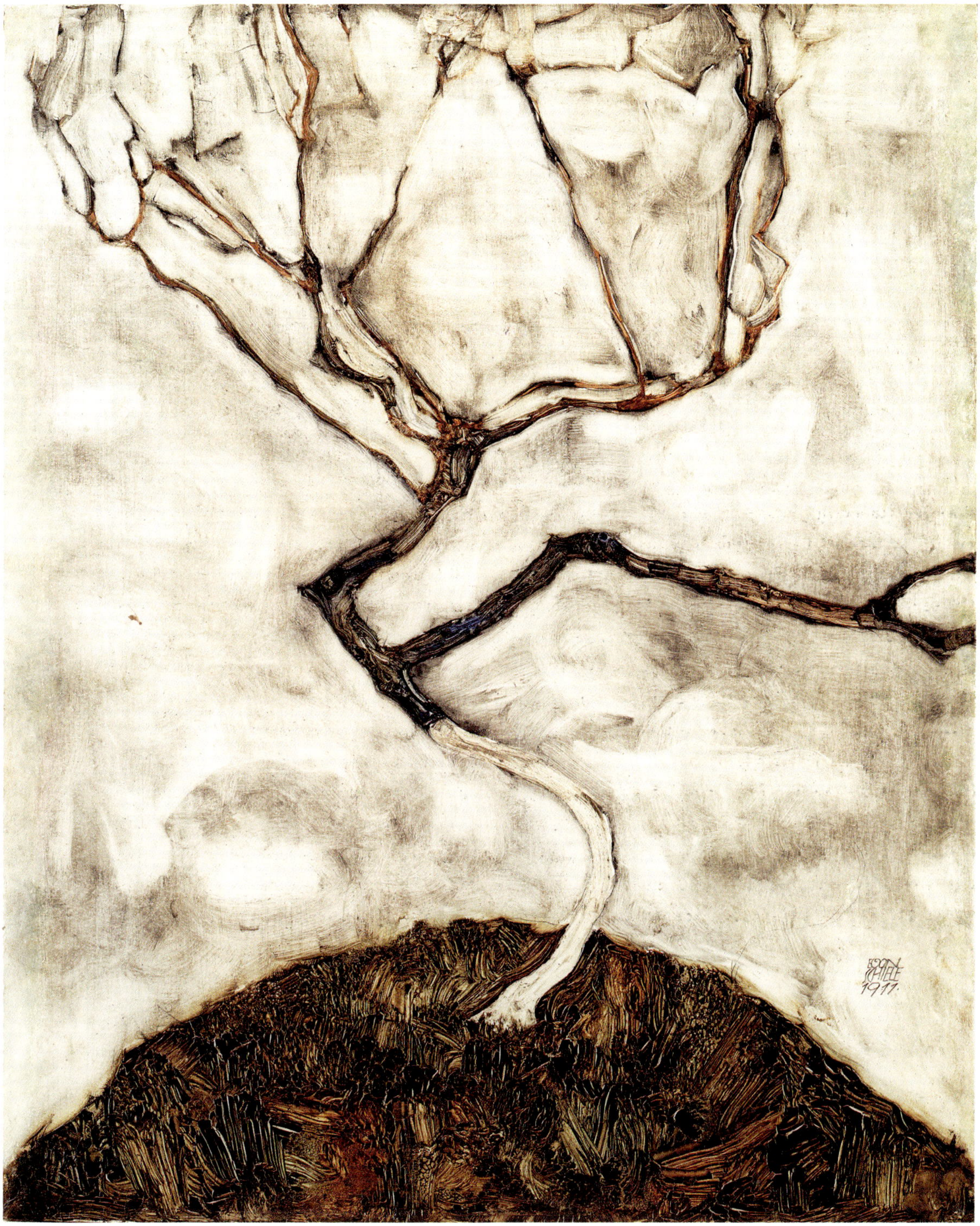
EGON
SCHIELE
1911.

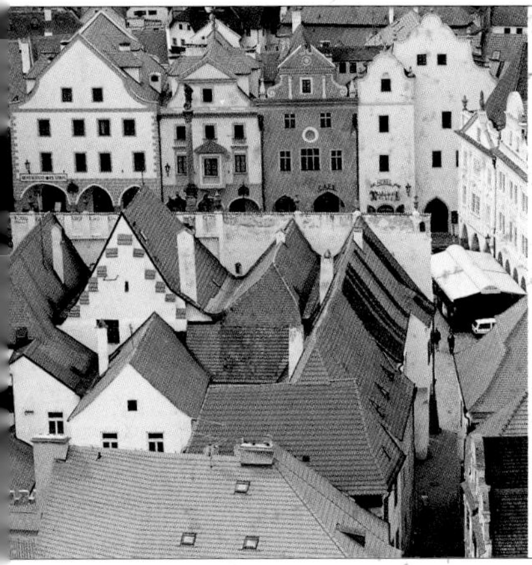

View across Roofs to Ringplatz Façades in Krumau ("Dead City" V) 1912

L 206 K 244
Oil on wood, 36.7 x 29.5 cm
Signed and dated lower right
Whereabouts unknown

Standing on the platform on Krumau Castle Hill, Schiele had this view over the roofs of the town to the houses on Ringplatz. Yet he has condensed the many tiers of roofs and walls between the Moldau and the former town hall into a somewhat amorphous, dark mass, and above its gable on Ringplatz, depicted four eerily illuminated façades. To reinforce the contrast, Schiele set them against an area of black. Two narrow lanes lead from Ringplatz to the bank of the Moldau. The one on the left does not exist in reality – it was apparently added as a compositional counterweight to the other. This right-hand lane was intended to represent Rathausgasse (Radnicí ulice), yet in contrast to its actual appearance, it remains very narrow even in its lower section, not growing wider until it reaches Bader Bridge over the Moldau. All in all, this is yet another of the ghostly nocturnal views Schiele produced in 1912.

View across Ringplatz in Krumau

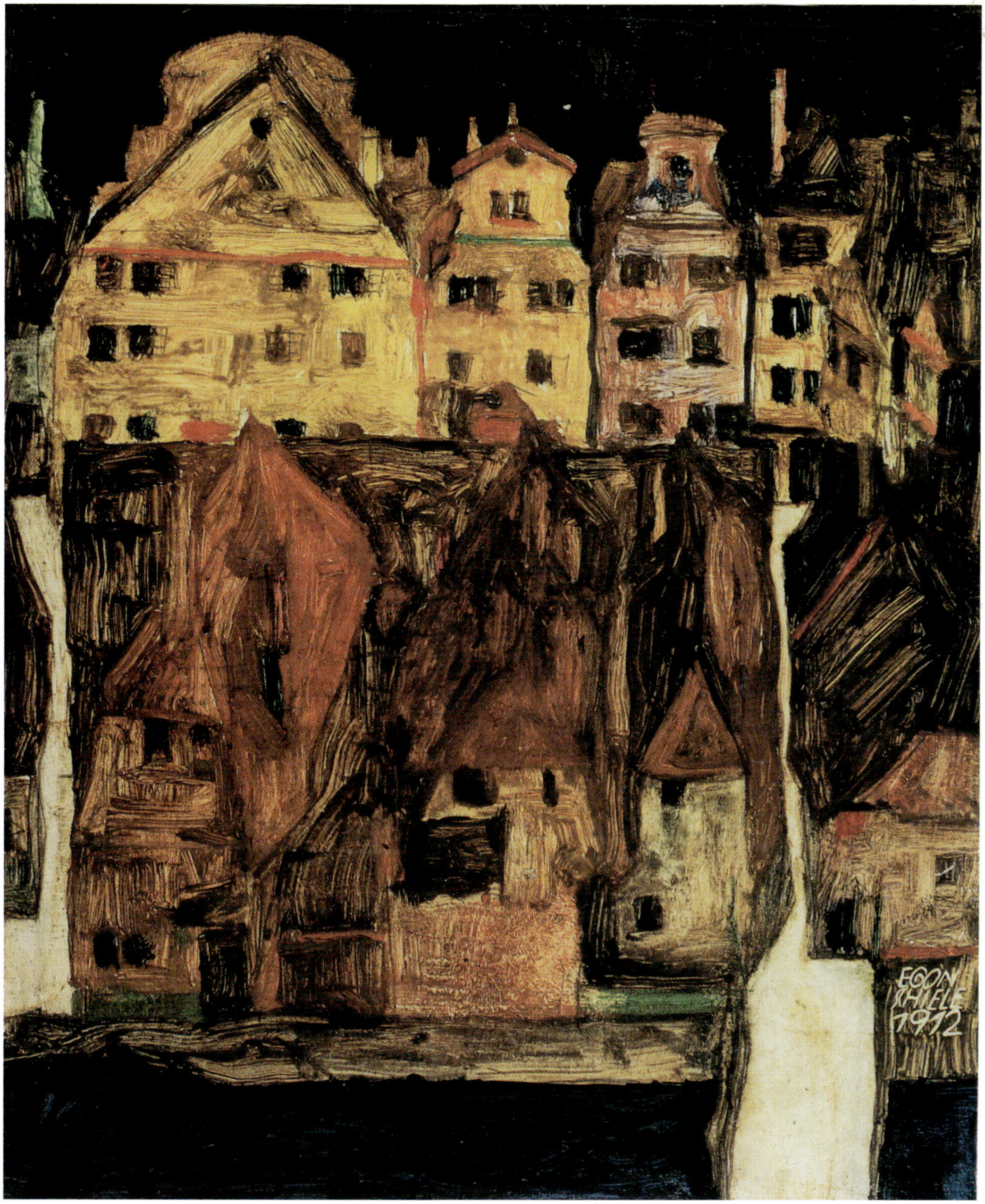
EGON
SCHIELE
1912

"The Old City" I (also known as "Dead City" IV) 1912

L 205 K 245
Oil on wood, 42.5 x 34 cm
Signed and dated lower left
Private collection

The motif here is an excerpt from the view of Krumau Schiele seldom used, but had selected the previous year for "Krumau at Night" (L 177/K 209, p. 77). Yet here everything appears simplified, even coarsened. This picture is painted in pure oils, whereas for the aesthetically more sensitive cityscapes of 1911, Schiele chose a combination of gouache and oils.

The 1912 picture, too, is dominated by the bare rear wall of the apothecary house, at 16 Ringplatz, but now rendered in a lighter gradation. Behind this, in contrast to the black night sky in the 1911 depiction, is a lighter plane (probably intended to represent Ringplatz) and above it, instead of the actually existing houses, only a textured surface painted with a dry brush in dark brown. A similar technique is used for the silhouetted house gables next to the apothecary and the amorphous mass of roofs in the lower area of the picture. These are only occasionally interrupted by lighter passages, such as a chimney at the left and the gable of the house at 49 Breite Gasse, cut off by the edge of the picture at the right. The impressive effect conveyed by this gable in the 1911 painting is entirely lacking here. None of the works of 1912 were actually painted in Krumau, but in Vienna, based on earlier sketches.

It was in quite different works that Schiele's artistic development became apparent. These include "Grieving Woman" (L 201/K 224), "Self-Portrait with Bent Head" (L 202/K 228), "The Hermits" (L 203/K 229), "Self-Portrait with Bare Shoulder" (L 209/K 227), "Cardinal and Nun" (L 210/K 232), the self-portrait and portrait of Wally painted as companion-pieces (L 211/K 233, L 212/K 234), and "Autumn Tree in Turbulent Air" (L 221/K 239, p. 103).

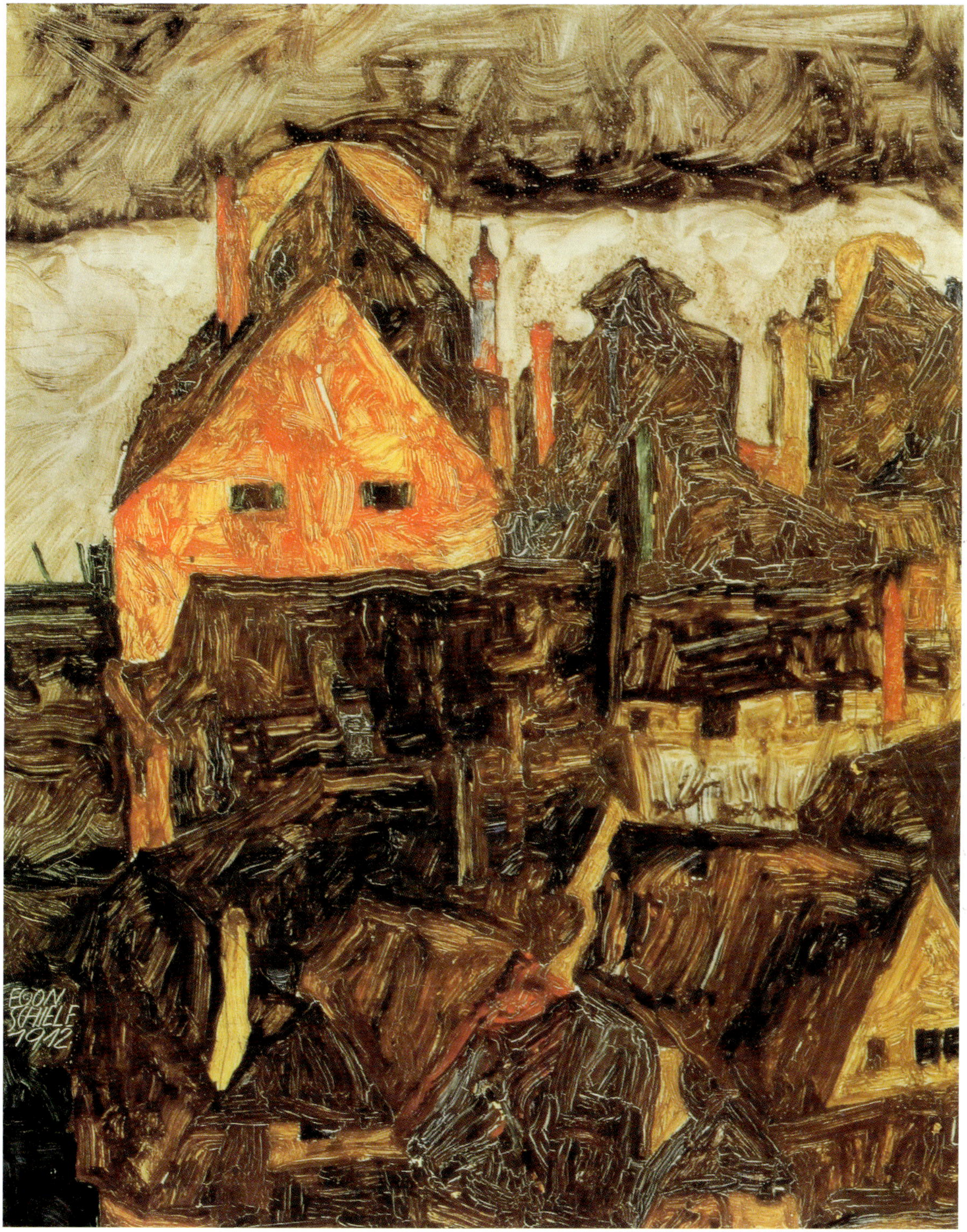
EGON
SCHIELE
1912

Landscape with Red Sky c. 1911

L 190 K 217
Oil on canvas, 69.5 x 82.8 cm
Unsigned, undated
Kunsthaus Zug, Sammlung Kamm, inv. no.: K. G 28

Despite the fact that nothing in this painting suggests the spring season, Otto Kallir gave it the title "Spring Landscape with Red Sky" (which was subsequently accepted without demur by his granddaughter, Jane, and other authors).

Schiele painted the picture over another, which was evidently in the early stages. This is indicated by the numerous pentimenti that show through the final paint layer and tend to disturb, or at least blur, the depiction. Judging by its style this work was probably executed in the final months of 1911. The special character of the lines running through the sky speak for this dating, as does the sonorous coloration of the ground area that occupies the larger part of the picture. The predominant dark hues have been enlivened by two tree props in a bright, luminous emerald green. This contrast is much more successfully handled than that introduced by the three rather awkward looking blue poles on the horizon.

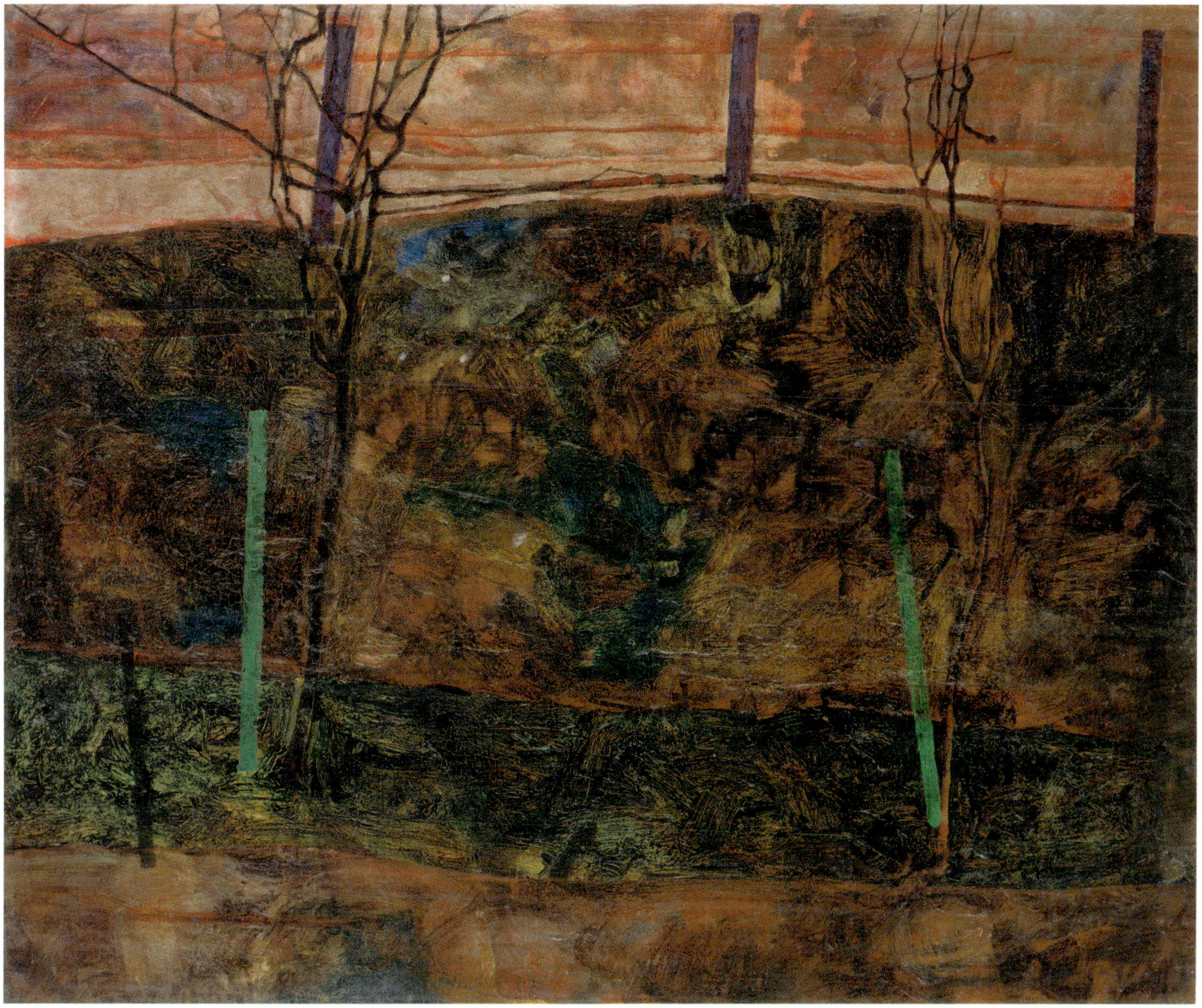

"Bare Trees" 1912

L 217 K 242
Oil and soft pencil on canvas, 80.3 x 80.5 cm
Signed and dated upper right
Kunsthaus Zug, Sammlung Kamm, inv. no.: K.G 30

Bare trees standing on bare ground – a subject Schiele repeatedly addressed and treated as an allegory of life. The fragile branches and slender, crooked trunks appear absolutely helpless, as if they would fall were it not for the props. The sky is gray. A few brighter lights and the two sunlike configurations that appear on the horizon – likewise gray, but somewhat lighter in tone – do not mitigate the sense of desolation but rather amplify it by the impression of unreality they convey.

The character of the textures in the sky shows a certain affinity with the drawing of the branches. On the other hand, the gestural brushwork of the blue, reddish and ocher flecks lends little vitality to the largely unarticulated ground, these color contrasts tending rather to reinforce its appearance of sterility.

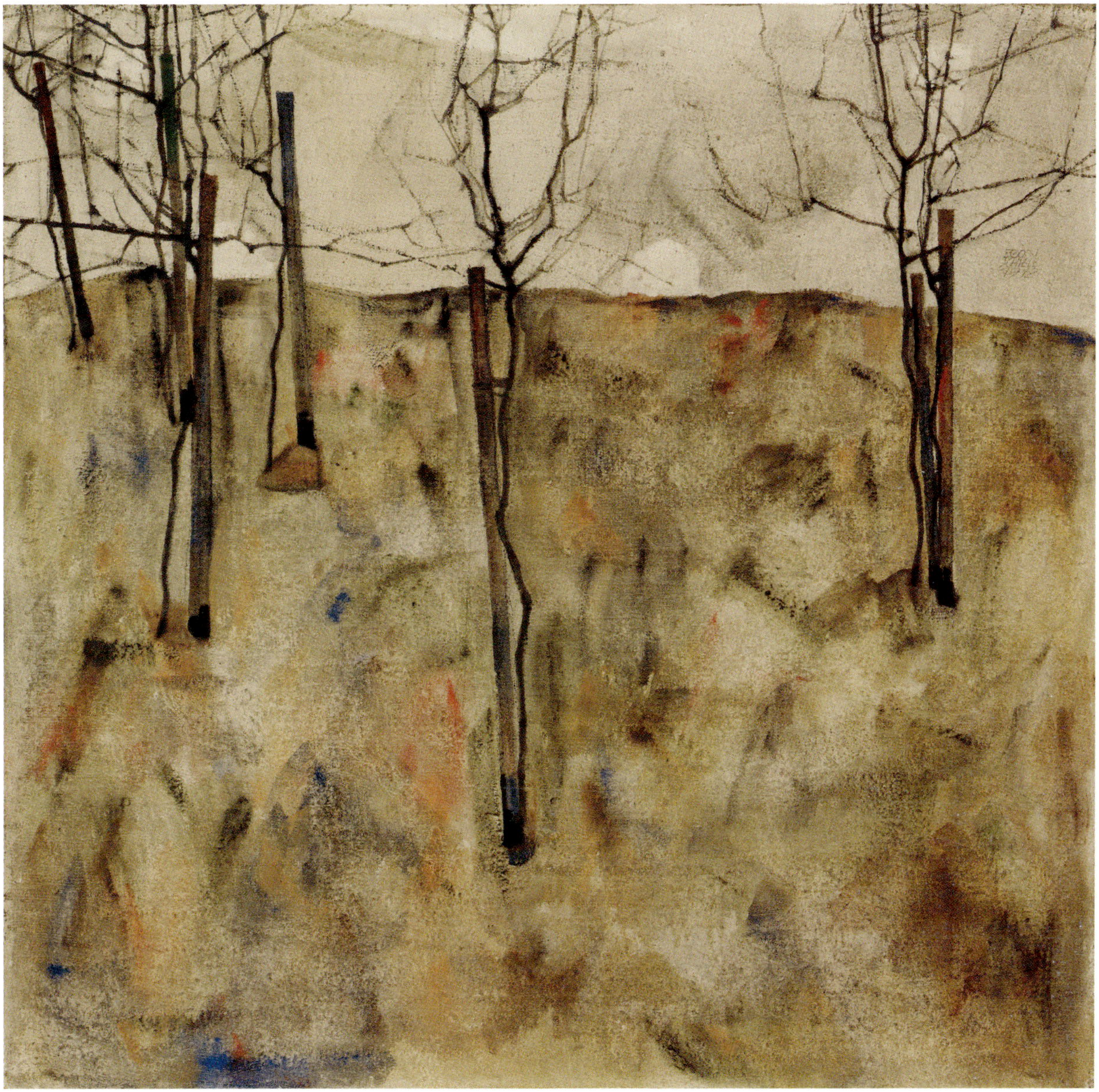

"Calvary" 1912

L 215 K 240
Opaque colors, oil and soft pencil on canvas, 81.7 x 80 cm
Signed and dated lower right
Leopold Museum, Vienna, inv. no.: LM 480

A rising sun is depicted in only two of Schiele's paintings. One is "Sun and Autumn Trees" (L 220/K 236), which the artist designated "Sunrise", among other titles. The other is likely "Landscape with Two Trees" (L 231/K 264), for which we have no Schiele title but whose atmosphere definitely suggests a sunrise. Otherwise this artist who was much more interested in depicting things coming to an end – whether a certain day or the late autumn season – concentrated almost exclusively on the mood evoked by the sun in the process of setting or thereafter.

Such is the case here, too. The meadows appear illuminated by the light of sunset, rendered in predominantly warm gradations of subsiding colors. Only a little blue has been added as a complementary color. A similar blue is employed particularly in the two lowest bands of cloud, where it is accented by a cool red. In sum, Schiele has contrasted the warm-hued foreground with the sky rendered in cool tones. In between, lies a zone of almost blinding white. Set against this are varicolored tree props with small leafless trees, a small station of the cross shrine, and above all, three crosses. Standing with bodies dangling from them in front of a hill evidently meant to signify Golgotha, these ancient symbols of Calvary appear on the verge of toppling, as if no one noticed or cared for them any more. The tree closest to them seems about to collapse. The many little trees with their props, which grow ever more oblique to the left, where they disappear behind a hill, all contribute greatly to the mood of demise.

Only in pictures of this period did Schiele depict the ground, among other things, in an entirely unnaturalistic way. A similar treatment is found, for instance, in "Winter Trees" (L 216/K 241), "Bare Trees" (L 217/K 242, p. 99) and "Autumn Sun" (L 220/K 236).

Heinrich Benesch was an avid Schiele collector who repeatedly visited the artist's studio. As his son, a later director of the Albertina, informed me, Benesch selected precisely the present "Calvary" from among the above mentioned stylistically related works. Viewed objectively it is indeed the most significant. Even regardless of what has been called its 'painterly painting', the compositional articulation here appears more successful than in the others.

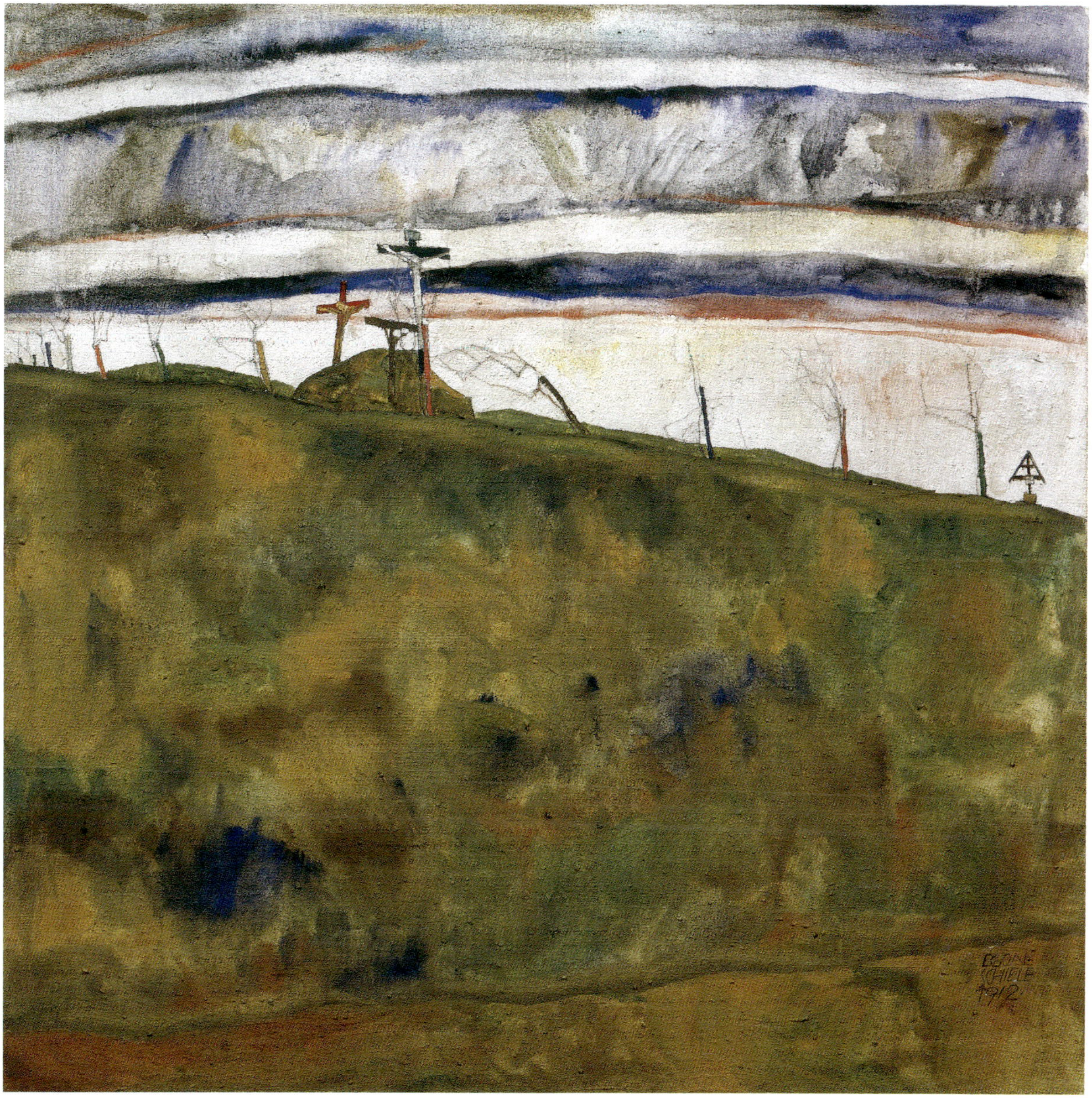
EGON
SCHIELE
1912

Autumn Tree in Turbulent Air (also known as "Autumn Tree" II and "Winter Tree") 1912

L 221 K 239
Oil and soft pencil on canvas, 80 x 80.5 cm
Signed and dated center right
Leopold Museum, Vienna, inv. no.: LM 449

The present picture might initially strike many a viewer as an abstract composition. This impression results from the treatment of the cloud formations in the background (which are perhaps not immediately recognizable as such) and the larger and smaller branches of a tree crown whose connection with the ground, the trunk, may not at first be evident. In fact, Schiele left this limed tree trunk uncolored in order to isolate its branches and the distant chain of hills and ground for the sake of chiaroscuro and color composition (and this even more strongly than in "Small Tree in Late Autumn", [L 199/K 222, p. 91]). The result is a striking formal juxtaposition.

The longer one views the painting, however, the more concrete it appears. With the irregularly shaped branches, Schiele attempted to evoke various states of life. The storm bends the upper main branches like whips, and causes the thin twigs that emerge from the slender branch protruding upwards at the upper left flutter like flags in the wind. Other branches have been crippled in the course of their struggle to survive, those dangling powerlessly at the right having apparently succumbed.

The crest of the hill above the light reddish-ocher of the plowed soil is clearly contrasted to it by means of bluish-black gradations, which also cause it to visually recede into the distance.

Neither earlier nor later did Schiele ever render a sky with such sensitivity, with a comparable richness of gray tones and carefully placed nuances. The outmost tree leaves are surrounded by the lightest lights, as if by aureoles. This luminosity – known colloquially as "snow lights" – frequently appears in the sky in this region on windy winter days and is a sign of an imminent blizzard. Yet even this phenomenon, like many elements in the picture, is not depicted in an entirely naturalistic way. Nevertheless, Schiele has very convincingly evoked a natural process here – the agitated unquiet air of a day in early winter. Beyond this he managed to create an allegory of an exposed, jeopardized existence, a symbol of life in general.

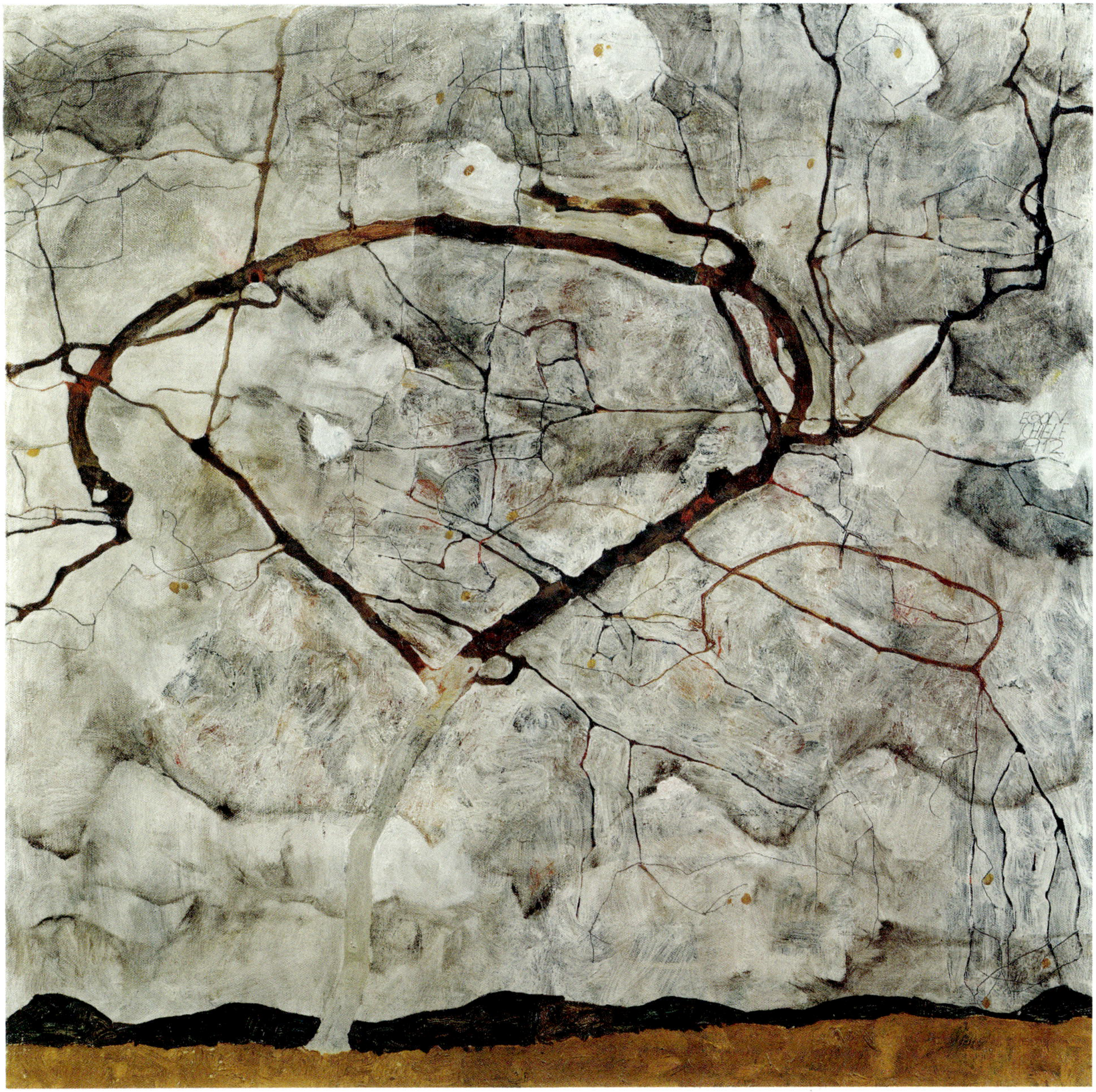
EGON
SCHIELE
1912.

House with Bell Tower 1912

K 1203
Hard and soft pencil, watercolor and opaque colors on paper, 48.2 x 32 cm
Signed and dated lower right
Professor Dr. Rudolf Leopold, Vienna

Very soon after his release from prison on 6 May 1912, Schiele undertook short trips in order to recover from his twenty-four-day sentence. He paid a visit to one of his collectors, Carl Reininghaus, in his country house in Knappenberg on the Rax. It was an old house on a hill, surrounded by a wooden fence. Schiele depicted it from a low vantage point, in perspective foreshortening, with all of its charming irregularities. He rendered the two lower windows in the gable side in blue – probably to create a contrast with the brownish-red on the chimney. He also added three small colored rectangles, apparently in order to heighten the romantic impression. Otherwise the wall surface, framed by the roof eaves and small hipped roof, is largely empty. The soft pencil lines characterizing the dilapidated wooden fence likewise reflect a superb sensibility.

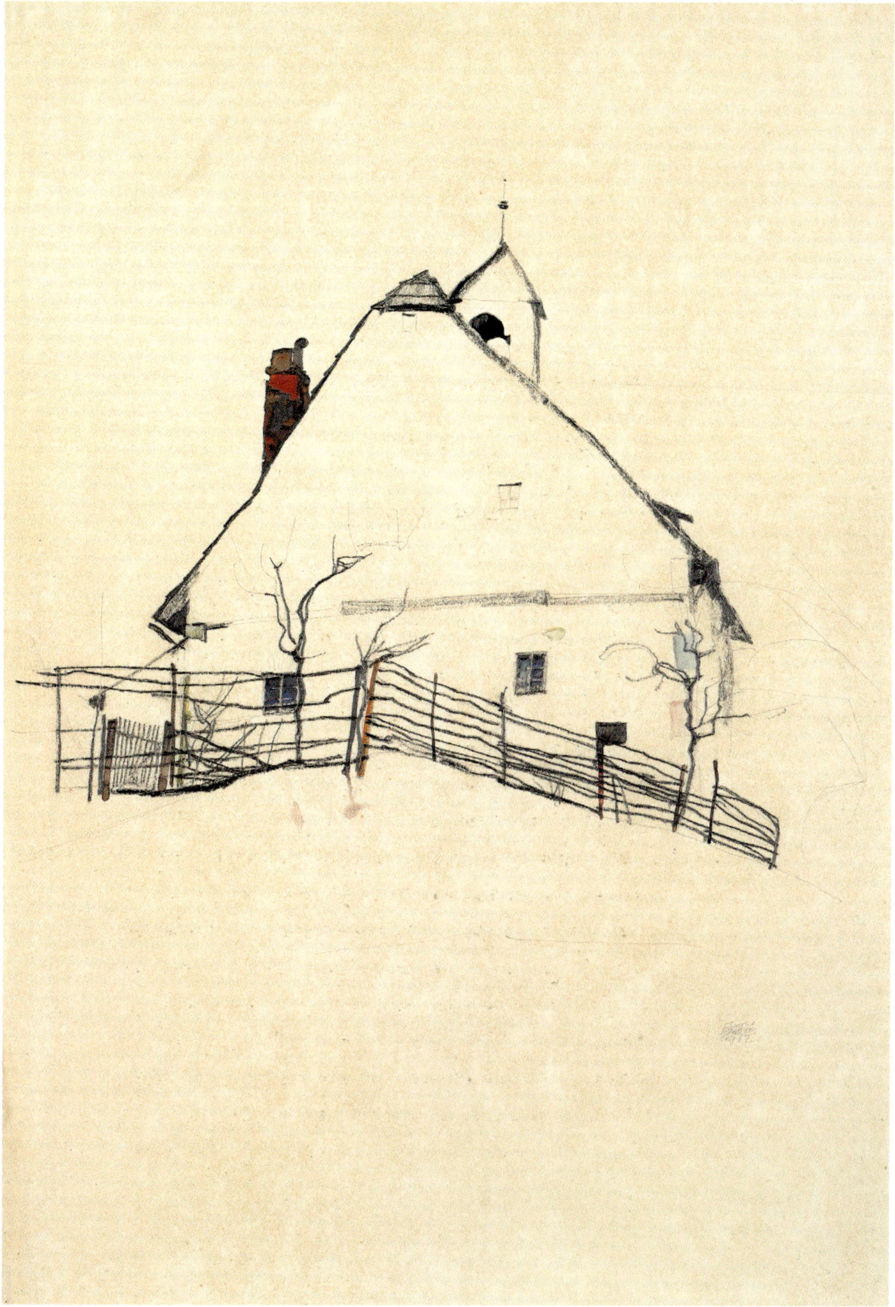

Little Tree (Chestnut Tree at Lake Constance) 1912

K 1215
Pencil, watercolor and opaque colors on paper, 45.8 x 29.5 cm
Signed and dated lower left
Private collection

The lake, the mountain chain rising on its far shore, and the sky are intersected by the trunk of a chestnut tree so slender that one wonders how it could ever support such a full crown.

Areas of the paper intended to represent lake and sky have been left unpainted, yet their meaning seems perfectly characterized by the vertical of the tree and the horizontal of the mountains in the background.

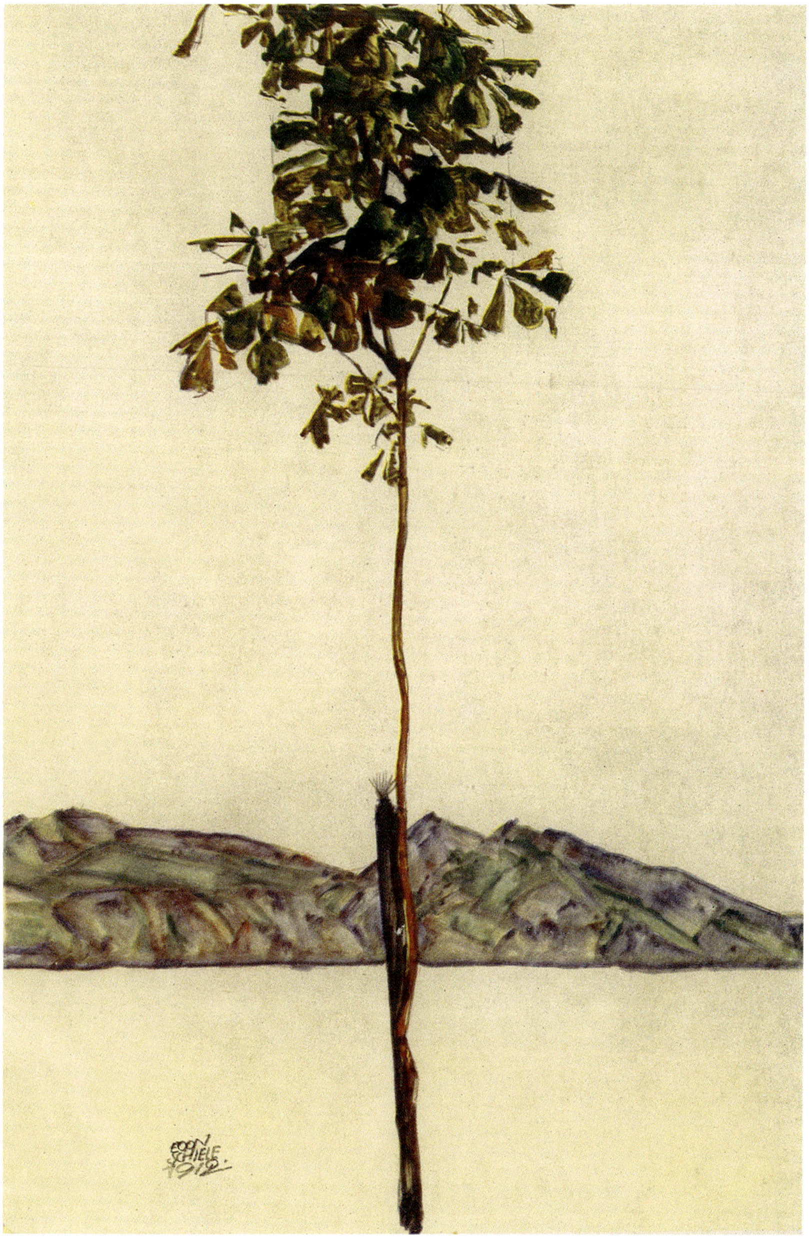
EGON SCHIELE 1912

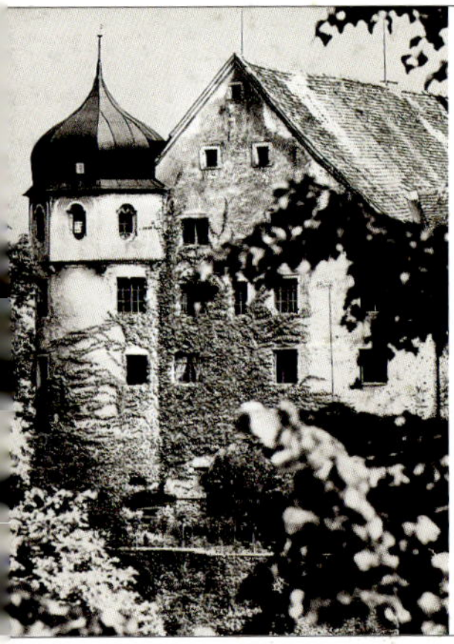

Deuring Castle, Bregenz 1912

K 1216
Pencil, watercolor and opaque colors on paper, 31.5 x 48 cm
Signed and dated center left
Leopold Museum, Vienna, inv. no.: LM 2373

Deuring Castle stands in the Upper Town of Bregenz. Schiele depicted it in August 1912 from the square in front of St. Gallus' Parish Church. At the left of the sheet is the tower with octagonal upper story which was built onto the original medieval building complex in the latter half of the seventeenth century.

The ocher walls and reddish roofs are contrasted mainly to cooler colors, various green gradations and ultramarine applied over an olive brown initial paint layer. With these vivid, energetically brushed colors, Schiele evoked the foliage that largely obscures the buildings almost in the manner of an Action painter.

Deuring Castle, Bregenz

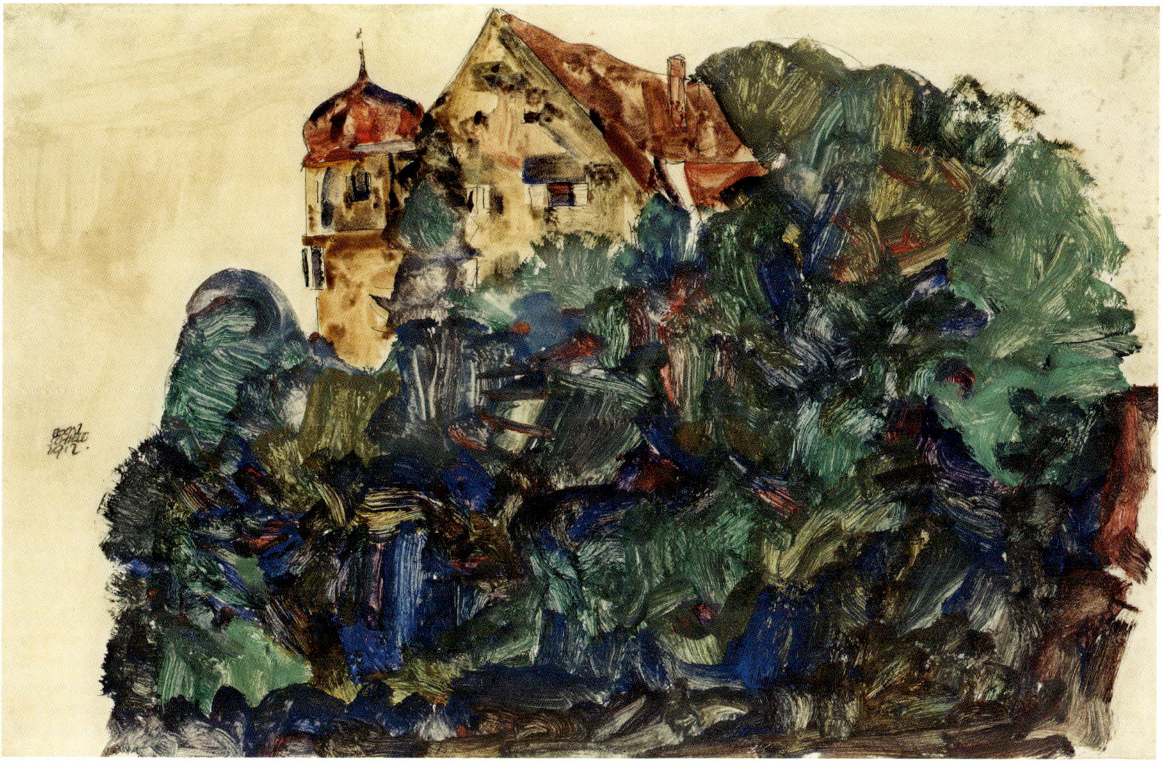

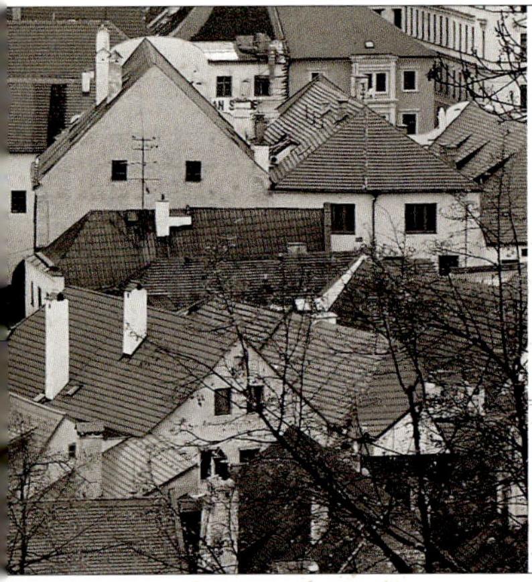

"Dead City" (also known as "Dead City" VI) 1912

L 222 K 246
Pencil, opaque colors and oil on canvas, 80 x 80 cm
Signed and dated lower right;
inscribed on the stretcher 'Tote Stadt – 1912'
Kunsthaus Zürich, inv. no.: 1964/1

Although the artist titled this work "Dead City – 1912" on the reverse, he included it in one of his painting lists as "Small Town" and in another as "Dead City".

The depiction was painted over an earlier one, which has left quite visible pentimenti in the dark roof areas, in the light gable wall and the false front, projecting above the roof. It was based on "The Old City" (L 205/K 245, p. 95), which in turn went back to the original version of this motif from the previous year (L 177/K 209, p. 77). Of the three pictures, the first is surely the most significant. (After a work on paper of 1910, it was the second depiction painted on wood to which Schiele applied the title "Dead City". In the following period he employed this designation so frequently that the 1912 picture under discussion was already the sixth to bear this title.)

The fact that in 1912 he twice repeated this motif of the apothecary house on Ringplatz in Krumau, in the second case painting over another picture, reflects the difficult mental and financial situtation in which Schiele found himself after his release from prison in early May 1912. This is also indicated by other paintings of the period, for which Schiele was forced to piece together canvases from narrow strips.

Based on a letter of the artist's to the Munich art dealer, Goltz, one may assume that "Dead City – 1912" was completed in August of that year.

View from Castle Hill, Krumau

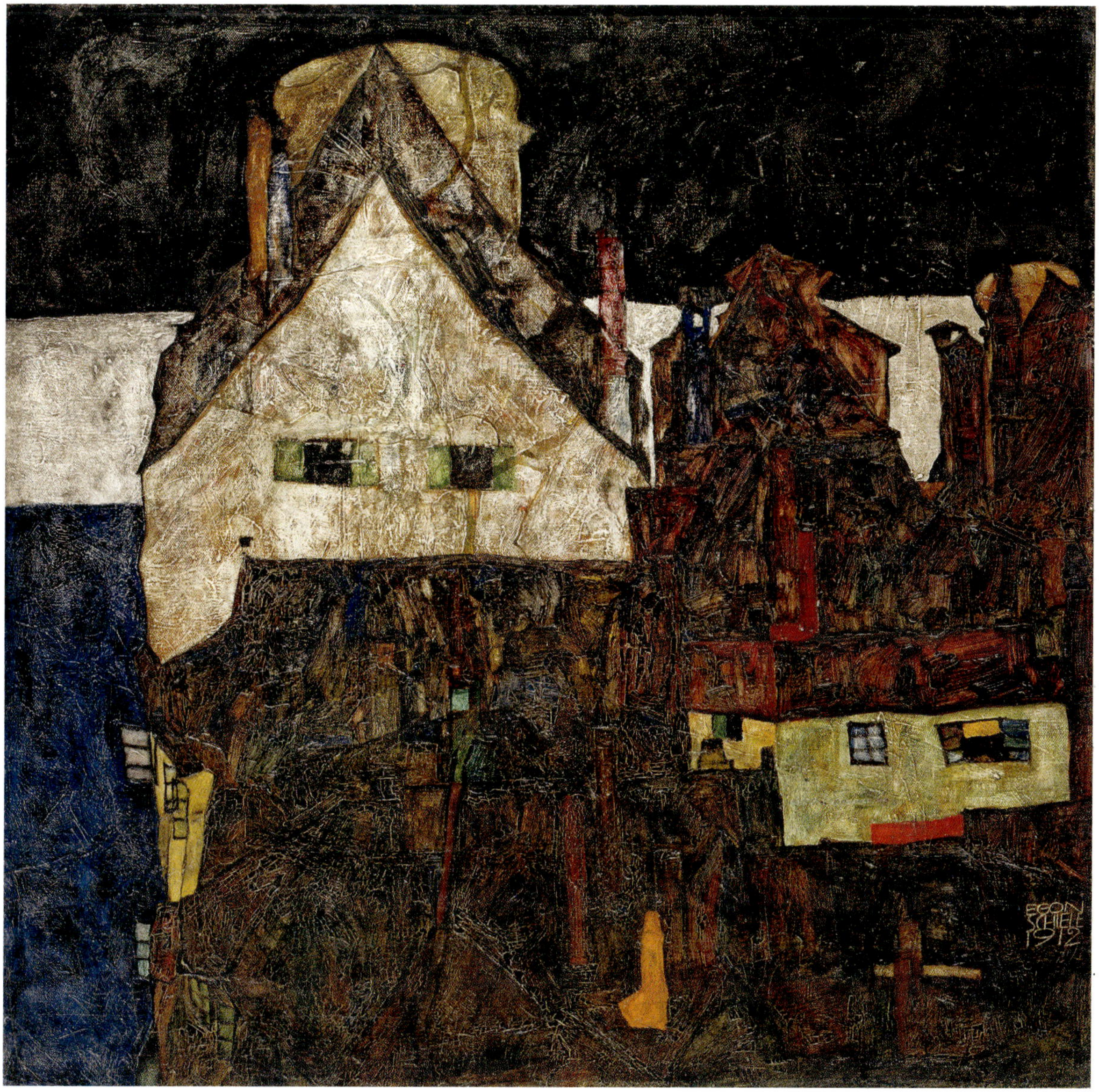
EGON
SCHIELE
1912

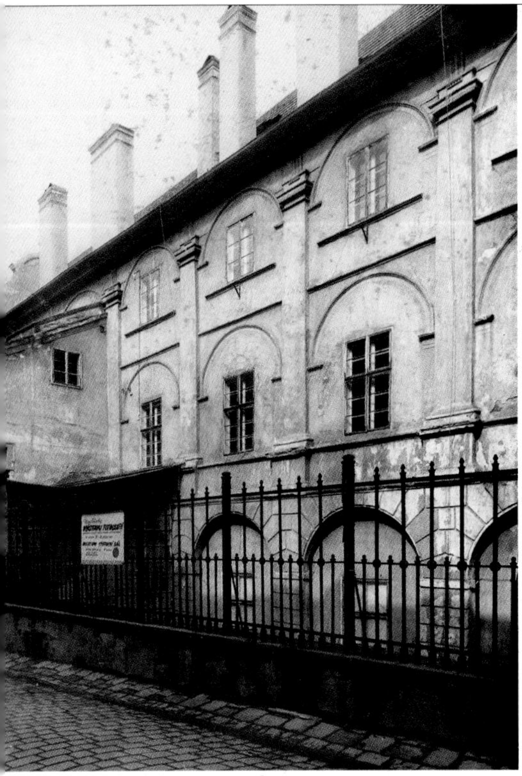

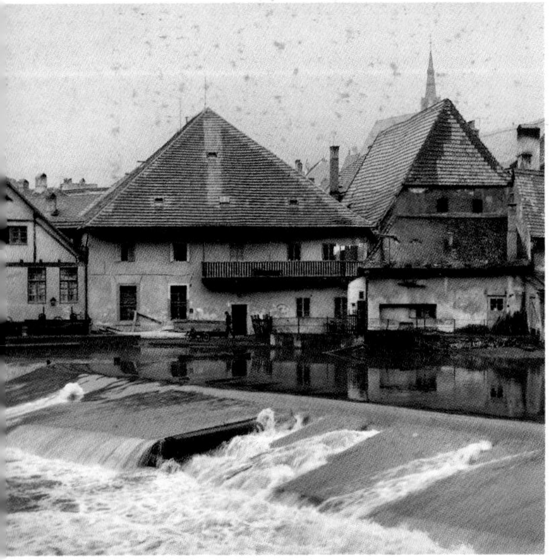

Façade of the Jesuit Seminar in Obere Gasse on the Moldau's right bank, Krumau

Former municipal mill, Krumau

"The Small City" II 1912/13

L 227 K 261
Soft pencil and oil on canvas
(two pieces sewn together), 89.9 x 90 cm
Signed and dated lower right; inscribed on the stretcher
'Die kleine Stadt' and 'Jung'
Leopold Museum, Vienna, inv. no.: LM 482

On 19 September 1912, Schiele wrote to Arthur Roessler, "Since March I have not been able to paint, and above all to think, like this until now ..." Apart from mental reasons for this block, Schiele lacked a suitable studio at the time. The 900 crowns he had received from Franz Hauer for three pictures on 19 July were apparently insufficient. So Schiele proceeded to paint a free reprise of the "Dead City" (L 222/K 246, p. 111) over another painting (which shines through in places) and was forced to use canvases stitched together of two pieces for his next three paintings ("City in Twilight" [L 226/K 260], "The Small Town" [L 227/K 261], and "The Bridge" [L 229/K 262, p. 116]). Concerning the two first-named pictures, he told Roessler in a letter of 16 November 1919 that, using "material of the most primitive kind ..." he had "almost finished a few pictures". Based on Schiele's stylistic development and a further letter, written to Carl Reininghaus on 20 December 1912 and describing cityscapes he had executed, it is highly probable that these in fact represented the two paintings mentioned. Since he frequently did not sign his works until some time after their completion, the fact that he did not sign and date these two until 1913 requires no particular explanation.

In view of Schiele's precarious situation at the time, it is understandable that he was unable to execute "City in Twilight" or "The Small Town" under the fresh impression of his journey to Krumau. Unlike all the other cityscapes of

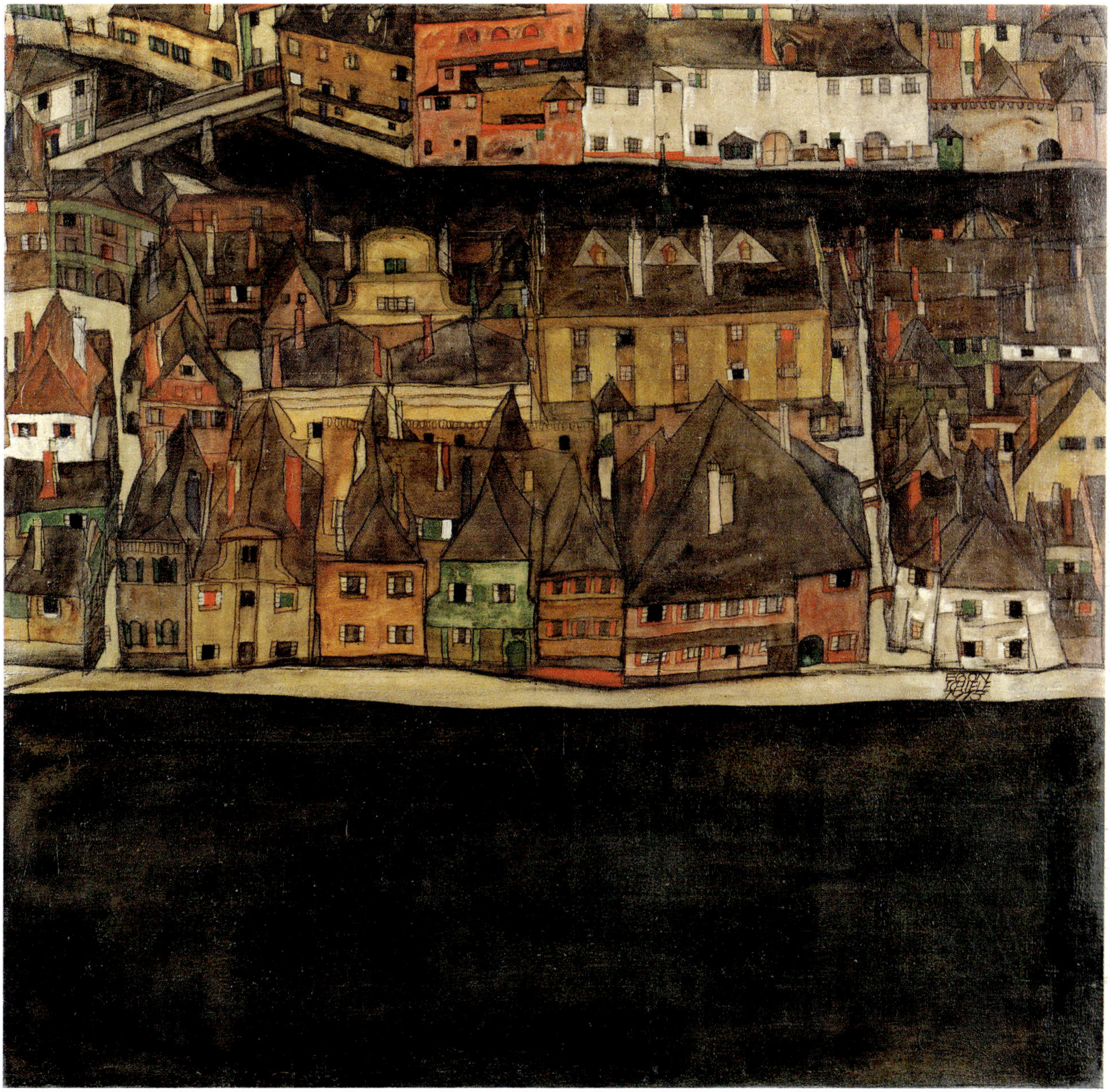

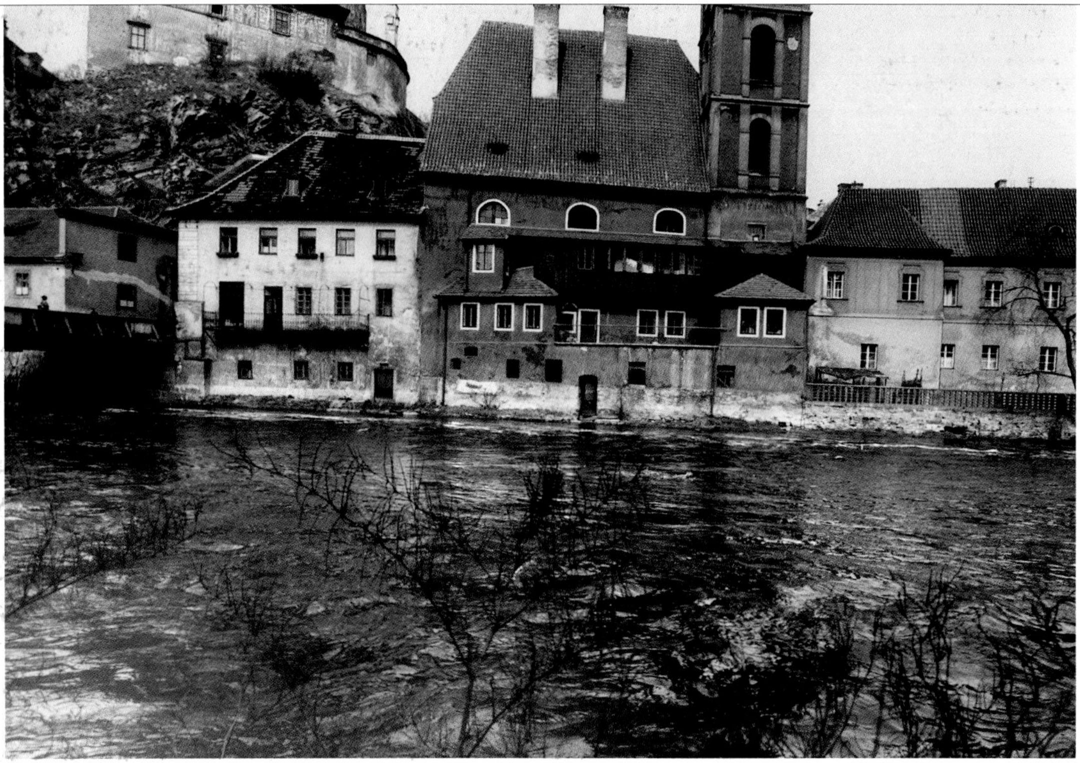

Former St. Jodocus' Church, on the left bank of the Moldau in Krumau

this period, these were freely composed in the studio, based on numerous separate motifs recorded in Krumau. Some of the houses depicted may be individually identifiable, but they cannot be seen together from any actual vantage point.

"The Small Town" is definitely the most impressive, especially in terms of color. Its most easily identifiable feature, despite its unrealistic red hue, is the wall of the former Jodocus Church with annexes, facing onto the Moldau. Likewise departing from reality, the adjacent house façades to the left do not lie in a line with the church but describe an angle to the upper left.

The buildings to the right of the church, and especially the adjacent fortified wall, appear considerably altered. Still, the unnaturally colored church wall and the houses along the Moldau are the only features which Schiele left in their natural context. The large, pale yellow house wall with two tall white chimneys above it to the right of picture center – despite several changes, including the three invented rooflines – was evidently derived from the Jesuit Seminar. Yet this building actually occupies a higher site, and there is no place in Krumau from which its roof and its façade along the upper lane could be seen from such a high vantage point. In the case of the crenellated wall to the left and below the building derived from the Jesuit Seminar, Schiele may have been thinking of Krumau Town Hall and its screen façade. This building, in use since about 1650, actually consists of four Gothic structures. In Schiele's pic-

City in Twilight 1912/13
L 226 K 260
Oil on canvas, 90.5 x 90.1 cm
Signed and dated lower left
Private collection

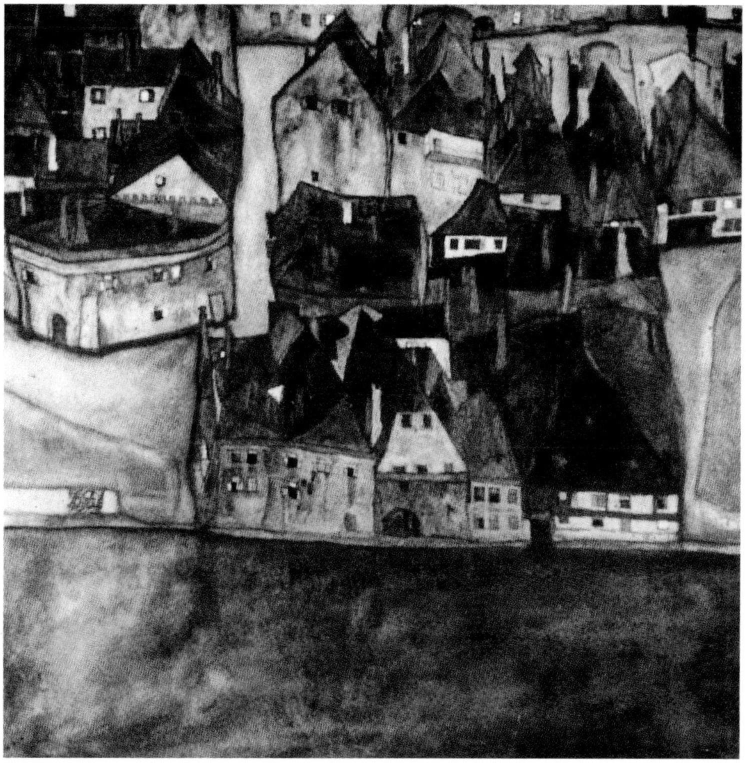

ture there are only three, which moreover have been shifted to the bank of a broad, black watercourse. On the other hand, we can detect a large building that actually did stand on the Moldau, the old municipal mill (no. 80 Breite Gasse). These and many other alterations with respect to the actual situation in Krumau are discussed in detail in the motif identifications in the present author's 1972 book on Schiele (p. 649 ff.).

It would surely be interesting to determine where Schiele found the various motifs, and how he changed them and combined them with his own inventions. More important, however, is the fact that he produced a compelling image of a venerable city on the basis of these diverse features.

The roofs are grayish-black, the façades varicolored. A black river runs through the town. Narrow at the top of the picture, it widens at the bottom, where restless reflections dance on the water. The river banks are lined by houses with high, pointed roofs. These call hats to mind, and many of the widows resemble eyes. The physiognomical character of the depiction cannot be overlooked.

The lovely colors of the house walls and the black of the river – both freely invented by Schiele – mutually heighten each other in effect. For all the diversity of the scene, it congeals into a harmonious and beautiful whole.

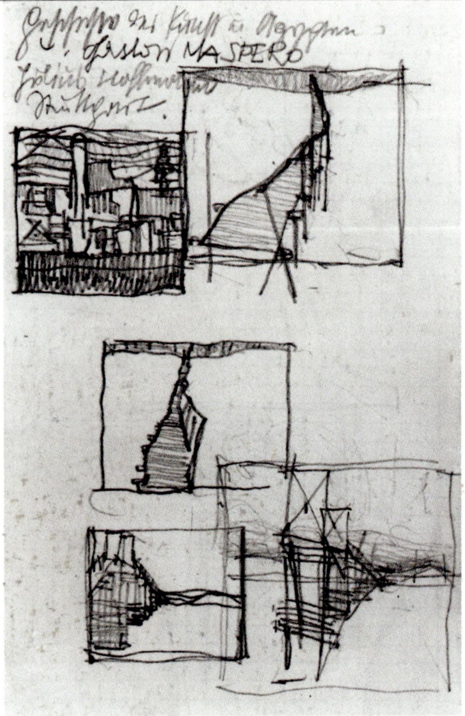

"The Bridge" 1913

K 1464
Gouache, watercolor and pencil on paper, 30.5 x 43 cm
Signed and dated center right
Private collection

On 24 December 1912 Schiele wrote from Györ, where he was staying with the Lederer family, to Arthur Roessler: "While exploring the town I saw an old wooden bridge over one of the three Danube branches, very high and rising at both sides, with many, many beams, quite Asiatic, as if Chinese." Based on four tiny sketches on a small sketchbook page and two watercolor-tinted drawings – the immediate preliminary work is reproduced at upper right – the painting was executed in the Vienna studio a short time later. But the aesthetically unprecedented thing lies in these constructive design sketches. Neither the watercolor nor the painting as a whole were executed with comparable inspiration.

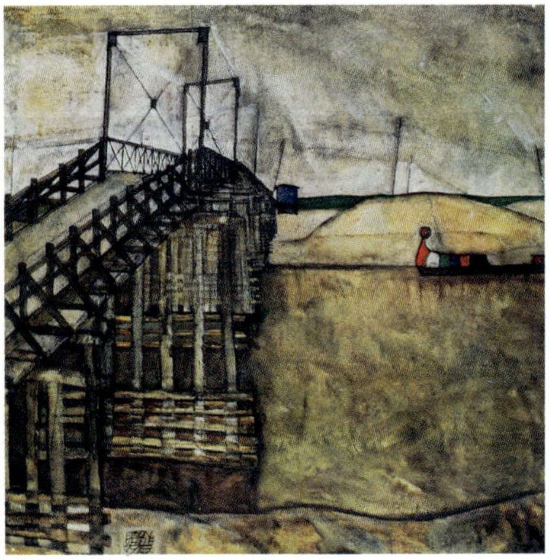

Sketches for *The Bridge*
(incl. a further sketch for *Stein on the Danube)*
Fourth sketchbook, 1912/13,
Albertina, Vienna, ESA 318 no. 2

The Bridge 1913
L 229 K 262
Oil on canvas (two pieces sewn together)
89.7 x 90 cm, signed and dated lower left
Private collection

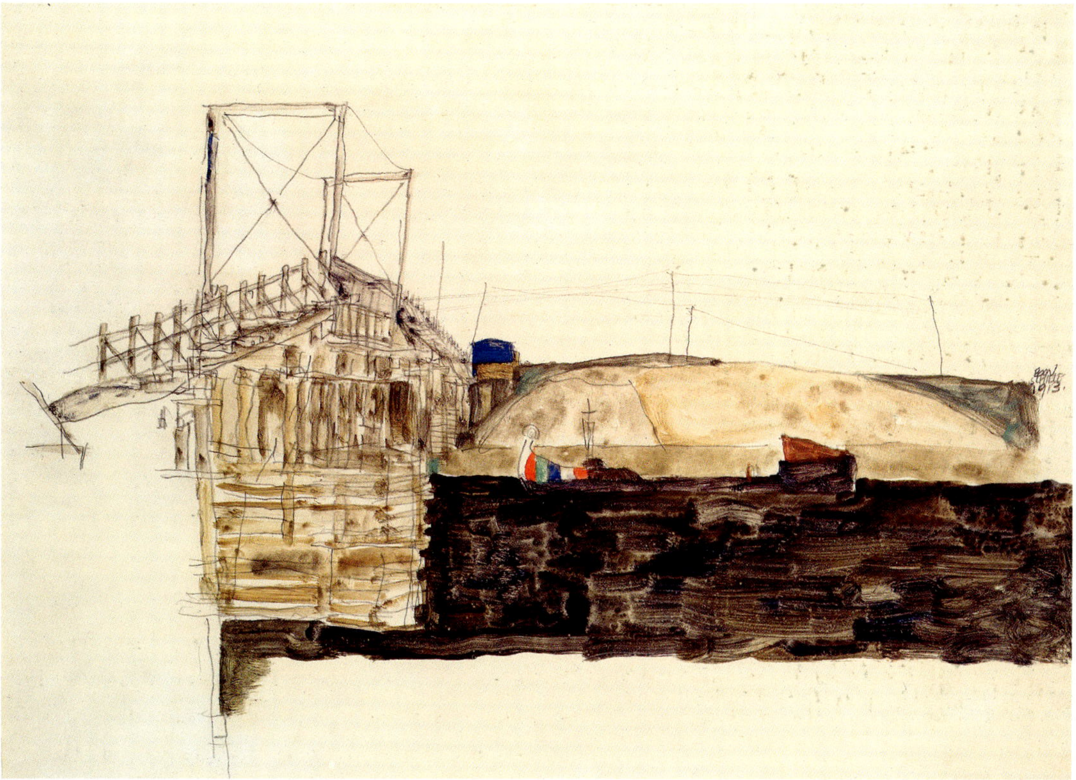

The staggering of the bridge piers and crossboards into the depths evokes a compelling sense of space. The remaining passages, however, are more or less disappointing. The uniform, stiff drawing of the bridge rail and the treatment of the river area appear all too flat and undeveloped by comparison with the bridge. (This is much more clearly evident in the original.) The brownish water is not notably distinguished from the bridge color. And the strong color accents on the boat strike one as merely decorative. More successful are the sky, which seems penetrated by unreal flashes of light, and the arc of the riverbank behind the boat. Its light ocher forms a lovely color contrast to the dark green strip of terrain behind it.

Except for the wavy outline of the bank, the lineature exhibits the new, harsher style Schiele adopted in 1913.

"Early Spring" 1913

L 230 K 263
Oil on canvas, 89.5 x 89.5 cm
Signed and dated lower left
Kunsthaus Zug, Sammlung Kamm, inv. no.: K.G 27

The very close formal relationship of this painting to "Landscape with Two Trees" (L 231/K 264) and also to "The Bridge" (L 229/K 262, p. 116) is quite obvious. Each of these works is built on a large foreground zone that appears inclined forward in space, and smaller middle and background areas. An influence from the composition of certain Klimt landscapes, such as "Poppy Field", 1907 (Dobai 149) and "Garden Landscape," before 1910 (Dobai 164) is highly probable, despite the fact that the various sections of Klimt's compositions are not sharply separated, as in Schiele's works, but flow into one another.

The close stylistic affinity between "Early Spring" and "Landscape with Two Trees" is reflected in the simple, homogeneous treatment of the tree trunks, props and crowns, which also recalls the rendering of the handrails of the bridge in the picture of that name. Moreover, the stylistic similarity of this "Bridge" with "Early Spring" becomes apparent when we compare the shadowed contours of the far bank of the Danube in the former painting with those of the river bank in the latter.

Quite different in character is the compelling multicolor treatment of the mountain chain in the background of "Early Spring".

The Munich art dealer Goltz wrote to Schiele on 1 April 1913 to confirm the receipt of two paintings. Then he went on to caution the artist not to allow "... the form to become petrified ... This merely to prepare you for a complete financial fiasco, which your pictures are bound to suffer at your present level." Very probably Goltz was referring here to "Early Spring" and "Landscape with Two Trees".

Yet Schiele was soon to find an artistically more convincing solution, in the new, as it were harsher style of pictures such as "Setting Sun" (L 235/K 265, p. 123), on which he already began to work in April of that same year.

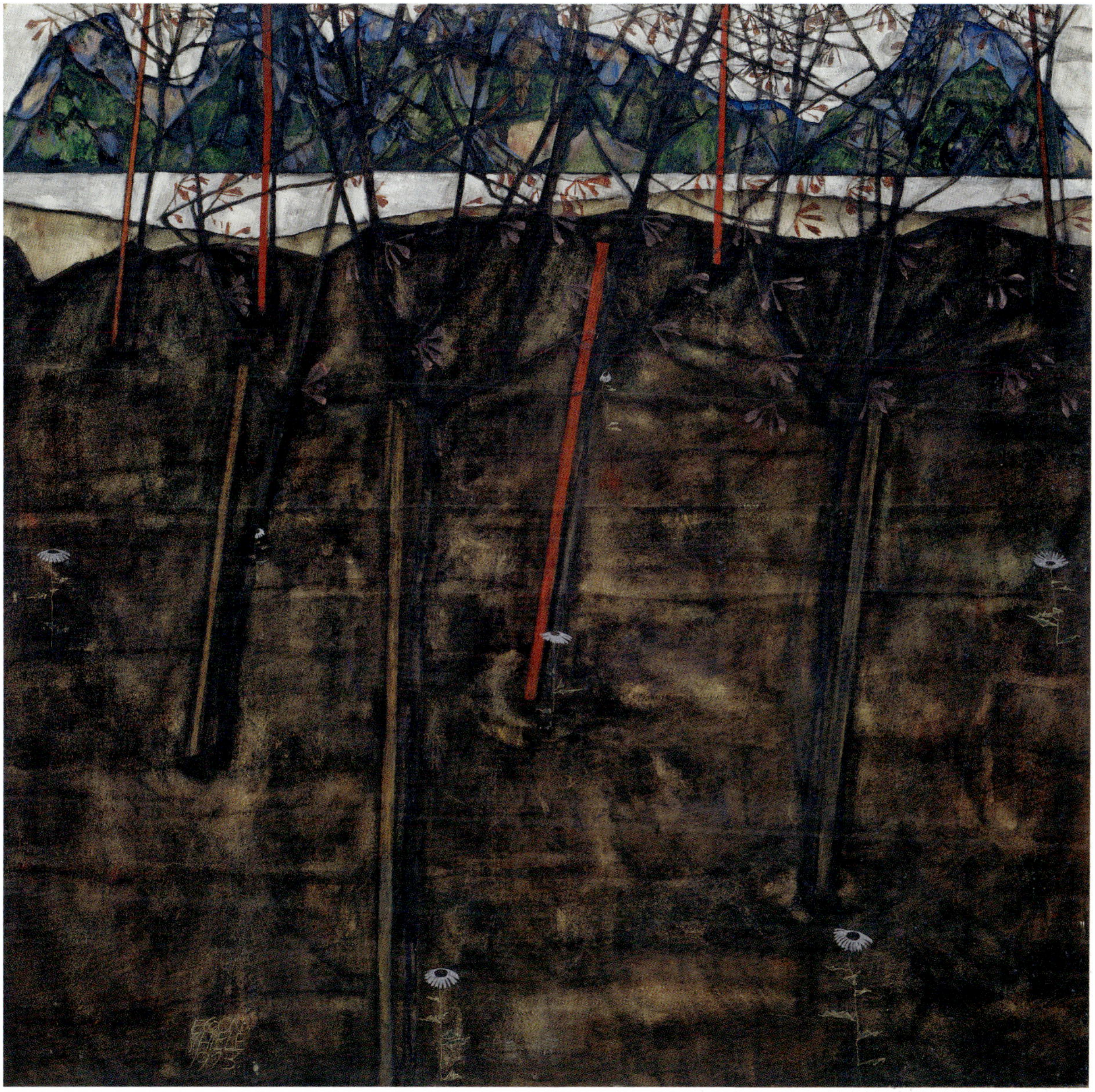

Vienna Woods Landscape 1913

K 1476
Pencil on paper, 28.7 x 43.8 cm
Signed and dated lower right
Leopold Museum, Vienna, inv. no.: LM 3666

The house outlines drawn in perspective and the two firs near them serve mainly to emphasize the foreground with respect to the background. Together with the almost empty middle ground, this evokes the distance to the far mountain without recourse to perspective lines in the landscape.

The houses are small, and the paper to either side of them is left empty. In contrast, the mighty line of the peak conveys a sense of natural grandeur. Yet it does not appear cold, thanks to the appealing, scribbled strokes with which Schiele depicts the many trees. The similar treatment of the firs in the foreground, together with the two rows of bushes in the middle ground, establish a link with the background. In general, these skillfully placed darks lend the drawing coherence. A further function of the group of houses might be seen in the contrast of its relatively simple, not very strong lines to the heavy strokes used to represent the shrubbery and trees. By comparison to his other depictions of houses, here Schiele has treated them quite straightforwardly and in abbreviated form. Their effect is secondary to the vital appearance of the vegetation.

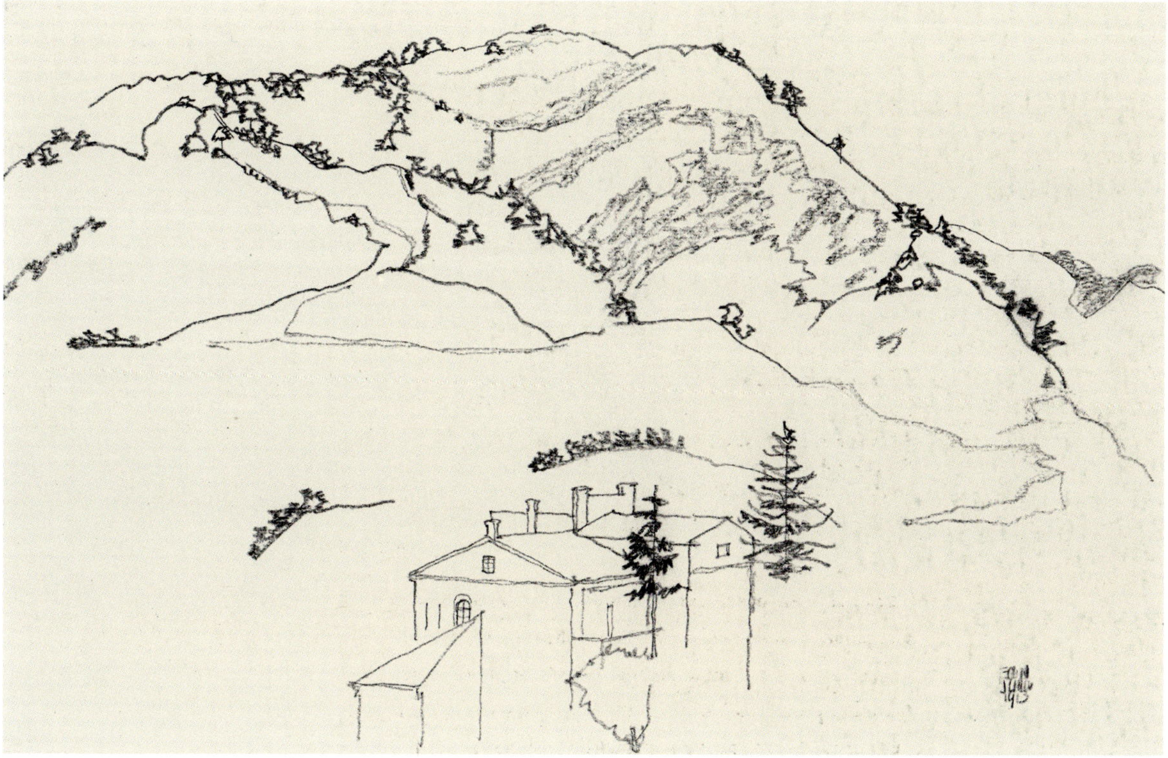

"Setting Sun" 1913

L 235 K 265
Black crayon, opaque colors and oil on canvas, 90 x 90.5 cm
Signed and dated center right;
titled on the stretcher 'Versinkende Sonne'
Leopold Museum, Vienna, inv. no.: LM 625

In Schiele's early years, the season depicted in his landscapes always conformed with their actual period of execution. In the case of his mature paintings, this connection no longer held. This is true of the present landscape, "Setting Sun." Based on Schiele's letters, it is safe to assume that this so profoundly autumnal depiction of 1913 was not done until April or early May of the following year – when spring was in the air.

The formal affinity with "Vienna Woods Landscape" from the same period (K 1476, p. 121) becomes apparent from the similar style of the lineature used to characterize the mountain there and that employed to articulate the terrain in the lower, darker section of "Setting Sun."

The motif that inspired Schiele to this painting was the coastline near Trieste and two outlying islands.

Two small trees project above the hilly area in the foreground, their crowns intersecting sea, islands and sky. Otherwise the painting is composed largely in terms of horizontal strata and lines. This lends it a sense of calm, but also of melancholy, to which the strange colors contribute.

Many artists before and after Schiele have depicted sunsets. Almost all have rendered the play of colors in warm gradations dominated by orange. Not so Schiele. Light carmine red and a compartively dark steel blue dominate the upper area of the composition, in an interplay that has a simultaneously cool and exciting effect.

Although by the laws of optics the isolated mountains would stand in shadow when the sun is in this position and be visible only as a black mass, Schiele has rendered them as if they were translucent, lending them a crystalline character. They are subsumed with sky and sea into a colored unity. This was done not only for aesthetic reasons but perhaps even more to find a compelling visual solution to the task Schiele apparently set himself. The overall brightness of the upper area, broken only by thin branches and foliage, is contrasted to the pervading darkness of the lower section. This is dominated by grayish-purple and dark green, only the small yellow flowers, rendered as circular ornaments in one last recollection of the Vienna Secessionist style, providing lighter accents. Otherwise everything is plunged in gloom and, one senses, it has grown cold – the leaves seem to have stiffened with cold and the nearly bare tree, as if with a shudder, has drawn its frail branches together into a narrow crown.

Only a few months separated the execution of "Early Spring" (L 230/K 263, p. 119) and "Landscape with Two Trees" (L 231/K 264). Yet in the meantime Schiele achieved an extremely refined differentiation in the rendering of trees, as in other respects. How distinctly are props and trunks, limbs and branches now characterized – compare the branches of the right-hand tree, their gradual thickening and thinning, their fine, arched form, with the stiffness of all of the branches in the two pictures named,

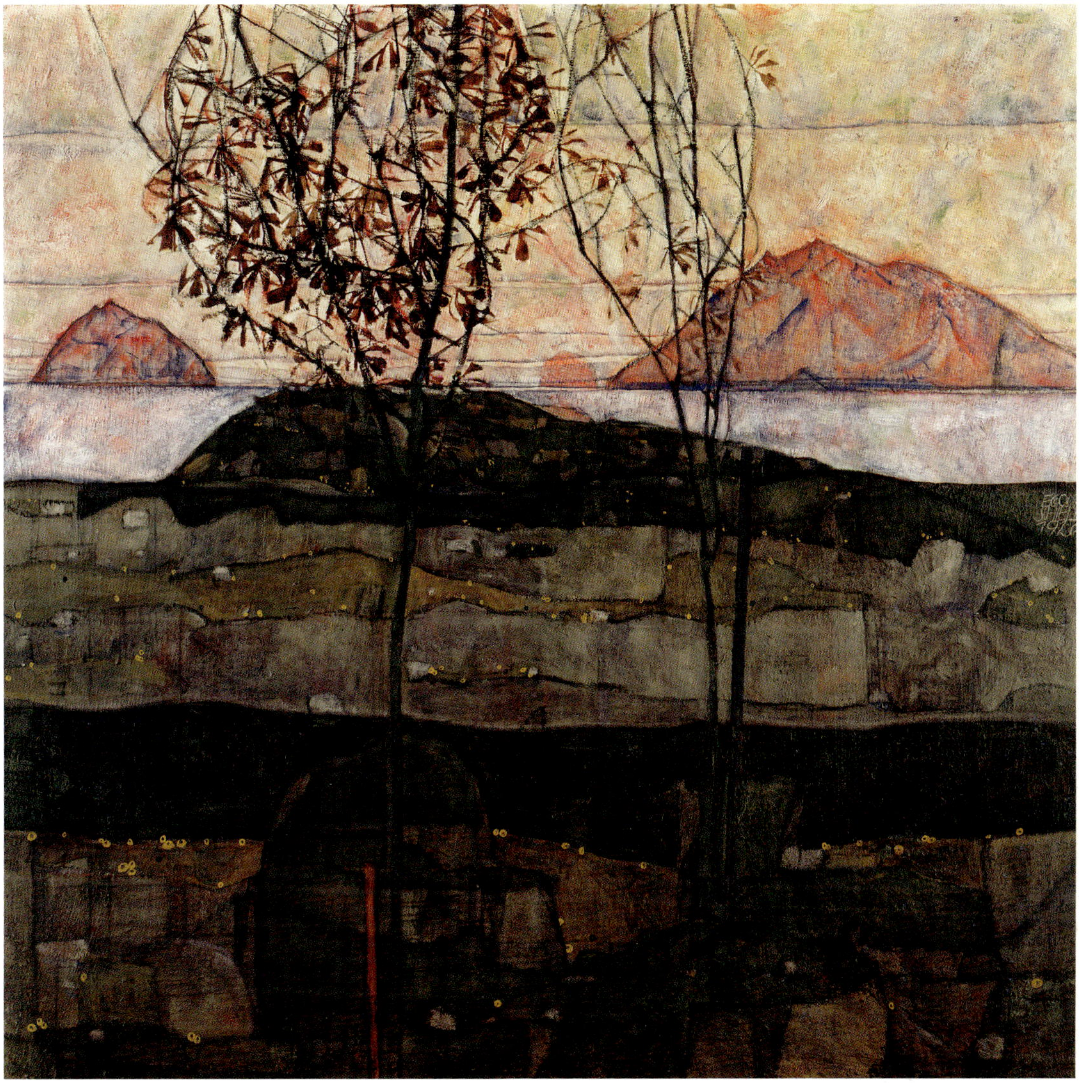

which were presumably done only a few months previously.

Differently than in 1911 and 1912 but with no less power of expression, in his new style Schiele managed to create an emblem of the transitory nature of all things. Everything seems to lie under a cloak of hopelessness and melancholy. Even the magic of the sky and the rocky islands is doomed to pass. Bluish veils have descended over the sun, whose light shines through only in two narrow bands. The question arises whether the light and warmth-giving sun might not sink into the sea never to rise again? This borderline situation is convincingly evoked here.

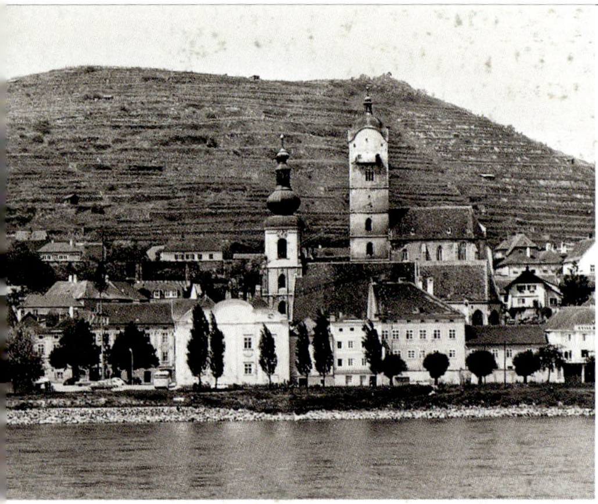

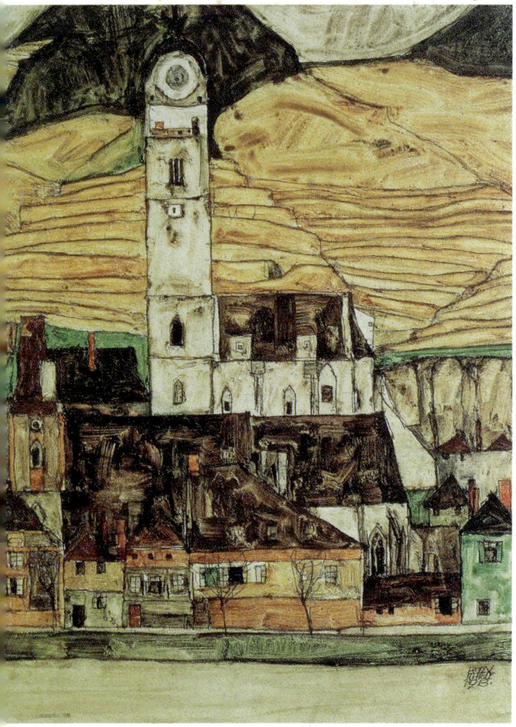

"Stein on the Danube" I 1913
(large version)

L 239 K 268
Oil on canvas, 89.9 x 89.6 cm
Signed and dated upper right
Neue Galerie New York

On 21 March 1913, Schiele was in the towns of Krems and Stein, where he made studies from nature. He might possibly have commenced working on his small-format paintings of Stein that same day; at any rate, he finished them in Vienna on 24 March. The large paintings were done at a later date, and all in the studio. These were compositions developed from studies and finished in June 1913.

The works L 232 and L 239 are views of Stein from the opposite bank of the Danube. In the small version, the excerpt is more constricted. The picture ends just beside the parish church, which has been strongly reduced in size and, likewise departing from reality, given an extremely simplified, small spire. Only a small portion of the building in front of it, Stein Town Hall, is visible. Simplifications, in fact, are found throughout the painting. For instance, the large house at center foreground, the parsonage (55 Steiner Landstrasse), has only one row of windows. An accent is set by an elongated and slender depiction of the Frauenberg church tower, rising to the left of center.

In the much more detailed large-format version, a quite naturalistic rendering of the parish church appears at picture center. Here the view of Stein includes the entire town hall square, Rathausplatz, and the round fortified tower at its left edge. The whitish gradations used for the square have been formally adjusted to the slightly tinted wall in front of the houses. In fact, the entire composition has a rather facile decorative effect which is not very con-

Stein on the Danube with Terraced Vineyards 1913
(small version)
L 232 K 266
Pencil and oil on wood, 39.9 x 31.3 cm
Signed and dated lower right
Private collection

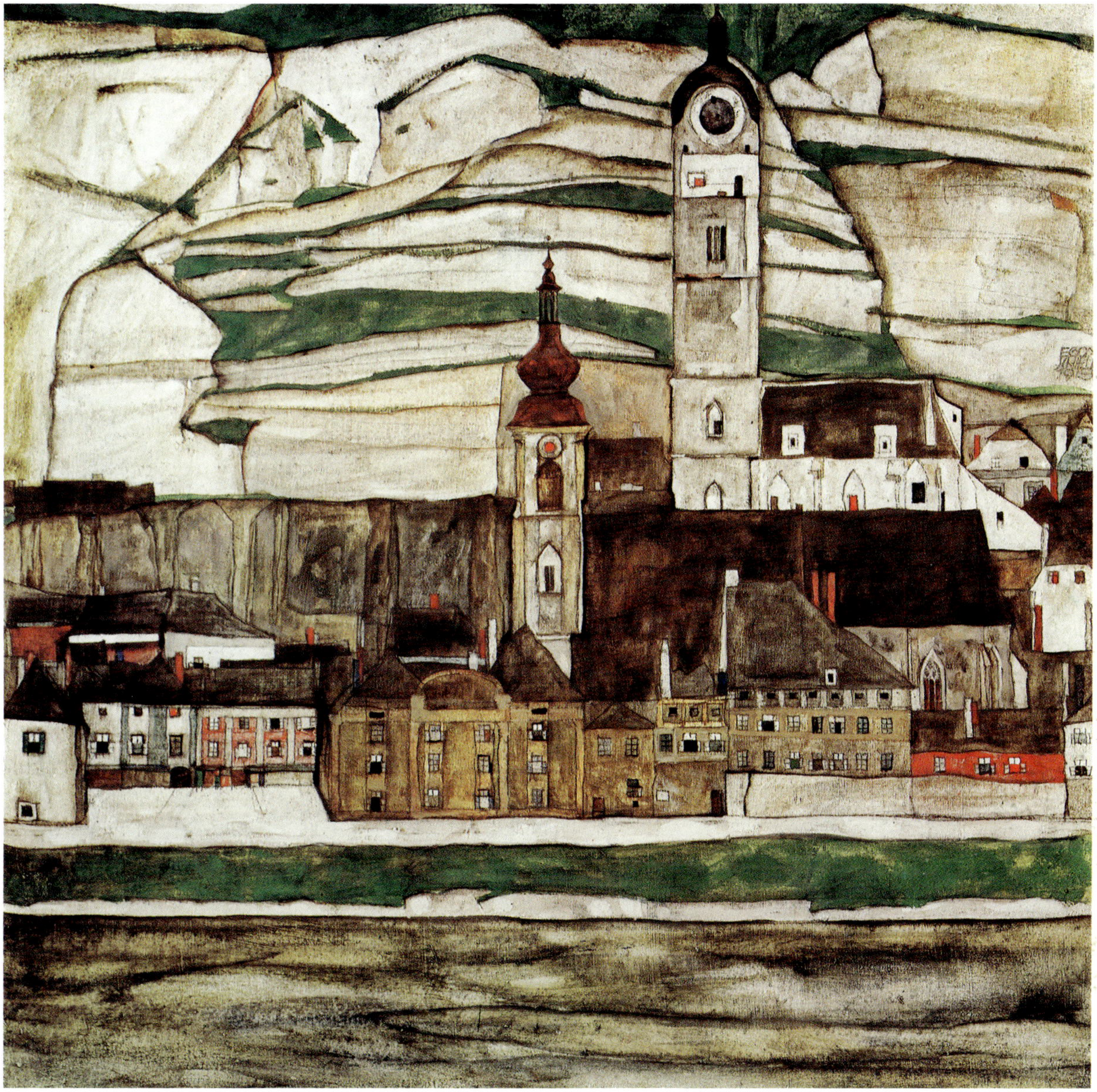

vincing, and the same holds for the treatment of the front city wall on the street alongside the Danube.

The majority of the color accents in the picture have no basis in reality. Yet although both their color (e.g. red and blue in the tower clocks, and red in several chimneys) and their form (e.g. the small red and blue rectangles on Frauenberg Church) are entirely imaginative, together with the grayish-white of the walls, the dark gray and reddish brown of the roofs, and the remaining passages, they convey a convincing impression of a hilly small town in the midst of a mountainous riverine landscape. The green of the meadows may occasionally appear too garish and therefore merely decorative. Yet on the whole, Schiele has composed the terraced vineyards on the Kreuzberg above Stein in a very free and interesting way. In contrast, the cleft in this hill, which from this vantage point falls in a steep arc behind the church spire to the eastern section of the choir, is depicted very faithfully, especially in the large version. The cleft finds a visual continuation in the edge of the choir and the house to the right and below it.

The green bands extending between the loess cliffs and terraces in the background, vaguely recalling arcades, round off the composition. This middle and upper area of the picture, and especially the predominating horizontals and verticals throughout, underscored by the strip of water in the foreground, might possibly have influenced a few works executed by Gustav Klimt a short time later – in particular, his painting "Church in Cassone" (Dobai 185). In an essay on Klimt's "The Kiss" (*Mitteilungen der österreichischen Galerie,* 1968, vol. 12, no. 56), Johannes Dobai wrote that Klimt's and Schiele's landscape art occasionally showed great parallels, for instance in 1913. The date of execution of the two large-format views of Stein, June 1913, is quite certain, as is that of Klimt's "Cassone", July and August of that year. So the time interval between them was not great. However, we should not forget that the small view of Stein, which also bears similarities with "Church in Cassone" despite its less rigorous composition, was painted as early as the end of May 1913. A further indicator for Schiele's influence on Klimt is found in a remark made by Dobai on "Church in Cassone" in his catalogue raisonné of Klimt's paintings: "… with this painting a stylistic change came about. Klimt began working with geometrically simplified forms."

Schiele's influence on Klimt is even more obvious in that artist's "Apple Tree", executed in 1916 (Dobai 195), whereas the composition of Schiele's "Early Spring" (L 230/K 263, p. 119) was inspired by Klimt. This painting

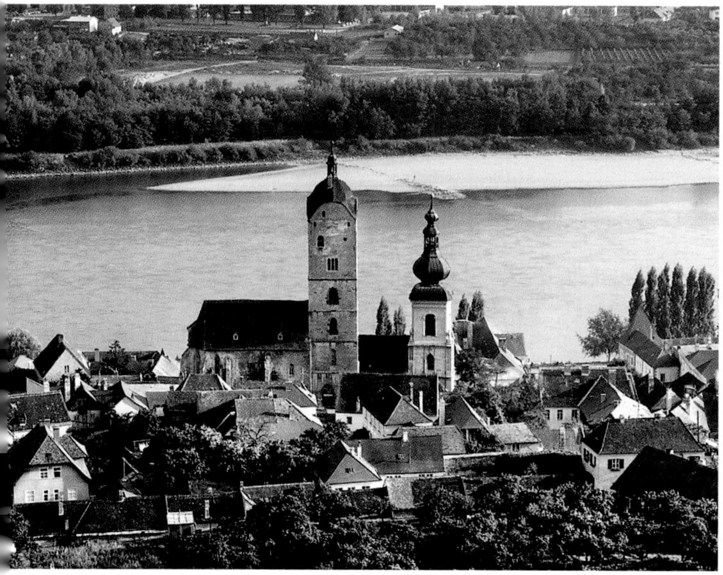

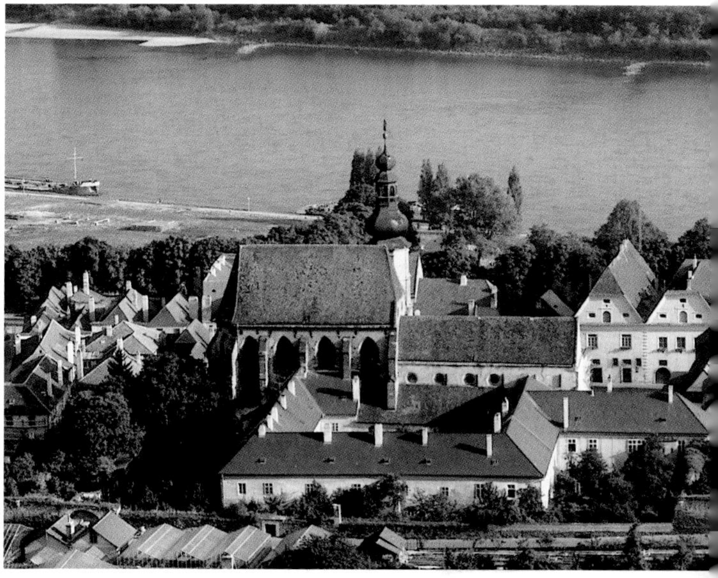

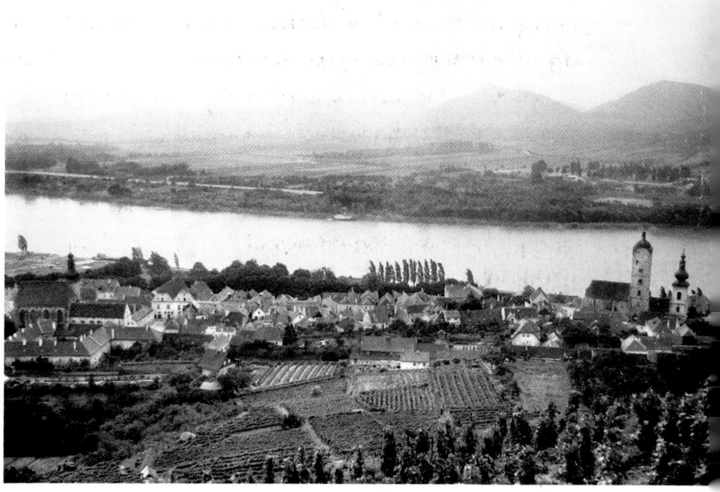

Frauenberg Church and Parish Church in Stein on the Danube, as seen from the Kreuzberg

Former Miniorite Church with Monastery in Stein on the Danube

Panorama of Stein with the former Minorite Church, Frauenberg Church and Parish Church in Stein on the Danube

strongly recalls Klimt landscapes done years earlier, for instance "Garden Landscape" (Dobai 164), even though individual compositional elements and even the manner of execution are entirely different in detail.

It goes without saying that Klimt, the mature master, decisively influenced the younger artist in his early years. Yet later this influence became reciprocal, especially, as mentioned, in the field of landscape painting.

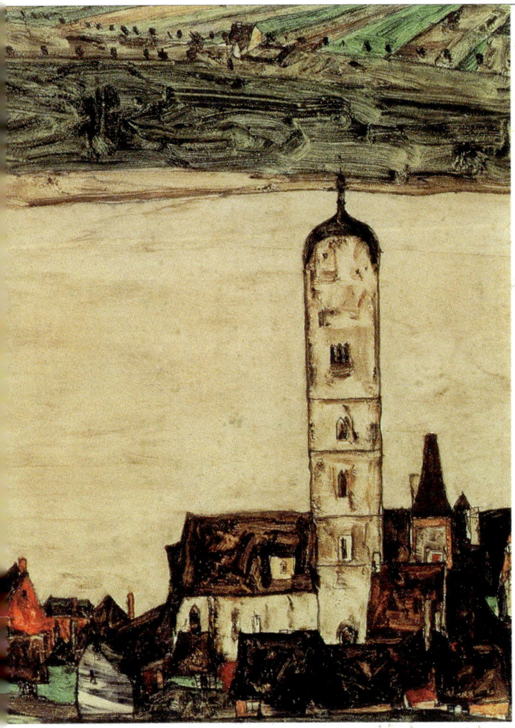

Frauenberg Church, Minorite Church with Monastery and the Danube 1913
(small version II)
L 233 K 267, Pencil and oil on wood, 39.8 x 31.5 cm
Signed and dated lower left, Private collection

"Stein on the Danube" II 1913
(large version)

L 240 K 269
Oil on canvas, 91.5 x 91.5 cm
Signed and dated lower right
Leopold Museum, Vienna, inv. no.: LM 479

Of the two works depicting the town of Stein as seen from the Kreuzberg, with the Danube and the far shore, only the smaller version (L 233/K 267) reflects the actual situation to any extent. As in the other small version showing Stein from the opposite bank of the Danube, Schiele has depicted the parish church only rudimentarily and with a schematically simplifed roof, perhaps with an eye to emphasizing the tower of Frauenberg Church opposite as the dominating element.

The large version, executed months later (L 240/K 269) – as the present author already pointed out in a publication of spring 1959 – is built up of several components. Visible in the foreground is the building complex of the Minorite Monastery and Church, and to the left, Frauenberg Church – which is in fact taller and, above all, lies approximately 250 meters farther west.

The three-aisle pilaster basilica of the former Minorite Church has round clerestory windows, depicted here as horizontal ovals, and is abutted by the choir on the east. Schiele has foreshortened both, and depicted the roof of the choir a great deal higher than it actually is. Visible at the southwest corner of the choir, as in reality, is a church tower with Baroque onion dome. Yet as we can see from certain details, this is not the dome of the parish church, as we would expect on the basis of the actual topography, but

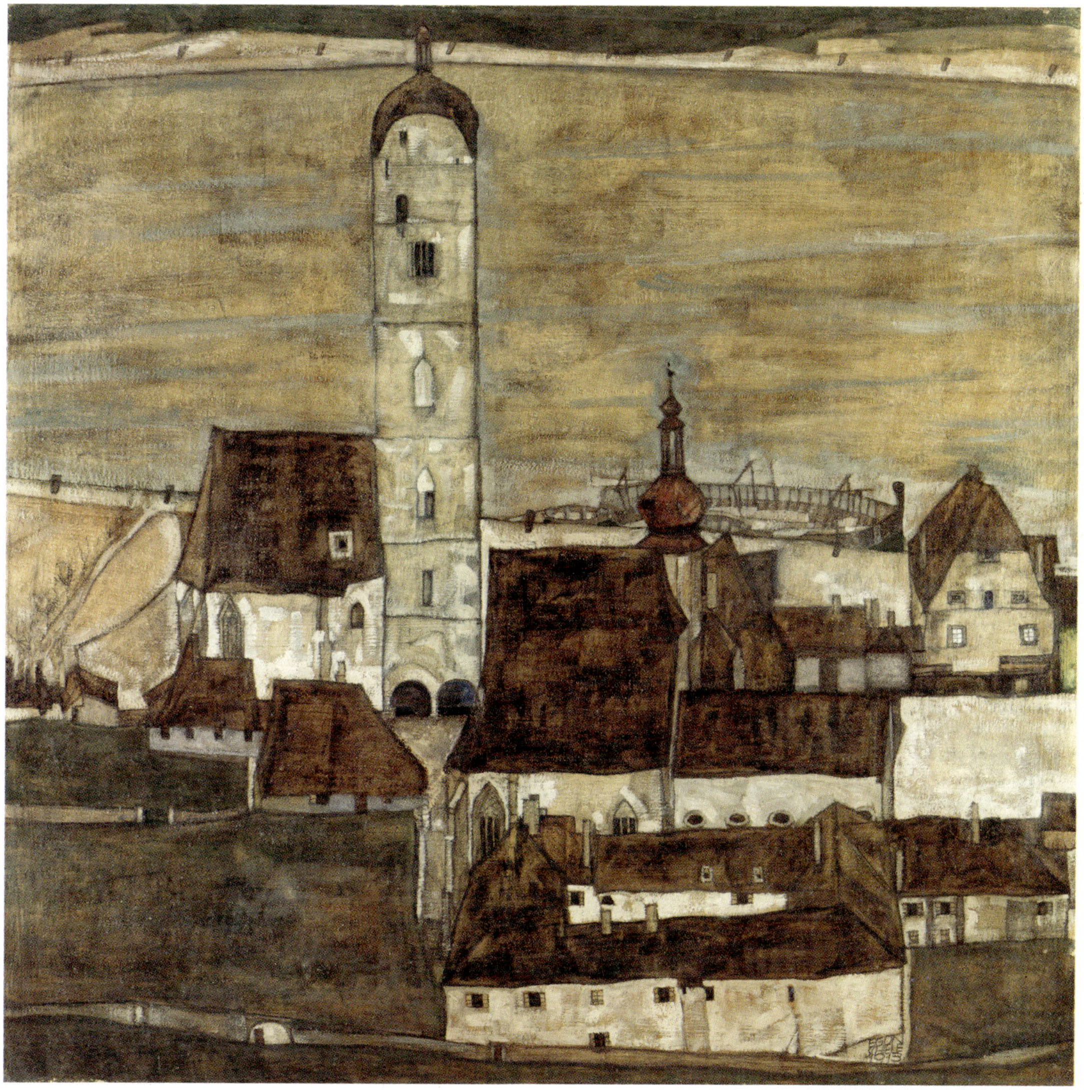

that of the Minorite Church. The main reason why Schiele chose to locate not the parish church but the Minorite Church to the right of Frauenberg Church, was recognized by my wife, Dr. Elisabeth Leopold. In order to emphasize the soaring tower of Frauenberg Church, which seems to extend over the entire width of the Danube, it was "necessary" to set a small church beside it – the Minorite Church, which appears to crouch behind the exaggeratedly high roof of the choir. Located adjacent to it on the west are two smaller buildings (the two "Salzstadel," built in 1598). Schiele has depicted only one of them, which rounds off the composition on the right. In reality, however, this building, too, does not stand west of Frauenberg Church but far to its east.

Schiele succeeded in blending these diverse separate motifs into a unity so convincing that viewing the picture, we feel that the local scene must have looked just like this and no differently.

Old Gable 1913

K 1473
Pencil and opaque colors on paper, 32 x 48.6 cm
Signed and dated lower right
Leopold Museum, Vienna, inv. no.: LM 1413

During his stay in Carinthia (Kärnten) in summer 1913, Schiele initially made a pencil sketch (K 1474) of this old brick shed with its crumbling masonry and dilapidated (K 1473), and included the ground floor. This he omitted in the pencil and gouache depiction reproduced here, but added narrow stripes in olive and orange at the lower edge in order to round off this carefully executed work.

The light-hued masonry seems framed by blackish tones, some of which are cut with blue. Behind the aperture the most intense brick red appears. Might this represent an open fire, one inadvertantly wonders for a moment. Thanks to the high gable, extending like a vault, the association with an old chapel might even arise.

Among all of Schiele's depictions of buildings in pencil, watercolor or gouache on paper, this and the rendering of the old house with miniature bell tower in Knappenberg on the Rax, done a year previously, are certainly the most impressive. Their delicate palette even surpasses the lovely study of old houses on the Flössberg in Krumau, 1914 (Albertina, inv. no. 31.158). All three works (K 1203, p. 105, 1473 and 1691, p. 141) were included in a Schiele portfolio published in color by Otto Benesch in 1950.

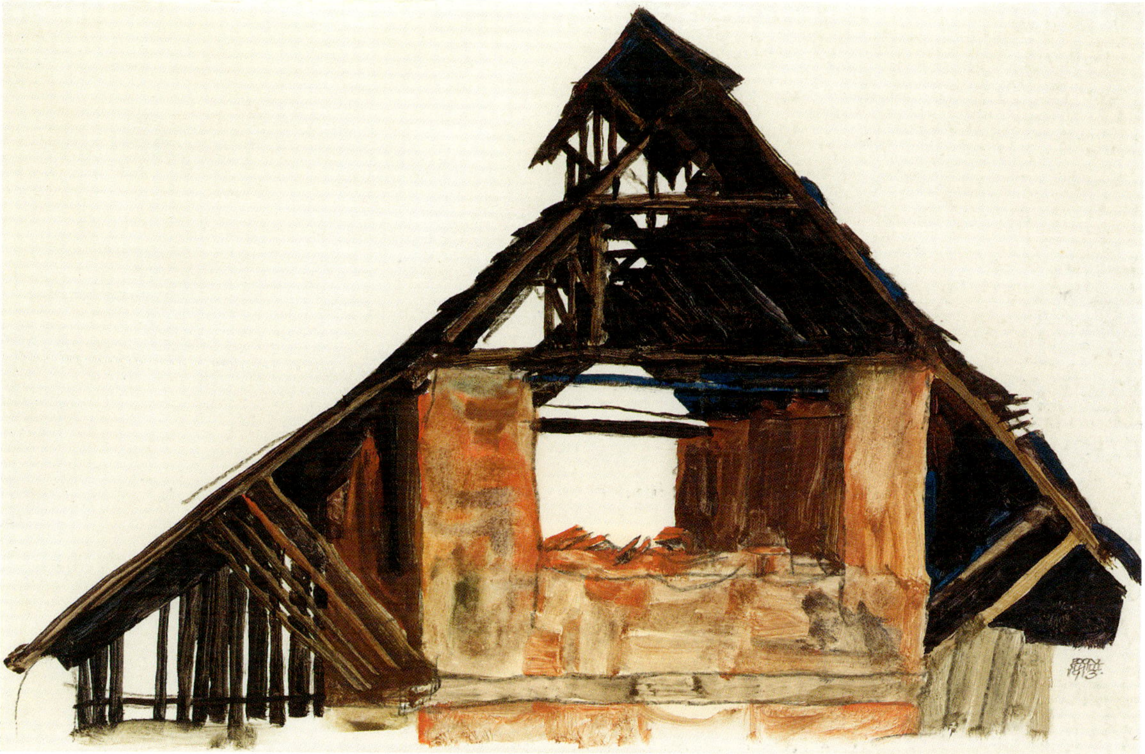
1913.

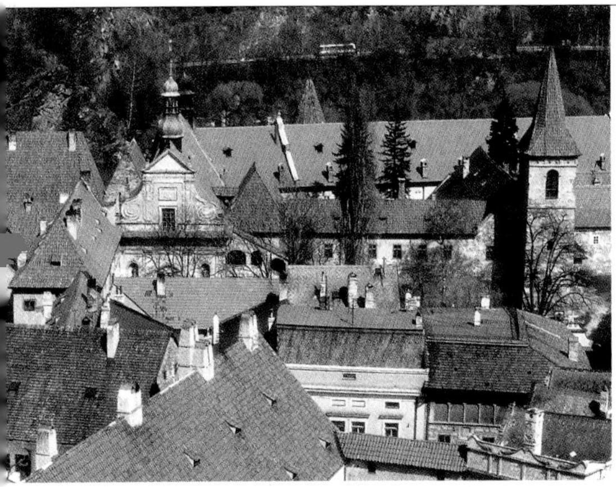

Clarissine Convent (Krumau) 1913

K 1468
Pencil on paper, 31.7 x 47.9 cm
Signed and dated lower right, titled 'Krumau' lower left
Private collection

Standing in the tower of Krumau Castle and looking northwest, one sees the district of Latron with the closed and abandoned premises of the Minorite and Clarissine orders. Visible is the front of the Minorite Church with its flanking volutes and two onion domes; to its left, the convent complex; on the right, the long monastery building (which contains a cloister and the Wolfgang Chapel); and to its right, the tower with steep roof.

Schiele sketched this view of Krumau in 1913 and has squared the sheet, probably intending to enlarge the depiction for a planned painting which was never executed.

At the lower right, Schiele has given a sketchy suggestion of the arches beneath the roof of the house at 53 Latron. (At the actual site, heavily weathered frescoes are still visible in these arches today.)

View of the Clarissine Convent, Krumau

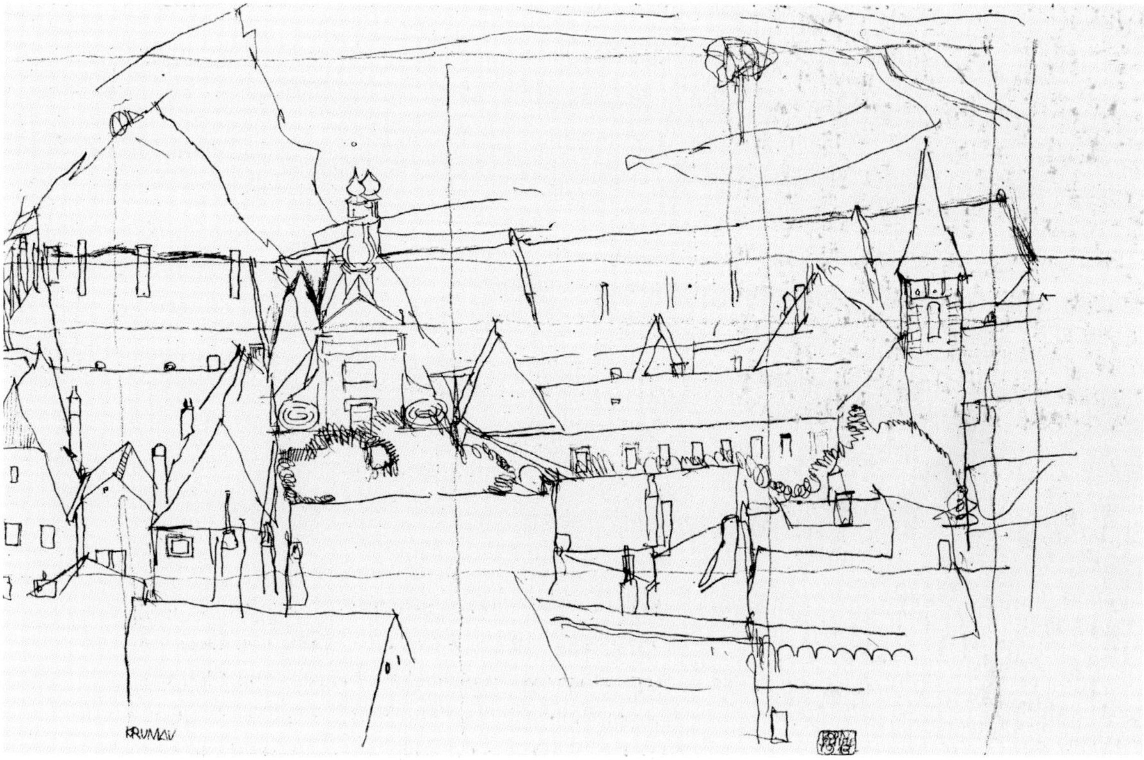
KRUMAU

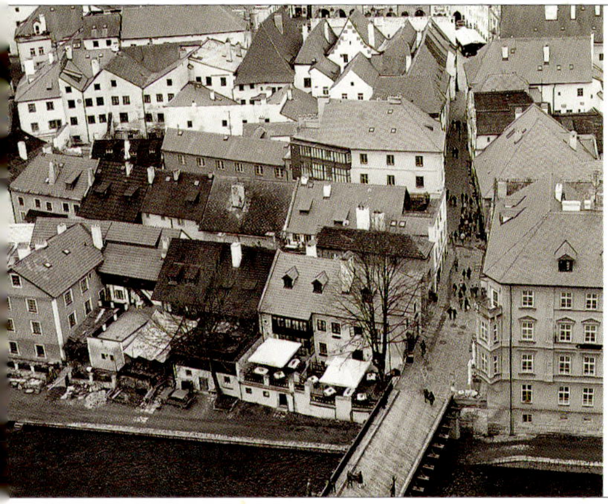

View from Castle Hill, towards Krumau

Krumau on the Moldau (also known as "The Small City" III) 1913/14

L 244 K 278
Black crayon and oil on canvas, 99.5 x 120.5 cm
Signed and dated lower right
Leopold Museum, Vienna, inv. no.: LM 655

Schiele first sketched these houses extending from the Moldau to the Rathausplatz, or town hall square, from the castle tower, a high vantage point subsequently exaggerated in the painting. He used the roofs and façades, together with the narrow lanes, to articulate the picture plane. Despite this purposely flat composition, the houses retain an effect of depth. This makes "Krumau on the Moldau" a fine and characteristic example of Schiele's new approach to composition, which began in 1913.

The plain row of houses in the foreground are depicted as if they were rising step by step to Rathausgasse. The house to their right, in turn, lies at a lower level, and has a yellow hue similar to that at the far left. With the similarly colored back wall of the Town Hall façade, these two houses serve to hold the composition together and are accordingly arranged symmetrically (resembling the angles of an equilateral triangle). At the very top Schiele added a band of green, not present in the actual scene, which serves to round off the composition at the top. At the bottom, the same purpose is served by broader zones running from left to right across the entire picture. The lowest, deep black zone represents the Moldau.

Above this quiet base, houses and buildings, some imagined, unfold a strange life with their white, orange, purple, gray and red façades and dark roofs. Two narrow lanes divide the massed houses like sharp incisions. The street façades of the smaller group of houses on the right are represented in daring perspective and with amazing variety. On the whole, they have a more multicolor appearance than those to the left, and their roofs, too (except for the uppermost one) are lighter in tone. Compared to this group, the houses between the two lanes, with their dark roofs and several strongly contrasting light walls, form a blocklike, massive whole.

The site of the medieval building depicted at the lower right is, in reality, occupied by an unprepossessing tenement from the latter half of the nineteenth century. Schiele included this building in all three versions of "Arch of Houses", because it made sense in the context of the paintings' statement.

In the present view of a medieval town, however, it would have been a foreign body, so Schiele replaced it by a completely different one, adapted to the character of the others.

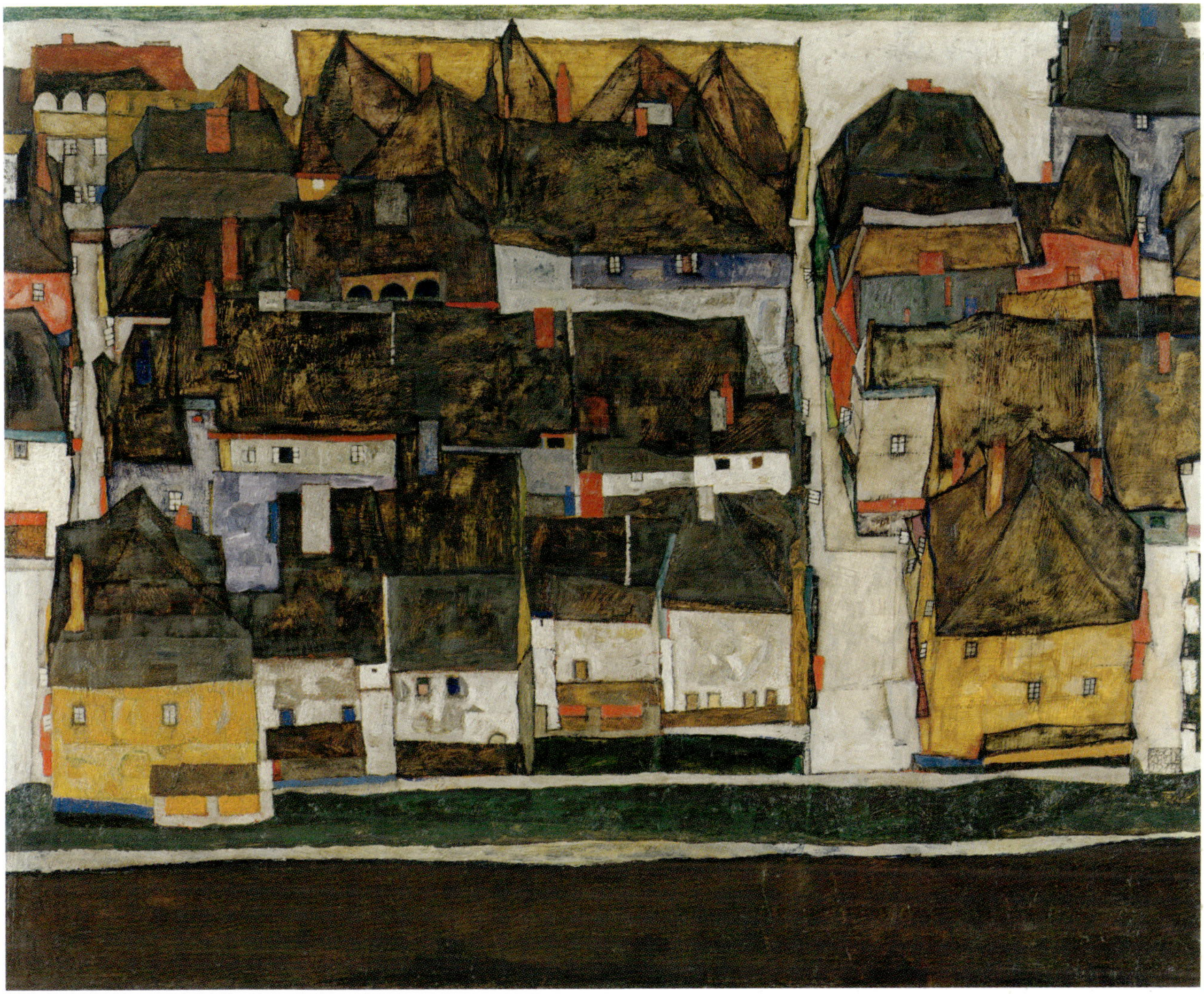

The physiognomic appearance of many façades is amplified by occasional pairs of windows – such as those shining from a dark purple section of wall under a great hat of a roof. Above this broad roof, at the back of the town hall's screen wall, project extremely pointed gables of different heights, depicted with great sensitivity. The picture is suffused by the dreamy mood of an ancient town, evoked by tipping walls and warped roofs, tiny windows, and not least by the freely invented colors. This may well be the only cityscape in which Schiele created an allegory of age that lacks all pessimism or sense of the tragic. The whole is suffused and transformed by a sense of quiet melancholy alone.

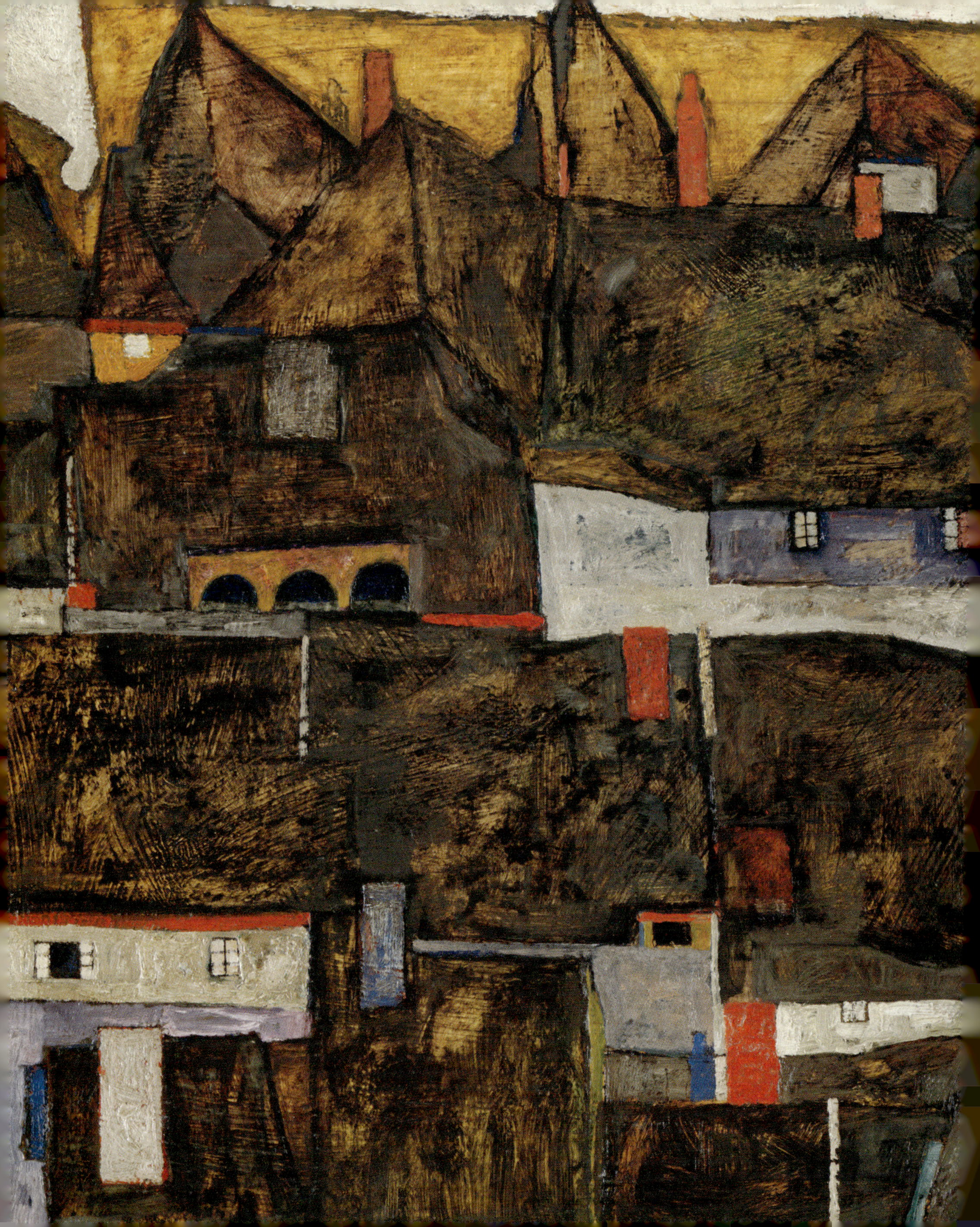

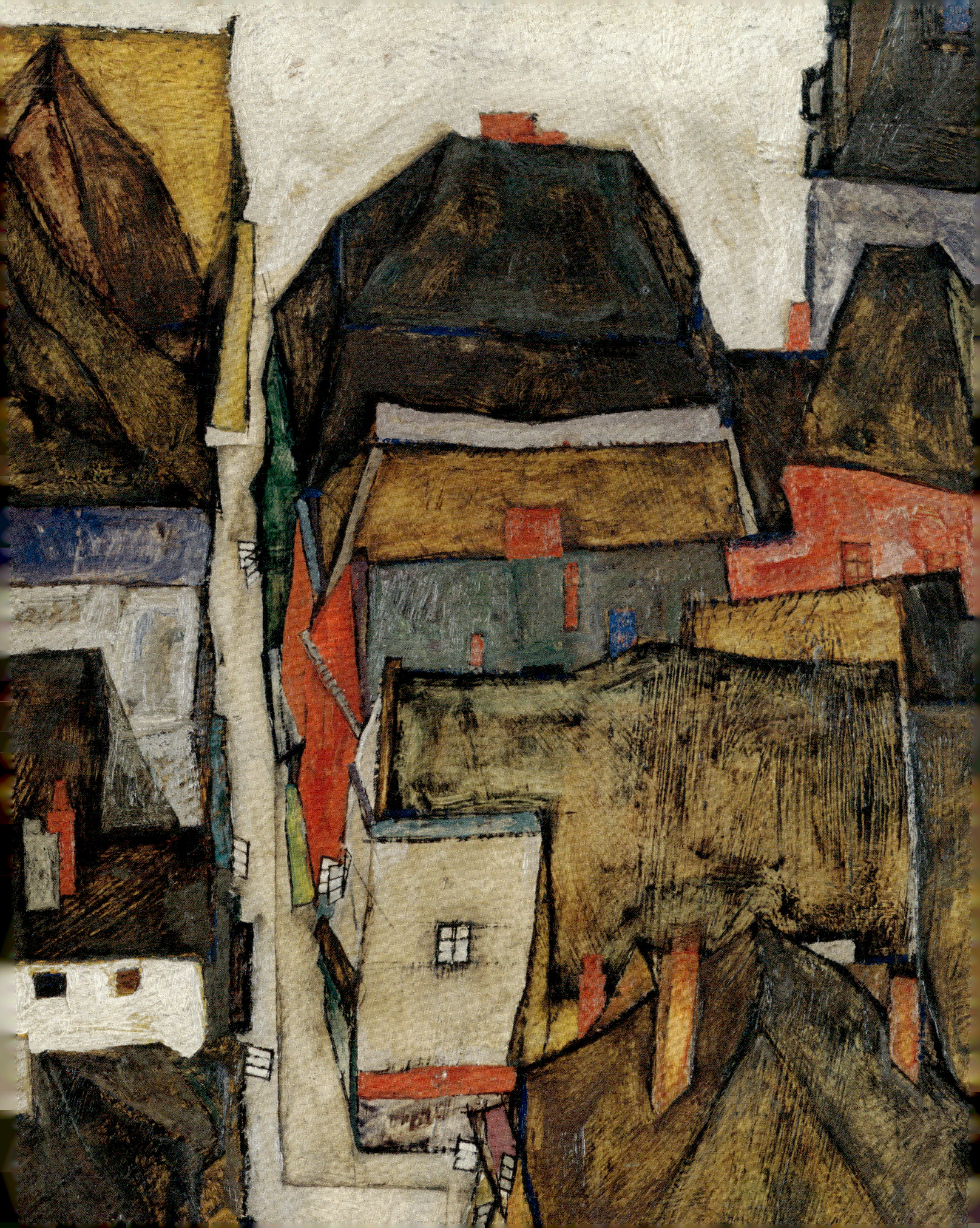

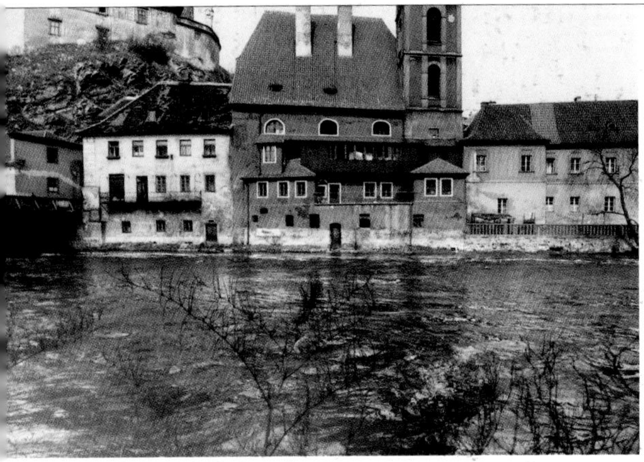

Houses by the River II* *(also known as "The Old City") 1914

L 245 K 279
Oil on canvas, 100 x 120.5 cm
Signed and dated upper right
Museo Thyssen-Bornemisza, Madrid

As I pointed out in my 1972 book on Schiele, this picture, previously described in the literature (catalogues raisonnés by Otto Nirenstein, 1930, and Otto Kallir, 1966) as "Wachau", was actually based on a motif from Krumau. It focusses especially on the former St. Jodocus' Church building and flanking houses. Bader Bridge has been omitted for compositional reasons, as it was in "Houses on the Moldau (Krumau)" (L 155/K 181, p. 57).

While the buildings immediately along the left bank of the Moldau have been more or less modified in form, those of a similar type behind them are purely imaginative. Schiele allowed himself equal license with the mountains in the background, omitting the spur with the walls of the castle.

Yet he did adhere to reality in the following features: The house upriver from Bader Bridge, at the height of Latrongasse, indeed has a rectangular screen wall, and the characteristic shape of the tall roof of the former St. Jodocus' Church, its three round-arched windows, and all of its later annexes on the Moldau, also appear in the painting. Admittedly, the tall church tower has been reduced to a

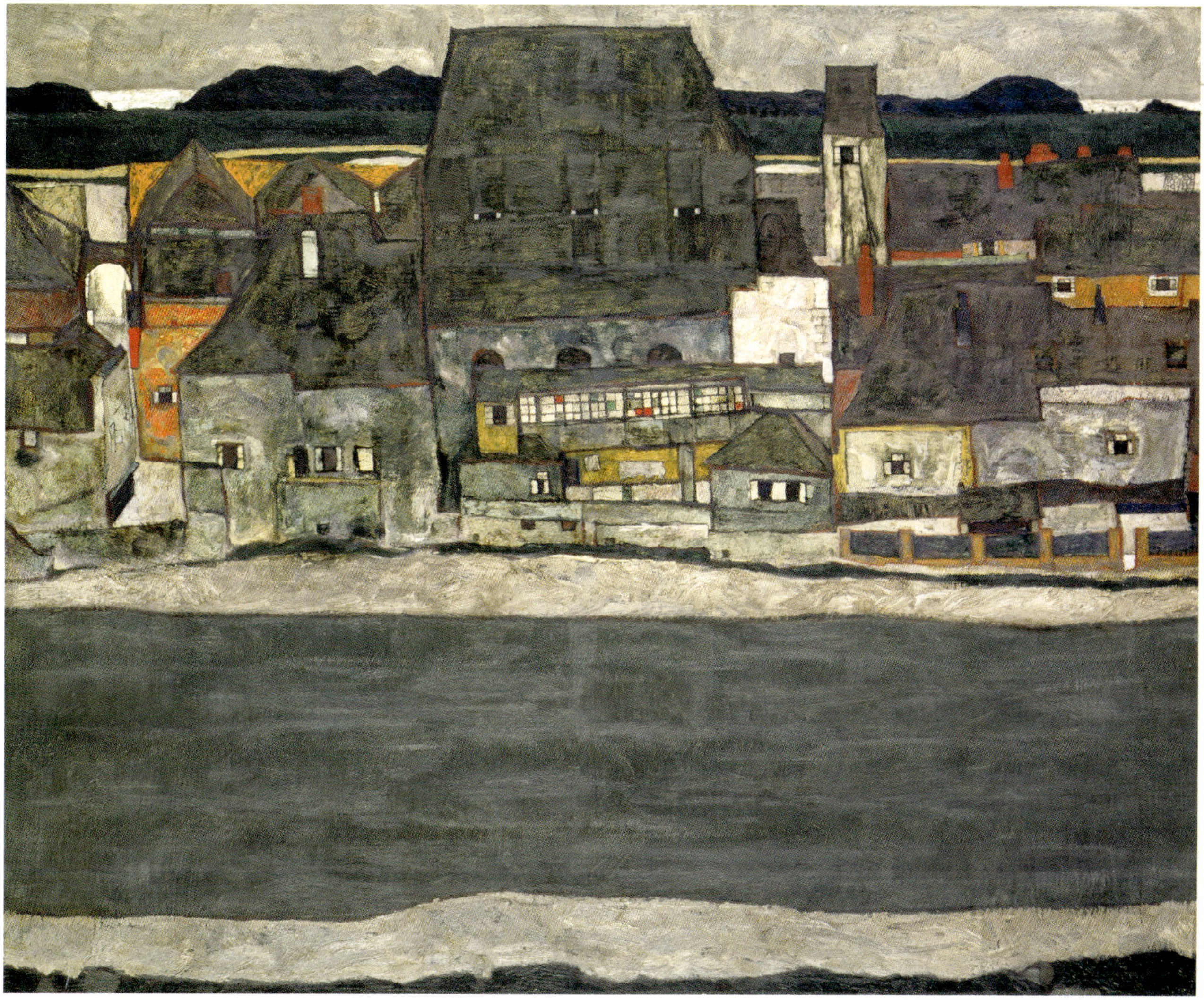

rudiment with a white-tinted wall. And to its right, behind the high roof of the former Royal Hospital Yard, Schiele has inserted a further, invented tower, which is narrower and taller than the real original.

The composition is articulated primarily in terms of horizontal strata. Its predominantly somber color scheme is relieved by a scattering of orange façades and red chimneys.

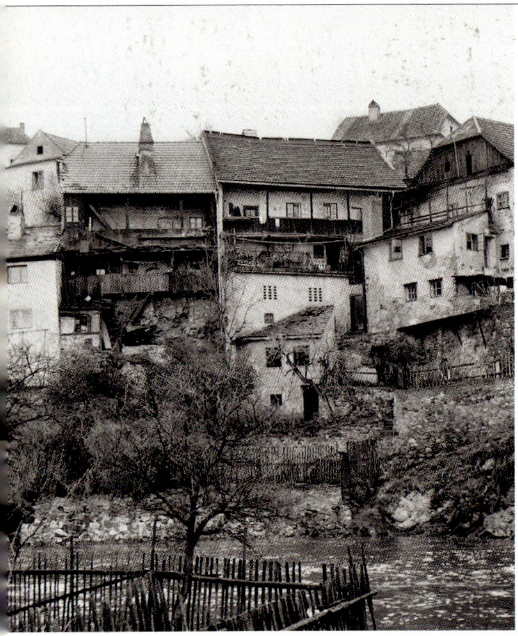

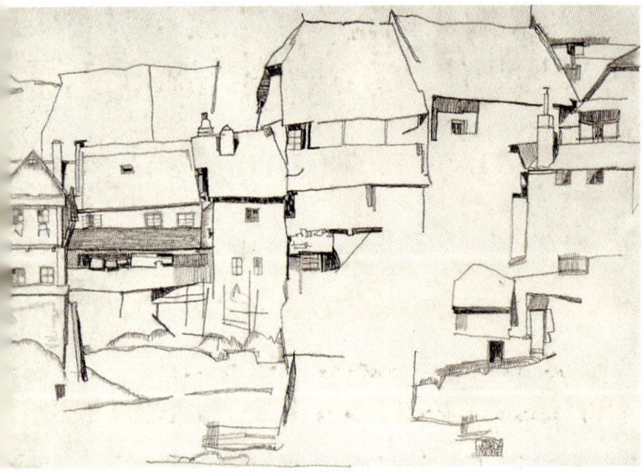

Houses on the Flössberg, Krumau

Old Houses in Krumau 1914
K 1690
Pencil on paper, 32.3 x 48 cm
Signed and dated lower right
Niederösterreichisches Landesmuseum, St. Pölten

Old Houses 1914

K 1691
Pencil and opaque colors on paper, 32.5 x 48.5 cm
Signed and dated lower right
Albertina, Vienna, inv. no.: 31.158

The suburb on a plateau south of Krumau was called "Flössberg" in German. It formerly went by the name of Fleiberg or Fleeberg (a Middle High German term for mountainside). In the course of time the meaning of these names was no longer understood and they were altered to Flössberg. (The original phonetic form lived on for a time in the Czech "na flaiperku", but this was later supplanted by a new Czech name: Plešivec). Since the romantic quarter attracted many artists, it came to be popularly known as "Painters' Corner". Today, the best-known depictions of it are those by Schiele.

The most beautiful of these is a drawing in the Albertina Museum, large passages of which the artist colored in gouache (Albertina, inv. no. 31.158). It is very likely one of the three most significant colored drawings by Schiele, as mentioned in connection with the work "Old Gable" (K 1473, p. 131). Admittedly some pure drawings, such as "Town Crescent" (K 1696, p. 157), hold an artistically equal

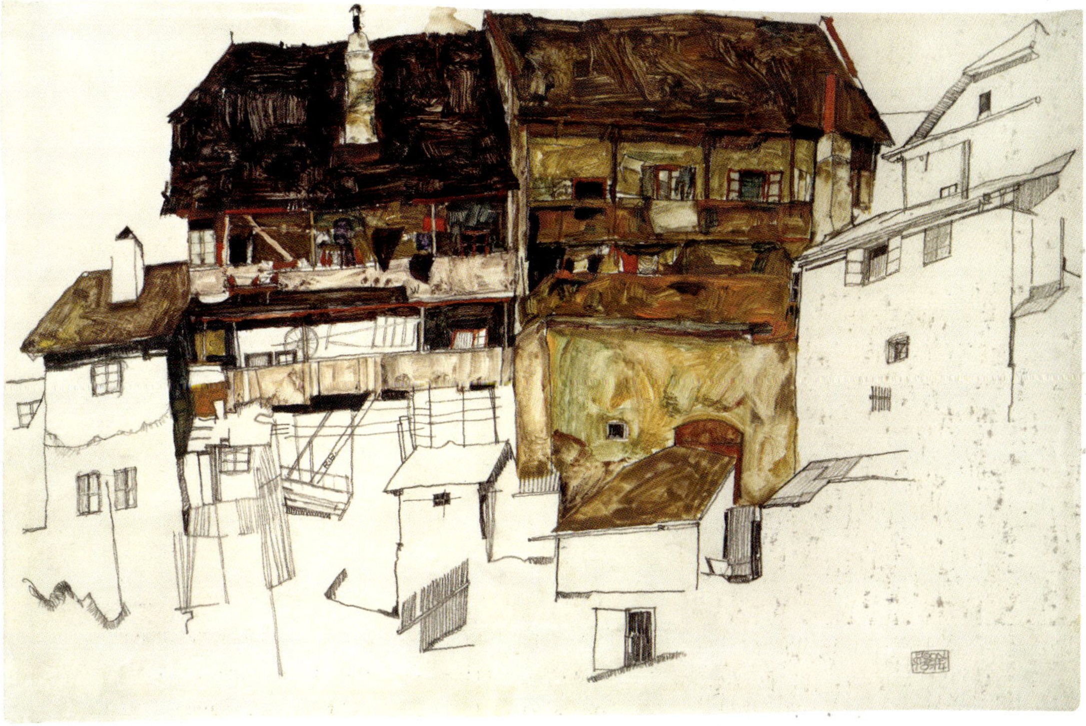

rank. This last-named drawing – like the uncolored section of the work reproduced on the left – contains a number of letters indicating the colors to be used for planned paintings based on these drawings. In the present case, only the composition sketch for a painting was ultimately made. In contrast, the drawing of the town crescent led a year later to a first painted version, which was followed by two more.

In the work illustrated above, Schiele purposely allowed the drawing to end irregularly towards the bottom and created graphic focal points with several windows, fences and other objects. The house depicted in perspective at the far right is further accentuated by the white of the empty sheet. The oldest of the houses is already recognizable from its unique balconies and projecting window and door frames, but is further emphasized by imaginative coloration. Wonderful touches are the black roof contrasted to a whitish chimney, and the pieces of laundry on this and other houses with their masterfully rendered balconies.

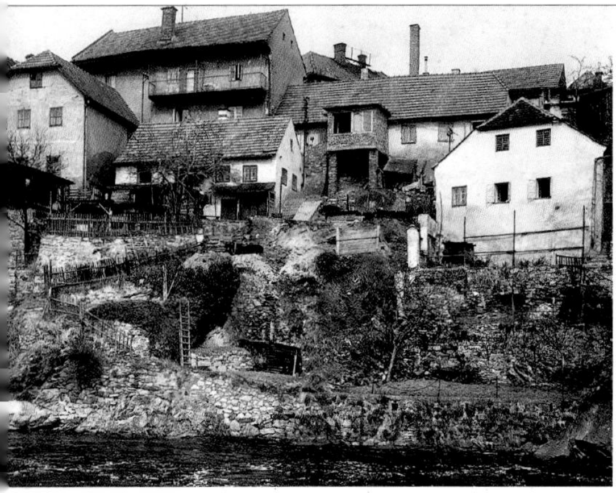

Houses on the Flössberg, Krumau

Row of Houses 1914

K 1692
Pencil on paper, 29 x 42.7 cm
Signed and dated lower right;
collector's stamp lower left: 'Sammlung Heinrich Böhler N:9';
inscribed in another (?) hand 'Krumau'
Leopold Museum, Vienna, inv. no.: LM 1393

These houses stand on a hill known as Flössberg in Krumau. Some of them have been considerably altered since Schiele depicted them, and others no longer exist. (This is why the present author had to resort to an old photograph to prove that Schiele in fact depicted a particular, identifiable row of houses in Böhmisch-Krumau.[1])

A street by the name of Na Stráni (which means "on the slope") begins at the left, with house no. 107. Converted in 1926, its original character was entirely lost, and today it has a modern hip roof. Next comes a longer, single-story house, no. 106. Visible to its right both in Schiele's drawing and in the period photograph mentioned, is a tiny building with a small window overlooking the Moldau, followed by a small, immediately adjacent house. Neither these two small houses nor the one with a porch depicted below them still stand today.

The essential traits of these buildings have been rendered with great sensitivity (see also the note on the related drawing "Old Houses", K 1691, p. 140).

1 Jane Kallir cited this statement verbatim in her catalogue raisonné. But as in many other, similar cases, she neglected to mention its source.

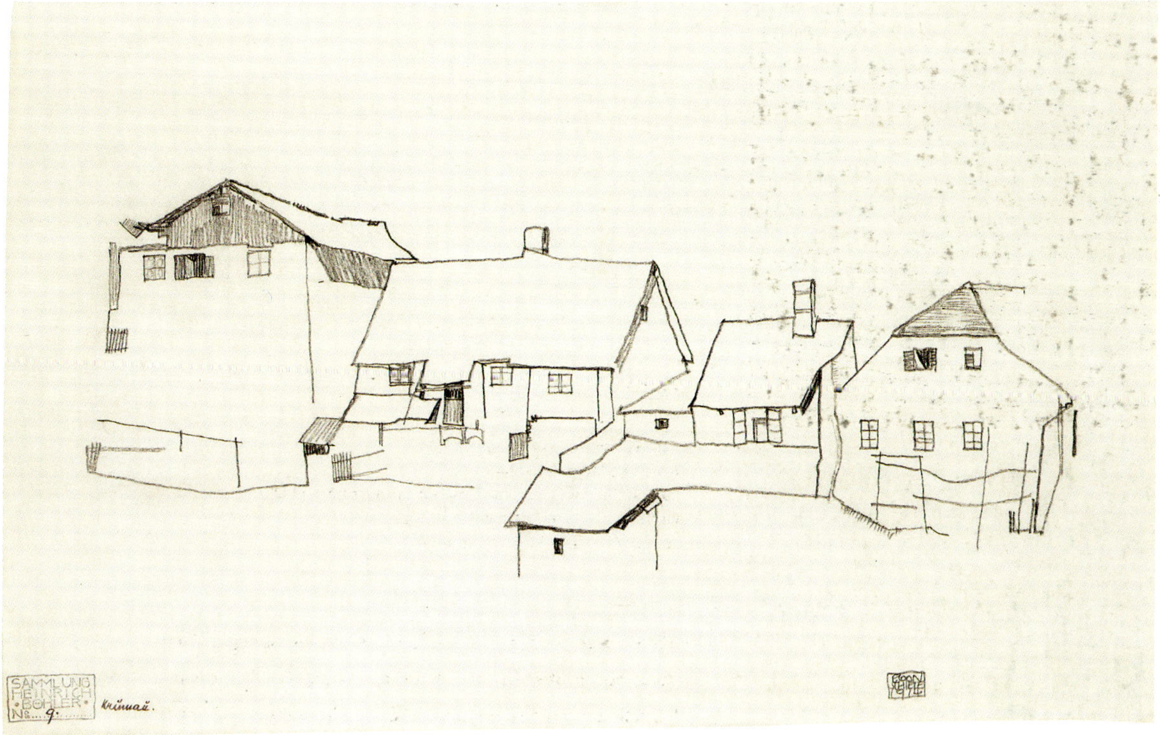
SAMMLUNG HEINRICH BÖHLER № 9.
Krumau.
EGON SCHIELE 1914.

Houses and Laundry (also known as "Two Blocks of Houses with Washing Lines") 1914

L 251 K 283
Oil on canvas, 100 x 120.7 cm
Signed and dated lower left
Leopold Museum, Vienna, inv. no.: LM 528

Here the effect of a shallow space tipped up into the plane, with which Schiele began to concern himself in 1913, is impressively handled. Although the boats on the river are seen strictly from above, the pictorial space takes on depth beginning with the zone of the laundry. This is equally evident in the area of the compact house blocks, whereas the zone behind them – formally linked with the river – has a spatially indeterminate effect (which, however, has its significance for the theme). Mountain peaks lie in the far distance. However, the bands of clouds above them appear to advance towards the viewer, more and more as they approach the top of the picture, effectively closing the composition at the top. This is further augmented by the uppermost, slightly arcing borderline between the clouds.

The horizontal layering of the composition, and the dominant gray and brownish-gray of the river, terrain and sky, create the impression of a certain monotony. Yet equally intended are the multifarious strong contrasts – in terms of color, the red accents of the small posts, the colorful laundry, and the brighter hues on the walls; and in terms of drawing, the house blocks extending not only horizontally but into the depths of the picture space, the arching, comparatively strongly shaded landscape contour behind them, and not least the lines formed by the pieces of laundry. The horizontal they describe is interrupted in places by pieces flapping up and down, for by no means all of them hang vertically. All of this, together with the diverse hues, adds up to produce a very exciting impression.

Many Schiele landscapes, whether with houses or with trees, can be interpreted as views of the world. Perhaps apart from its formally interesting composition, the present work was intended to express something along the following lines. The colorful laundry, infused with much more motion than its surroundings, may in Schiele's eyes have symbolized the still innocent and carefree lives of children and young people. Grown old, they remain in their dwellings, crowded into a constricted space. This idea is suggested by the interlocking character of the houses, and is underscored by the physiognomic suggestion of the two house walls on the right with their "window eyes." Just behind the houses begins an open, empty no-man's land. The mountain peaks emerging from the clouds – perhaps

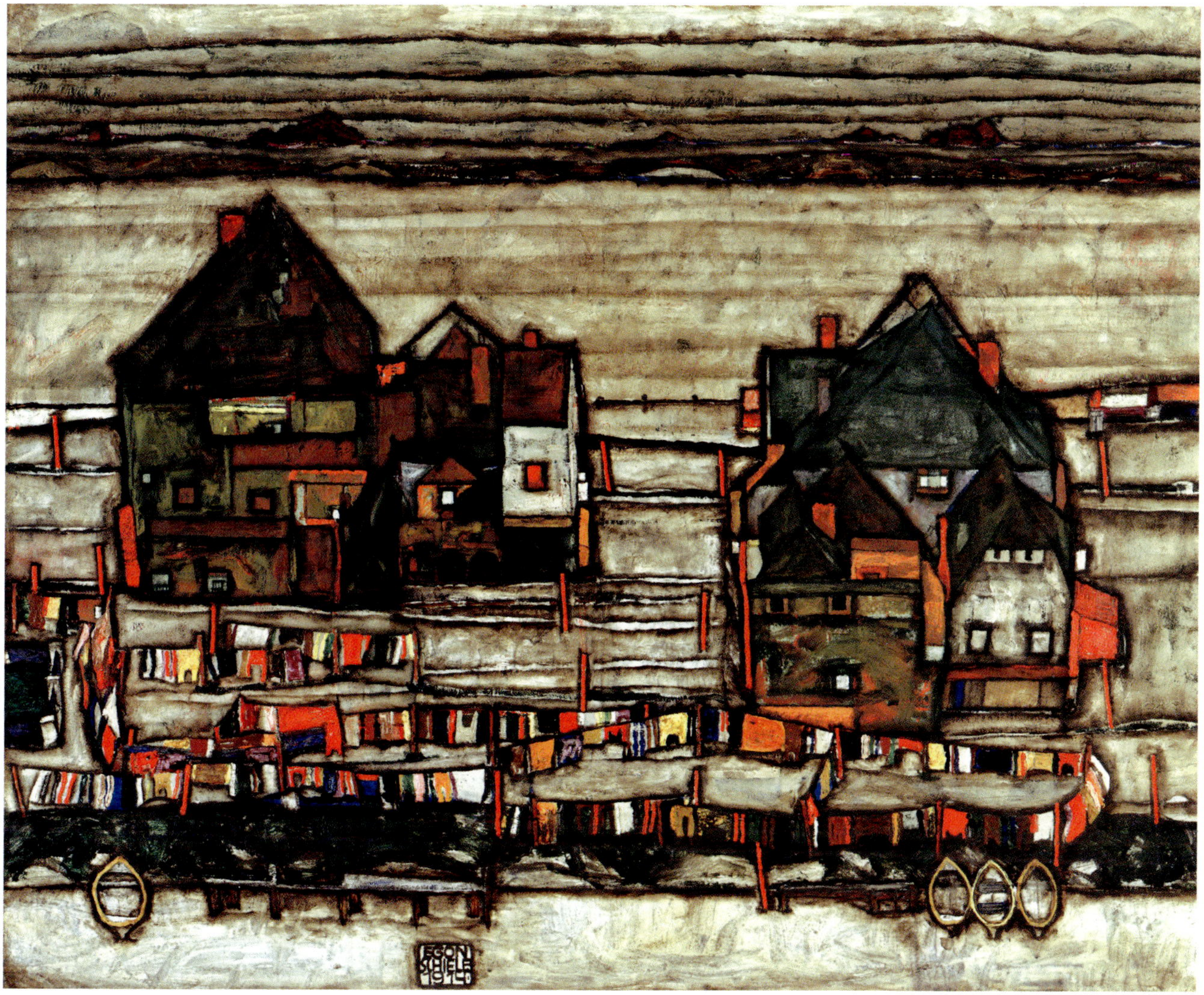

meant symbolically as the goal of human longing – appear inaccessible.

As becomes quite evident from the original, the no-man's land was formerly occupied by a row of houses. Schiele painted them over in a quite uniform way, emptying this zone – principally, perhaps, for compositional reasons, but surely also for the reasons of content just described. Only a few of the upper outlines of house façades were left standing, to enrich the distant strip of meadow. (Not many artists are able to bring themselves, as Schiele did, to paint out finished sections of a picture simply because the composition or perhaps the subject in hand seemed to require it.)

Sunflowers II (also entitled "Wilted Sunflower" and "Autumn Sun" II) 1914

L 246 K 280
Oil on canvas, 100 x 120.5 cm
Signed and dated lower left
Whereabouts unknown

Schiele produced three highly expressive paintings of sunflowers, the first in early 1910, the second in late 1911, and the third, present one in 1914.

In the foreground we see a group of sunflowers and a meadow dotted with flowers, behind it a low chain of hills and a mountain in the background at the far right. The wildflower blossoms, primarily in strong reds and blues, may seem all-too naively and decoratively depicted. Yet possibly Schiele consciously intended them as a contrasting foil to the sunflowers. In fact, it would be hard to imagine a greater contrast than that between the wildflowers and the sunflowers with their drooping, wilted leaves. Cut off by the picture edges above and below, they stand like a wall in front of a gray-clouded sky that is only slightly articulated by fine horizontal lines. A much more striking feature is the small, bright disc, its interior tinted a delicate pink, which appears between the sunflowers in the sky. This was doubtlessly intended to represent the sun – but a sun so weak that the heads of the sunflowers do not even turn to follow it, as they would in nature.

In his first catalogue raisonné, published in 1930, Otto Nirenstein, who later changed his name to Kallir, described this painting as representing "… sunflowers. Visible between them is the full moon …" In 1951 I pointed out to Kallir's assistant, Vita Künstler, that the disc in the painting must represent the sun. To her objection that it could not be the sun because sunflowers always naturally turn towards it, I replied that the opposite reaction, seen here, conformed with the tragic idea of painting: the autumn sunrays were so feeble that the sunflowers no longer felt them and even turned away (see Leopold, *Schiele*, 1972, p. 581).

It was not until about a decade later that I discovered a letter of Schiele's in which he gave this painting two titles: "Sunflowers" and "Autumn Sun". In his second catalogue raisonné, of 1966, Kallir corrected his earlier misapprehension by simply designating the picture "Sunflowers with Sun," thus giving the sun much greater prominence than its actual, small and quite inconspicuous appearance in the painting would warrant.

As in the 1911 "Sunflowers," the depiction points beyond its mere appearance to an allegory. There, the blossoms of the young sunflowers in the lower area evoked children extending their arms, a carefree impression like

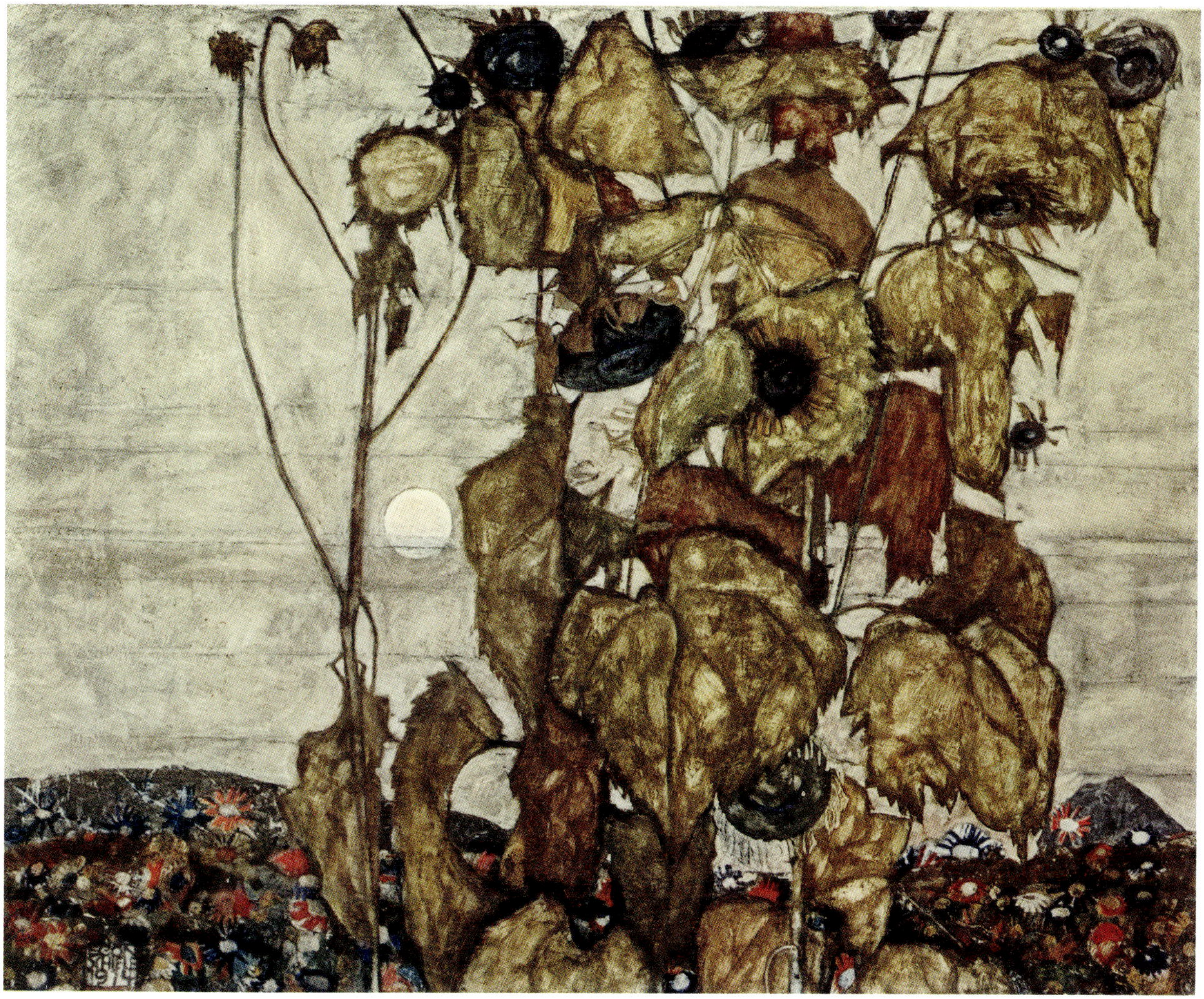

that suggested here by the colorful flowers in the meadow. In contrast, while the sunflower blossoms in the upper area of the earlier picture appeared windblown and drooping – like people bent under life's burdens – in the 1914 painting the full tragedy of approaching death becomes clearly manifest. With the drooping sunflower heads in subdued blue, contrasted to the highly colorful meadow flowers, and the even more deeply hanging, dessicated leaves in gradations of olive and reddish-brown, Schiele created a poignant symbol of ageing and death.

Landscape with Fields 1914

K 1679
Pencil on paper, 30.9 x 47.9 cm
Signed and dated lower right
Leopold Museum, Vienna, inv. no.: LM 1396

Except for a small passage at the lower left, Schiele has left the foreground open. He has drawn only the fields extending over a long, low hillcrest. As arbitrary as their size, boundaries and arrangement may appear on first sight, the fields have been combined into an unobtrusive but well-considered composition which nonetheless retains the charm of the accidental. The focal point of the composition lies just left of center, and the diagonals of the field boundaries to the left and right accordingly possess a certain symmetry. (Complete symmetry would have appeared unnatural, apart from the fact that it could hardly have been present in the actual topography.)

Long and short lines, hatchings in various directions and densities, and spiral scrawls providing numerous accents, combine to produce an effect of great vitality. The irregular surfaces of the fields are characterized with considerable graphic ingenuity. Yet everything is subordinated to the larger, overall form. The fields extend across the entire sheet from left to right – without beginning or end. Standing against the empty zone signifying the sky, the gently curving horizon, together with the series of meadows and fields, convey a sense of the vastness of the world.

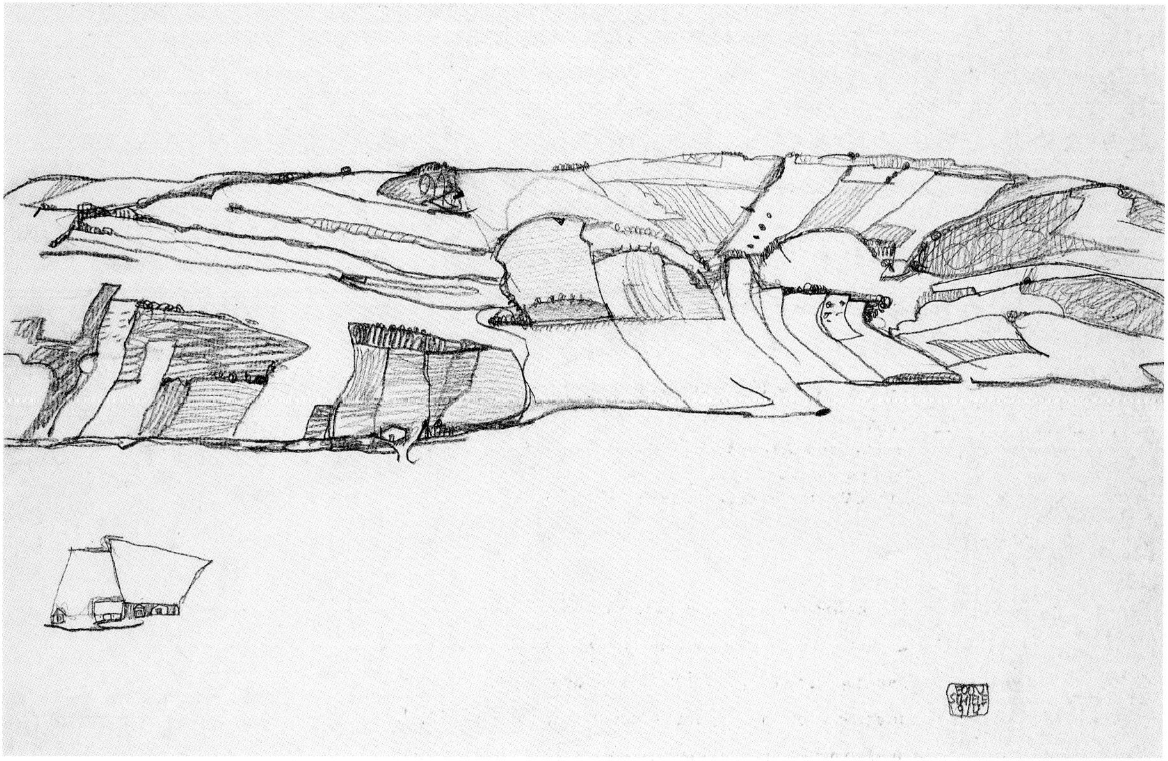
EGON
SCHIELE

"Windows" 1914

L 252 K 284
Oil on canvas, 110 x 140 cm
Inscribed on the stretcher as 'Eigentum von Hans Böhler, Wien I, Elisabethstraße 12'
Österreichische Galerie Belvedere, Vienna, inv. no.: 4278

It was a quite new and daring idea to make a house wall – in fact, not even the entire wall – the principal subject of a painting. Visible apart from this are only a small section of pavement at the lower left and a glimpse of sky at the upper right. (Since the sky has a quite similar color to the wall, it is difficult to identify as such, despite the bands meant to indicate cloud formations. Its function in the picture is merely to set a contrast to the bare wall in front of it.)

Schiele has articulated the wall by means of numerous windows and two rows of shingles. Eye level lies at about the window with the wide open outer casements, that is, a bit lower than picture center but considerably shifted to the right. This results not only in a high vantage point to the lower windows but an extremely oblique view of those on the left. These are also seen from quite varying points of view. Especially in the case of the upper left window, the vantage point from below and the side combines with the arcade-like shadows on the wall to produce a highly interesting configuration.

The warped windows and their dilapidated state suggest poor living conditions, as do the bare house walls with their flaking stucco and blue stripes below. These stripes were probably added – apart from compositional reasons – in order to provide a conclusion to the wall at the bottom and, at the same time, to create a correspondence with the nearly horizontal purple band underneath the upper row of shingles. Yet these formal and substantial considerations cannot prevent the harsh blue, the white of the wall, the garish yellow and blue-green on the lower windows from making the broad row of shingles immediately above, with its delicate hues, appear somewhat empty. Nor has the advancement in space of these shingles on the wall projection been pictorially achieved (apart from the perspective drawing of the shingles' sides).

In this large painting Schiele concentrated mainly on configuring the windows, pulling all the stops of his inventiveness in the process. In addition to being depicted from various angles, they are arranged in the wall in a very balanced way, and their variety of colors and shapes reflect Schiele's fertile imagination. The view of, and into, the windows, and their highly differentiated rendering, have been exploited to the point that we can speak of marked individuality. It was for good reason that Schiele called the "Windows".

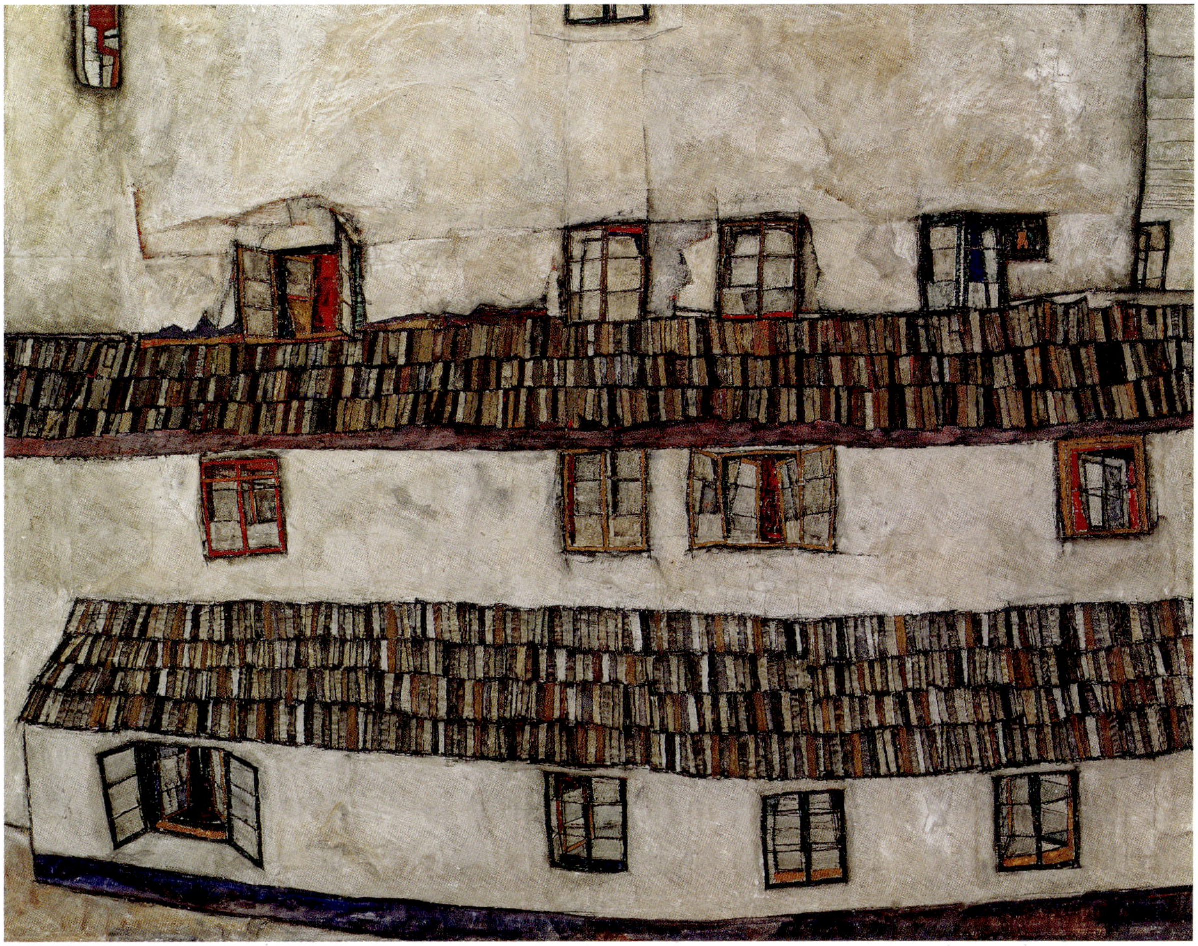

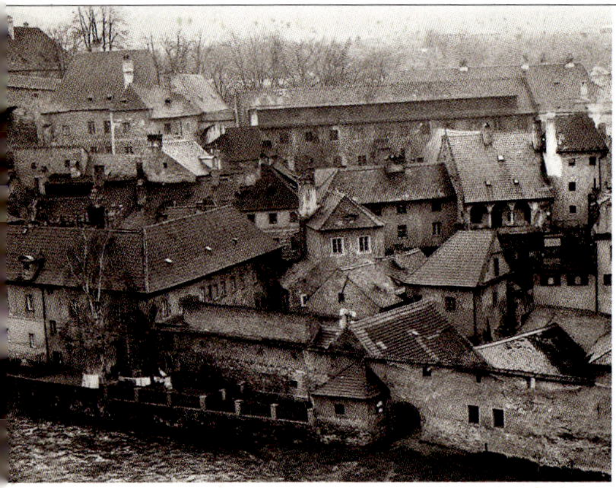

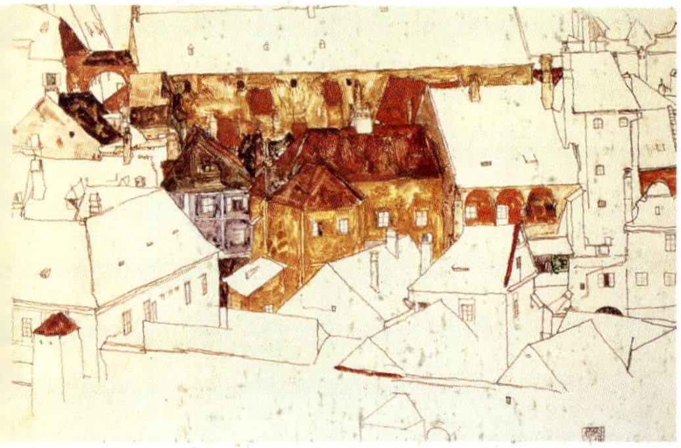

"Yellow City" 1914

L 255 K 286
Black crayon, gouache and oil on canvas, 110 x 140 cm
Signed and dated lower right
Whereabouts unknown

The study for this painting was presumably made from the vantage point of the former Jesuit Seminar, which lies on a rise on the right bank of the Moldau. Depicted is an excerpt from the Krumau district of Neustadt, or New Town, whose early fortifications are cut off by the lower edge. Almost all the smaller and larger buildings of the district are identifiable, even details such as the three arcades of the building to the right of center (21 Latron). Yet as so often, Schiele has altered the number and placement of the windows.

The very large building at the top of the painting is the former "Schüttkastengebäude", or granary, whose site is now occupied by police headquarters. While in the topographically more precise study this building is depicted in its full width, here, like many other features, it has been strongly foreshortened for compositional reasons and the windows reduced to peepholes. To round off the picture, Schiele added an imaginary landscape of fields and a row of trees whose green forms a counterpoint to the reddish-brown of the large roof below. (Formerly this was the site

Latron district, in Krumau

Yellow City 1914
K 1695
Pencil and opaque colors
on paper, 30.5 x 34.5 cm
Signed and dated lower right
Private collection

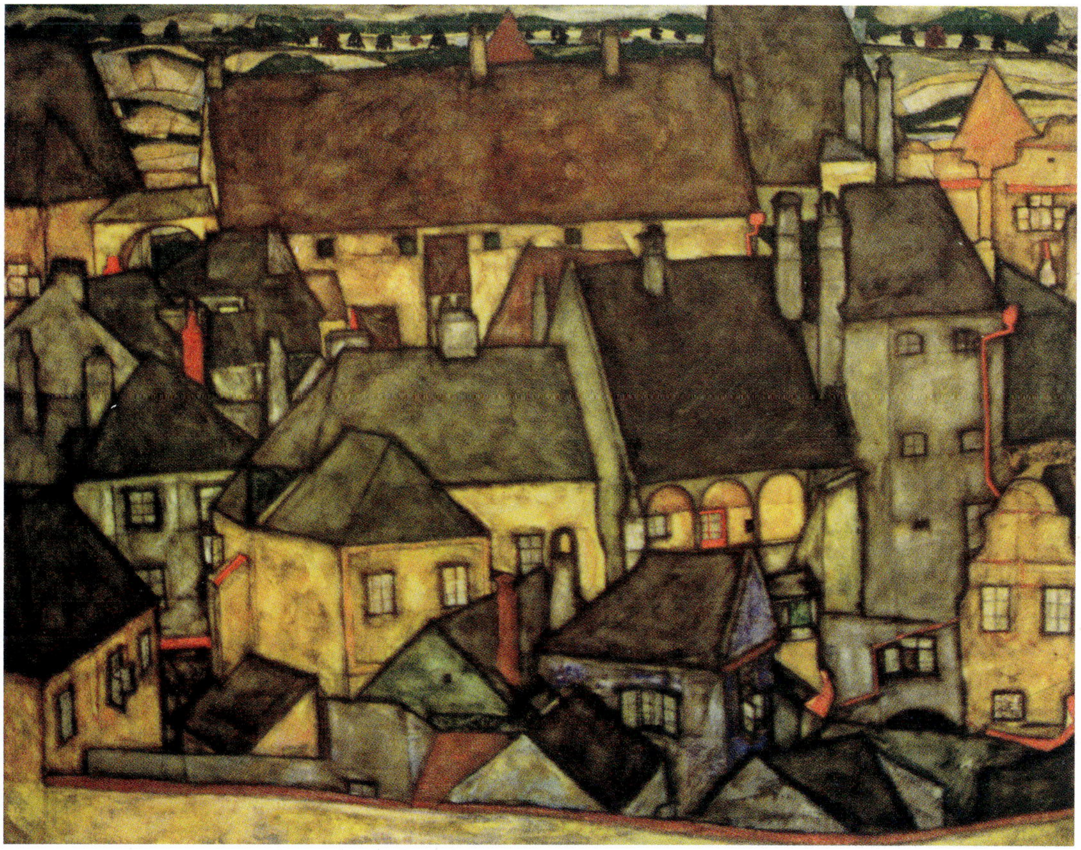

of the castle tilting yard.) The erstwhile granary has been fitted with a high narrow roof on the right, which in reality belongs to a broader building behind it (known as the "Saltbox", a storage building for salt). Visible to the left of the granary is a round-arched portal through which, coming from the castle, one arrives in Latrongasse at Bader Bridge. The building at the lower left is part of the former Royal Hospital Yard adjacent to St. Jodocus' Church. Much more of it is visible in the study, where it is not so strongly curtailed by the picture edge.

While the shapes of the houses and roofs are depicted quite faithfully, if in strongly reduced geometric terms, their colors have little in common with the real motif – predominating yellow and orange gradations that prompted Schiele to entitle the painting "Yellow City".

Last Houses (At the Edge of Town) 1914

K 1806
Pencil on paper, 19.6 x 31.6 cm
Unsigned, undated
Albertina, Vienna, inv. no.: 23.591

Judging by the small front yards, and especially by the wooden fence on the right and the trees behind it, we can assume that the title given in the literature for this drawing is justified. More importantly, the artist succeeded in characterizing every object in the depiction by apparently simple means. The houses and a few of the windows appear contoured with a single stroke, while other windows, the tufts of grass, and the fence are emphasized by means of heavier graphite strokes applied with greater pressure. The distribution of these darker passages in the composition, too, is only seemingly simple; in fact, it is quite inspired.

A date of execution between the end of 1914 and the middle of 1915 can be assumed. This dating is suggested by a comparison not only with drawings dated to 1915, but with paintings of house groupings, such as "Yellow City" of 1914 (L 255/K 286, p. 153), the paintings of individual houses, or the two "Town Crescents" of 1915 (L 259/K 292 and L 258/K 291, p. 159, L 260/K 293, p. 161), especially with regard to the way the house windows are graphically depicted here. The most obvious stylistic affinity is between the contour and interior drawing of the trees in the second "Town Crescent" and those in the drawing reproduced here.

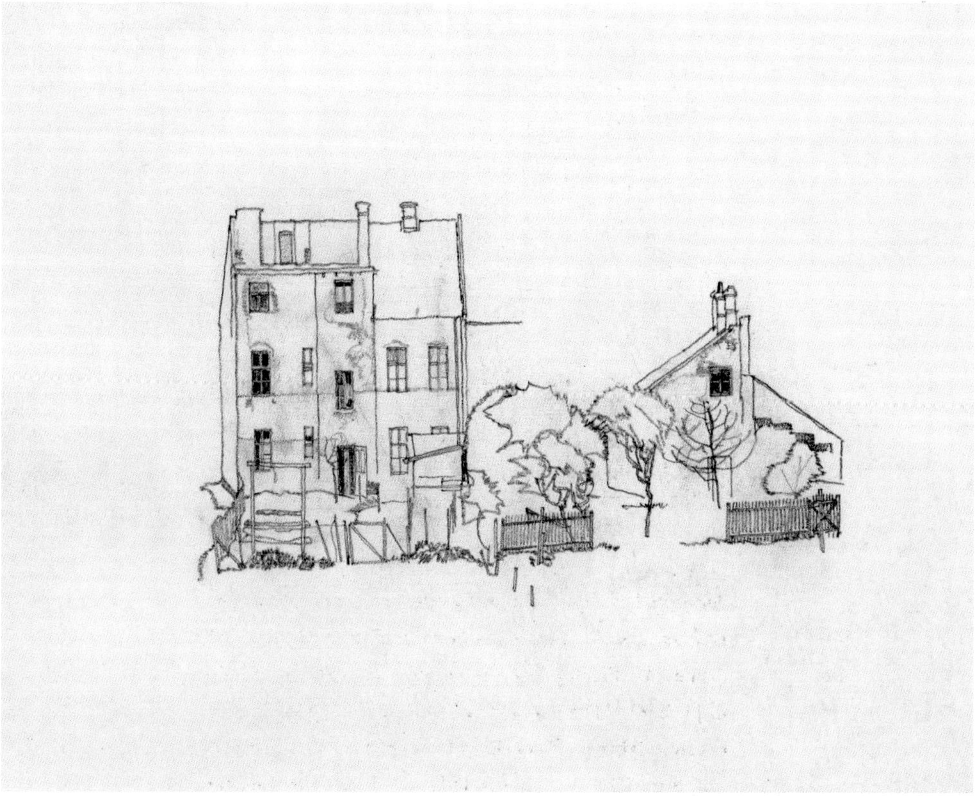

Town Crescent (drawing) 1914

K 1696
Pencil on paper, 43.7 x 31.9 cm
Signed and dated lower right
Leopold Museum, Vienna, inv. no.: LM 2308

Seen from Krumau Castle Hill, this row of houses built along a gently curving lane is clearly distinguishable from the many other buildings in the town. To emphasize the crescent shape, Schiele has omitted other buildings or depicted them only fragmentarily. Nevertheless, such features as the roof outlines in the foreground and the strongly foreshortened wall of the house at lower center play a key role, serving to reinforce the effect of the high vantage point and emphasize the distance to the crescent. And the device is extraordinarily successful. The houses appear to stream upwards and into the distance. The many oblique lines leading towards the river create a formal overbalance on the left, but this is counteracted by the Bader Bridge and the nearby houses on the left bank of the Moldau. The buildings jutting off at an angle to the right of the tall double house at upper center also serve to take up the leftward motion of the crescent and anchor it in the composition.

The outlines of houses and roofs are only apparently simple. Actually they are delineated with great sensitivity, both as regards their course and the varying pressure of the strokes. These in themselves are sufficient to evoke the houses' volume (although the masterfully handled perspective does help). One imagines that the effect of space could have been achieved more easily with the aid of multiple shadings, but this would have diminished the effect of the superb lineature. The few indications of shadow merely form accents in this wonderful drawing. The various letters on the house walls evidently represent color notes for paintings Schiele planned to make after this drawing. The first two painted versions of the town crescent were done in 1915.

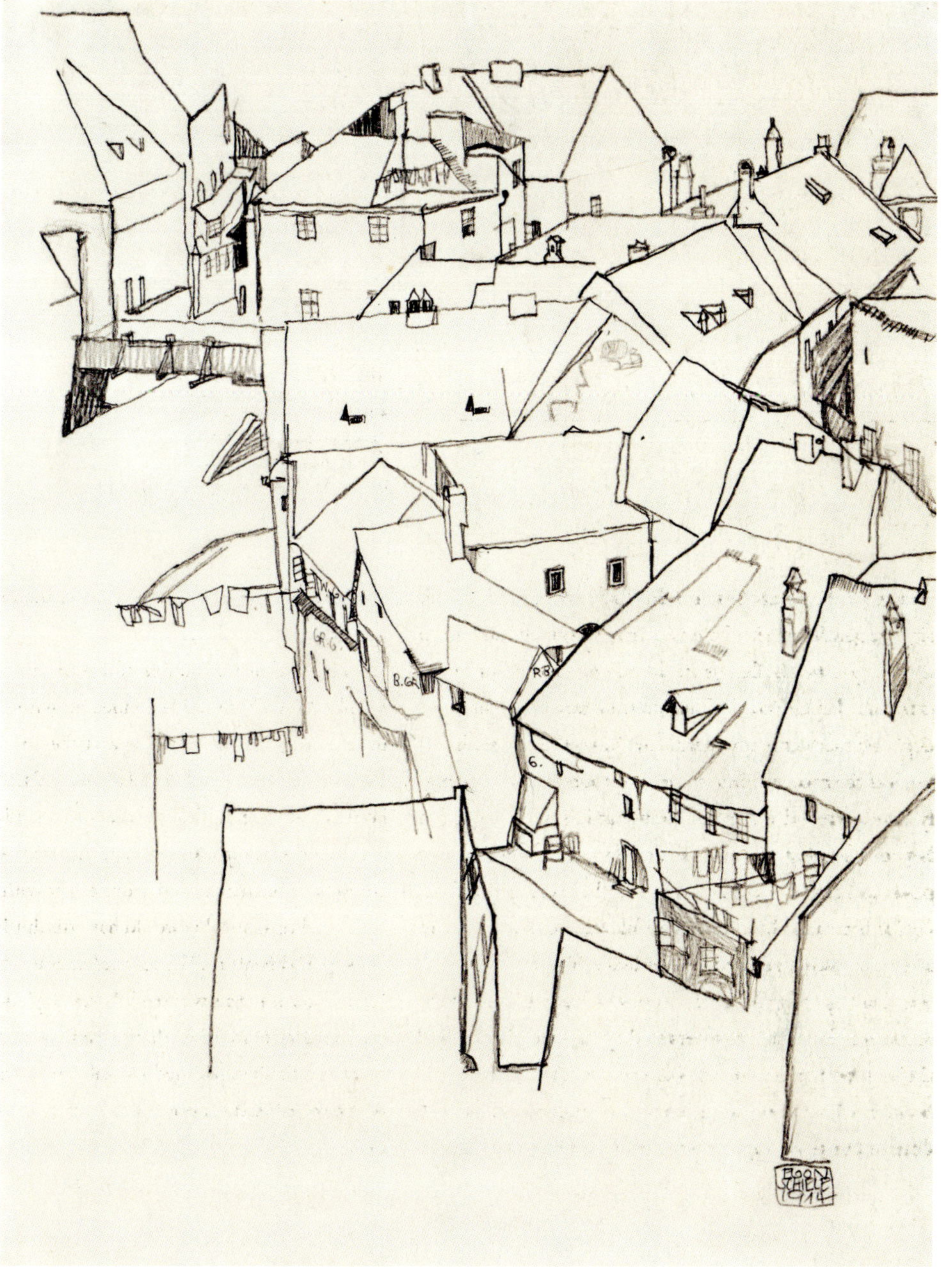
EGON
SCHIELE
1914

Krumau Town Crescent I (Krumau Town District I) Entitled by Schiele "Town" III as well as "Small Town" V 1915

L 258 K 291
Black crayon, gouache and oil on canvas, 109.7 x 140 cm
Signed and dated lower right
Israel Museum, Jerusalem

Schiele painted three different versions of this Krumau motif, based above all on his 1914 drawing (K 1696, p. 157). As in this drawing, in the second and third versions of 1915 and 1917/18 he placed greater emphasis on the fundamental visual idea: a crescent of houses viewed from a high vantage point. None of the three paintings includes the roof outlines and the single house wall depicted in perspective in the foreground of the drawing. Schiele apparently relinquished the *repoussoir* effect employed to such advantage there because in a painting, the roofs would have had to be filled in, which might have detracted from the essential subject: the view of these old houses and walls in the foreground.

In the drawing, and especially in the second painted version, one has the feeling that the crescent is in motion. Although the overlapping of the houses into the distance seems somewhat more obvious in this first version than in the second, the overall effect – augmented by the distribution of lights and darks – is basically static. The calm center is formed by a section of the courtyard with whitish walls enclosed by the darker roofs of house nos. 92 and 93 Lange Gasse. The distribution of the three reddish-yellow to orange façades also serves to anchor the dynamic components of the crescent.

The motif depicted consists principally of the row of houses between Lange Gasse and the millrace below the castle, seen from a low vantage point, looking obliquely upwards. The 1914 drawing and the first painted version of 1915 reflect the actual situation most faithfully. (The correspondence extends even to the clothes today still being hung out to dry in virtually the same places.) Here the houses – 89 to 100 Lange Gasse – are arranged approximately in an arc. The not directly connected group of houses at the upper left, near Bader Bridge (for this motif, see p. 156), differs clearly in type from the old houses. Today their crescent arrangement is interrupted by a new building at a crucial place, especially as regards the first painted version. Back then their static center was formed by a section of courtyard framed by roofs. The light wall of the hip-roofed house facing the viewer at that point is also visible on the card Schiele sent to Arthur Roessler on 15 January 1915 (WSB 180601). On it Schiele outlined a group of

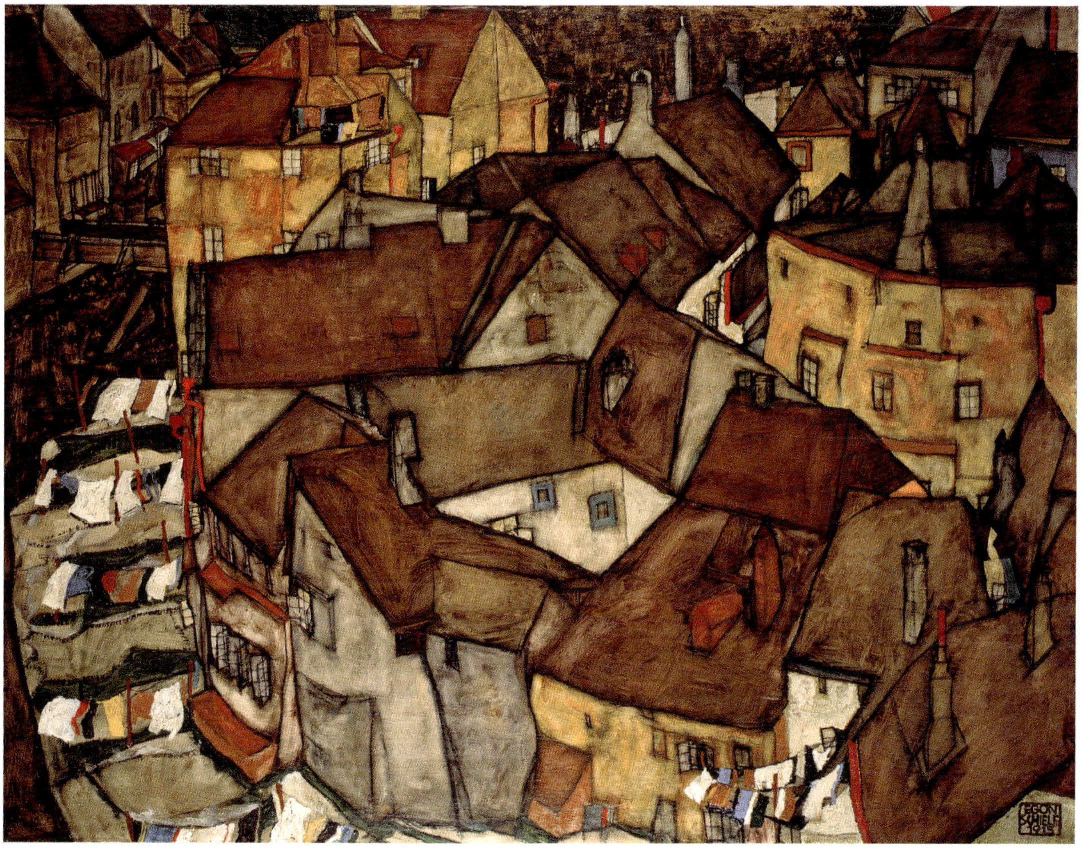

houses that corresponds to the first version of "Town Crescent". The house with the hip roof mentioned has since been demolished, as have the two houses that once stood between the courtyard from the millrace. A new building now occupies this lot.

In contrast to the second and third painted versions, in the first, much as in the 1914 drawing, Schiele depicted Bader Bridge and adjacent buildings at the upper left. The St. Jodocus' building is just recognizable, even though Schiele has replaced its three round-arched windows with two rows of windows. All of these structures cut off by the picture edge are rendered in dark gradations, and the Moldau skirting the building complex to the right of Bader Bridge in a gentle arc in a blackish-brown. All of these darks serve to make the building complex in light orange tones stand out by contrast. Its color is replied to by the similarly brilliant orange of the tourist hostel to the right of the crescent.

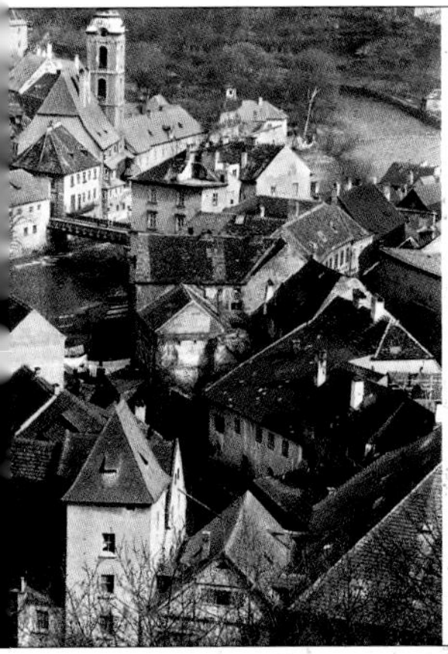

View of Krumau

"Island Town" (also known as "Krumau Town Crescent" II) 1915

L 260 K 293
Black crayon, gouache and oil on canvas, 110.5 x 140.5 cm
Signed and dated center right
Leopold Museum, Vienna, inv. no.: LM 456

This second version of the "Town Crescent" was likewise done in the first half of 1915. Here the houses have been entirely divorced from their topographical setting.

The courtyard with whitish walls and two green-framed windows, an essential feature in the first version, has grown smaller here and been rendered in broken gradations that diminish its significance. The courtyard no longer functions as a static center. Otherwise it would have "stopped the movement" which Schiele aimed to evoke at this period, even in certain townscapes.

The houses in this painting give the impression of flowing viscously into the background, a movement that seems even to communicate itself to the light band of ground behind the orange-yellow building complex at the top. This impression of gradual motion is underscored by the way the house façades diverge from the vertical to various extents and in various directions. The first two appear to lean forwards; the walls adjacent to the little white house set like a capstone tip backwards; the following, in this version overlapping walls tend to lean forwards, while the larger part of the tall houses appears to turn in the opposite direction as if leaning into a curve. The sense of motion is even clearer in the row of trees, whose middle portion seems to be pushed left as if by centrifugal force.

While in the first version the idea of a town crescent was subordinated to a more complete depiction of the district, the second is treated in a more focussed and symbolically evocative way. Here the arc configuration is surrounded by dark waters and set on a spit of land resembling an island. This is likely the source of Schiele's title, "Island Town".

In part these houses with their bays, roofs and chimneys have the appearance of geometric solids. The façades are accompanied by green and purple bands which relate to them and to each other like the parts of a fugue. In order to emphasize the arc configuration, Schiele omitted the decorative laundry lines of the first version and replaced them by the row of autumnal trees mentioned, which is continued on the right by a few smaller trees in the background. Like borderlines between land and water, all of the trees and the numerous textures in the terrain are arranged in the form of an arc to underscore the direction of the massed buildings.

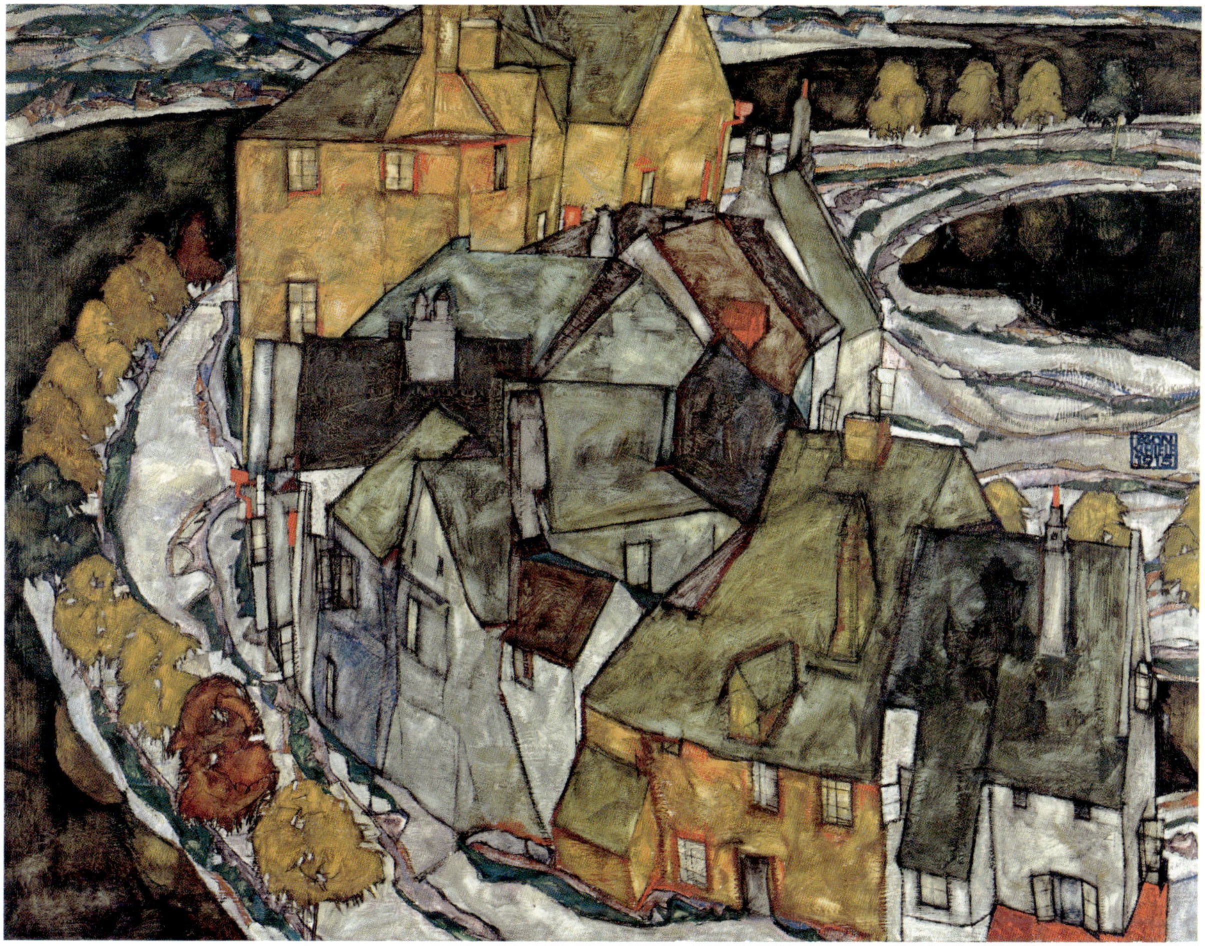

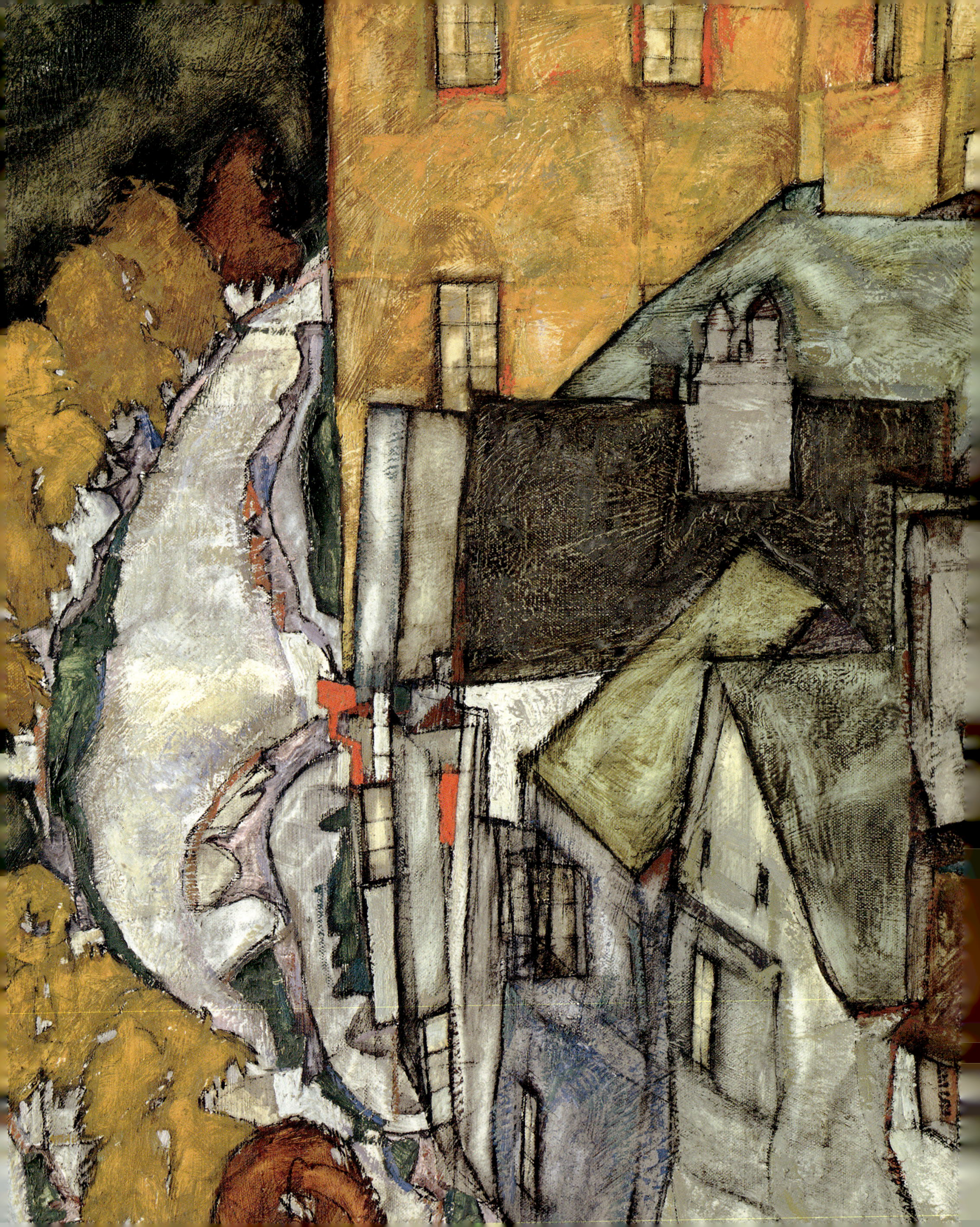

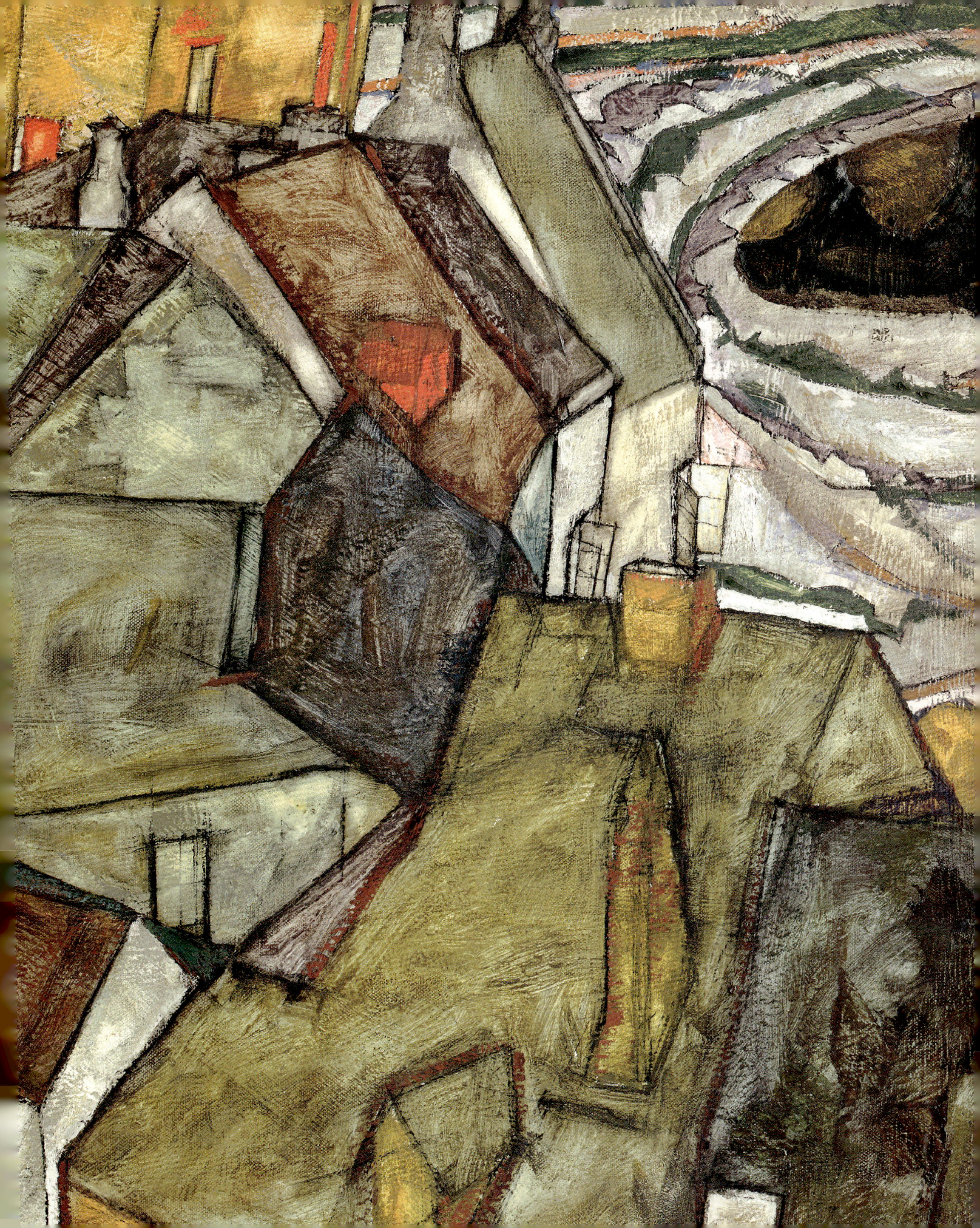

House with Shingle Roof (drawing) 1914

K 1694
Pencil on paper, 43.3 x 31.8 cm
Signed and dated lower right
Leopold Museum, Vienna, inv. no.: LM 1428

The motif for this study was provided by a building that still stands in Krumau (30 Rooseveltova ulice, formerly Adalbert-Stifter-Gasse). Its site between other houses is indicated both in the first sketch for the painting (L 262/K 295, p. 167) and in this sheet-filling sketch. (In the painting, Schiele omitted the buildings next to and behind the "House with Shingle Roof" for reasons explained on p. 166).

Especially this drawing of houses is enriched by pencil strokes applied with lesser or greater pressure, and a window hatched entirely in black supplies an eccentrically located point of reference.

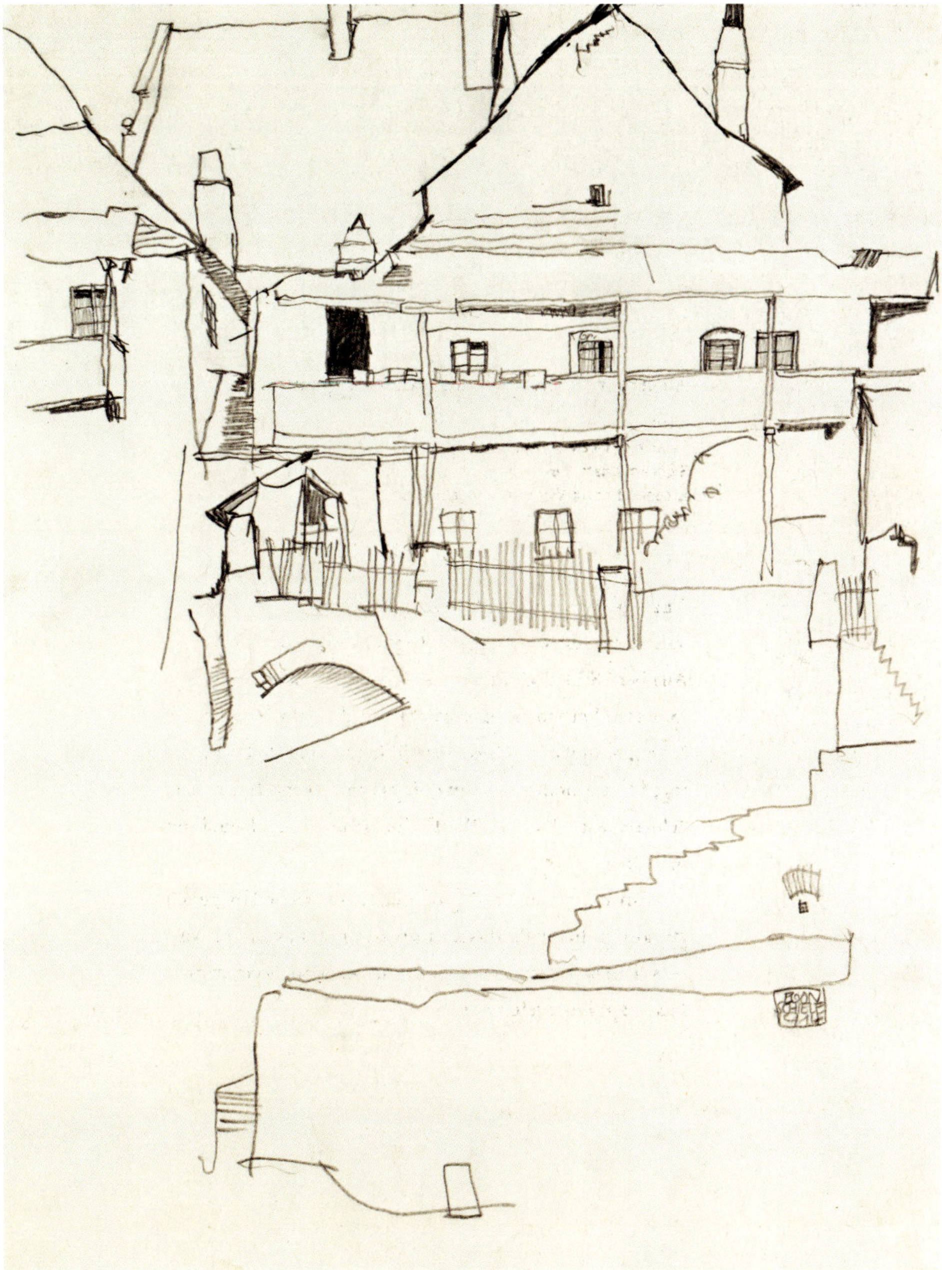

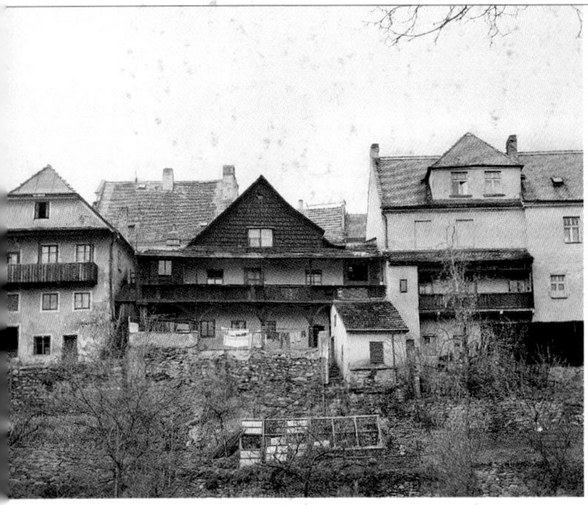

House with Shingle Roof
also known as "Old House" or "House" I 1915

L 262 K 295
Black crayon, gouache and oil on canvas, 110 x 140 cm
Signed and dated lower right
Leopold Museum, Vienna, inv. no.: LM 469

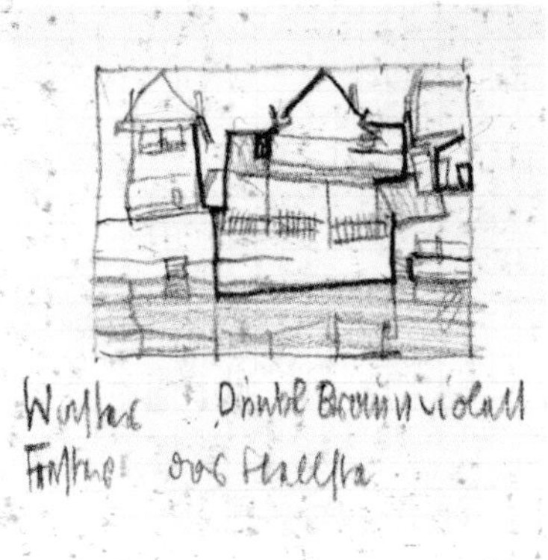

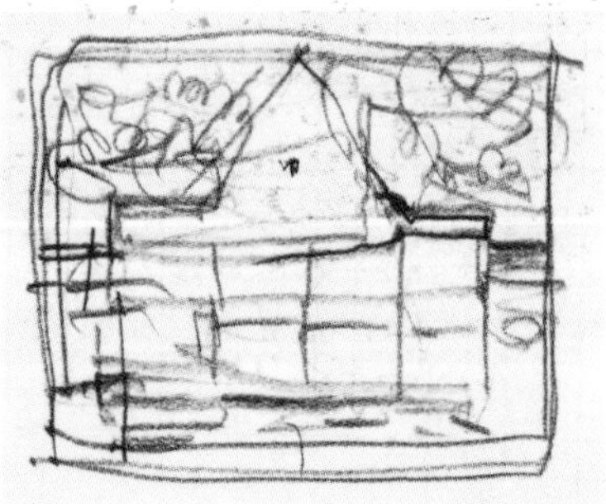

Sketches for House with Shingle Roof

Sixth sketchbook
Albertina, Vienna, ESA 322

In the first sketch for the present painting (left) the passage below the fence is foreshortened, and beneath it, a river – the Moldau – is sketchily indicated. Below this Schiele wrote in German script, "Water dark brown-violet (!), window the lightest." In his second design (bottom) the artist formulated a new idea: an isolation and monumentalization of the house. To this end he spirited it into an imaginary landscape in which nothing of the actual surroundings remains visible.

The rendering has the effect of a penetrating portrait of a house that, so to speak, has succumbed to senility. Each of its sections reflects a unique fate: the decaying fence and the crumbling wall by the pillars, the warped windows, the weathered boards and the many shingles. Never before or after did the artist depict shingles with such eloquence. (Compare, for instance, those in the painting "Windows" [L 252/K 284, p. 151]). In reality, the color of the shingles would cause them to recede with respect to the foliage of the trees. Here it is just the opposite. The shingles (and, analogously, the laundry hung outside the upper story and

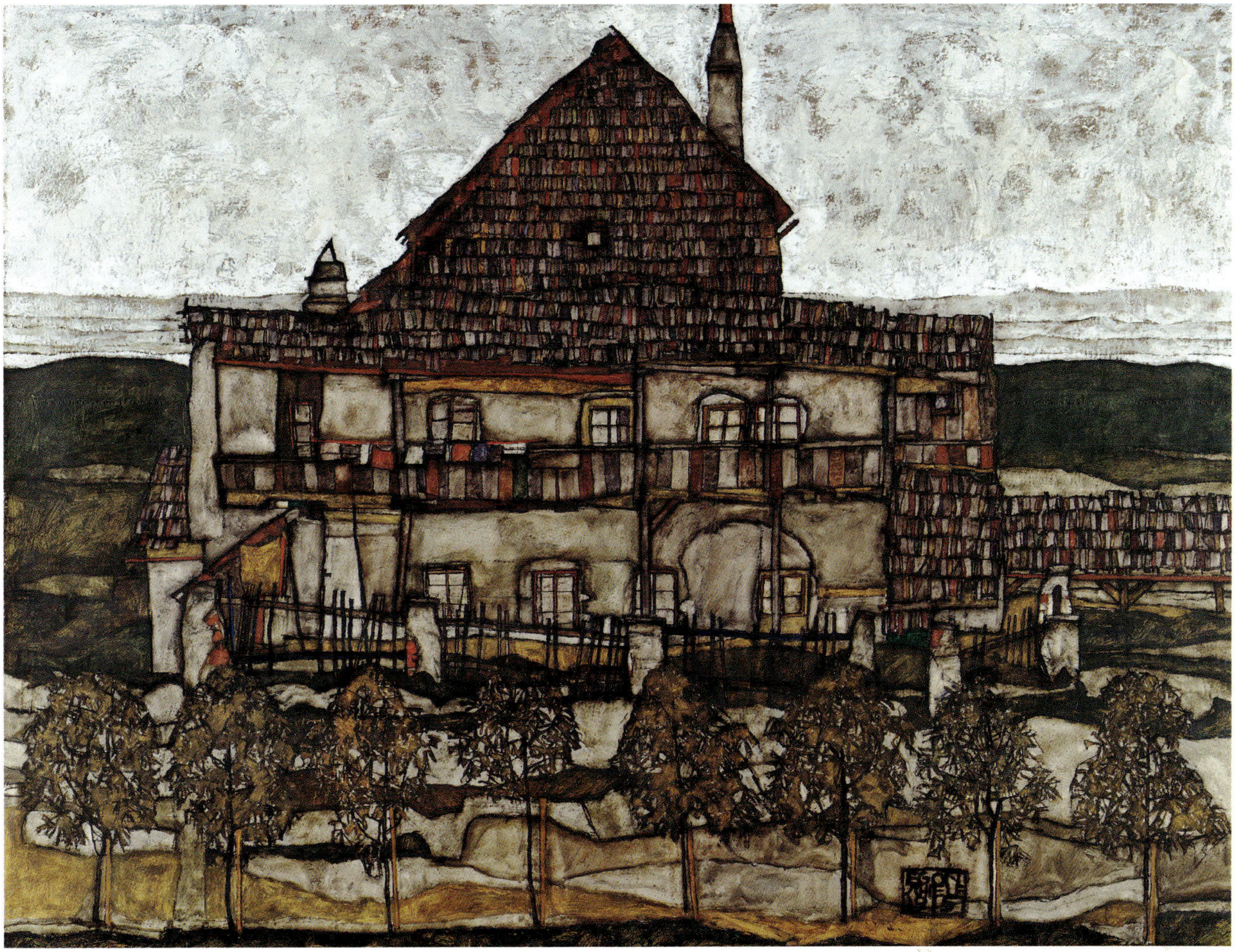

the boards behind it) are rendered in a variety of enigmatically luminous tones. This reflects an Expressionist penchant to amplify essentials and subordinate everything else to them. The row of trees, for instance, serves merely to provide a pedestal for the "house monument". Its steep gable rises into a sky – painted entirely differently from the rest of the composition – which leaves no room for hope. The image becomes an allegory of loneliness and decay.

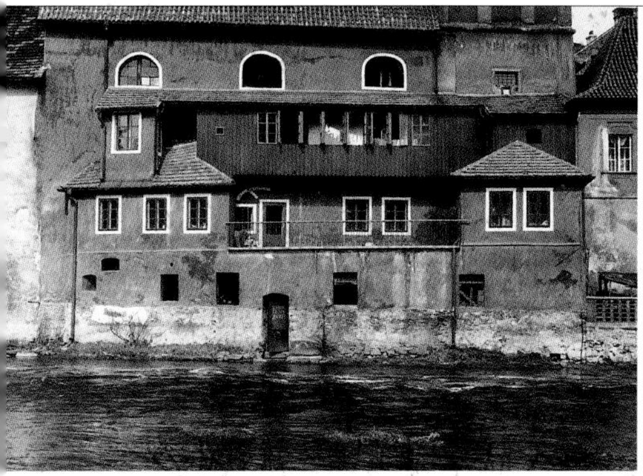

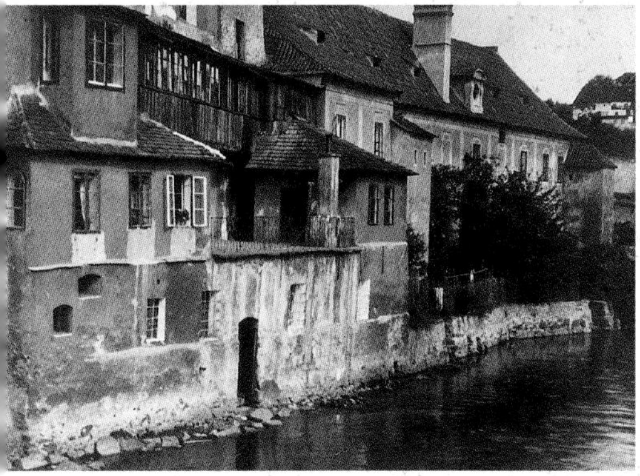

View of the former Jodocus' Church, Krumau

Postcard of Krumau

House on a River 1915
L 263 K 294
Black crayon, opaque colors and oil on canvas, 109.5 x 140 cm
Signed and dated lower right
Leopold Museum, Vienna, inv. no.: LM 468

As in the 1914 work which Schiele called "Windows" (L 252/K 284, p. 151), a house wall is the sole subject – augmented here by a river in which door and windows are reflected. The motif was provided by the façade of the former St. Jost's or St. Jodocus' Church on the left bank of the Moldau, a section of the adjacent house upriver, and the river itself. (The church, first mentioned in the records in 1347, was converted in 1596. The tower with onion dome was added in the Baroque period. After the Jesuit Order was abolished, the church was closed in 1788 and converted in 1791/92 to a residential building with annexes on the Moldau. These annexes and the connecting wooden veranda were once roofed with shingles.) In 1964 the Moldau-side façades and all annexes were repainted. In the course of work, numerous windows, a door, and the three round-arched windows of the former church were given an incongruous colored framing.

In the 1915 painting, Schiele reproduced the earlier view quite faithfully, including the chimney on the terrace, which had since been torn down. (It is likewise visible on the postcard reproduced at the lower left). Since he wished to concentrate on the wall, Schiele purposely omitted the roof that begins above the round-arched windows.

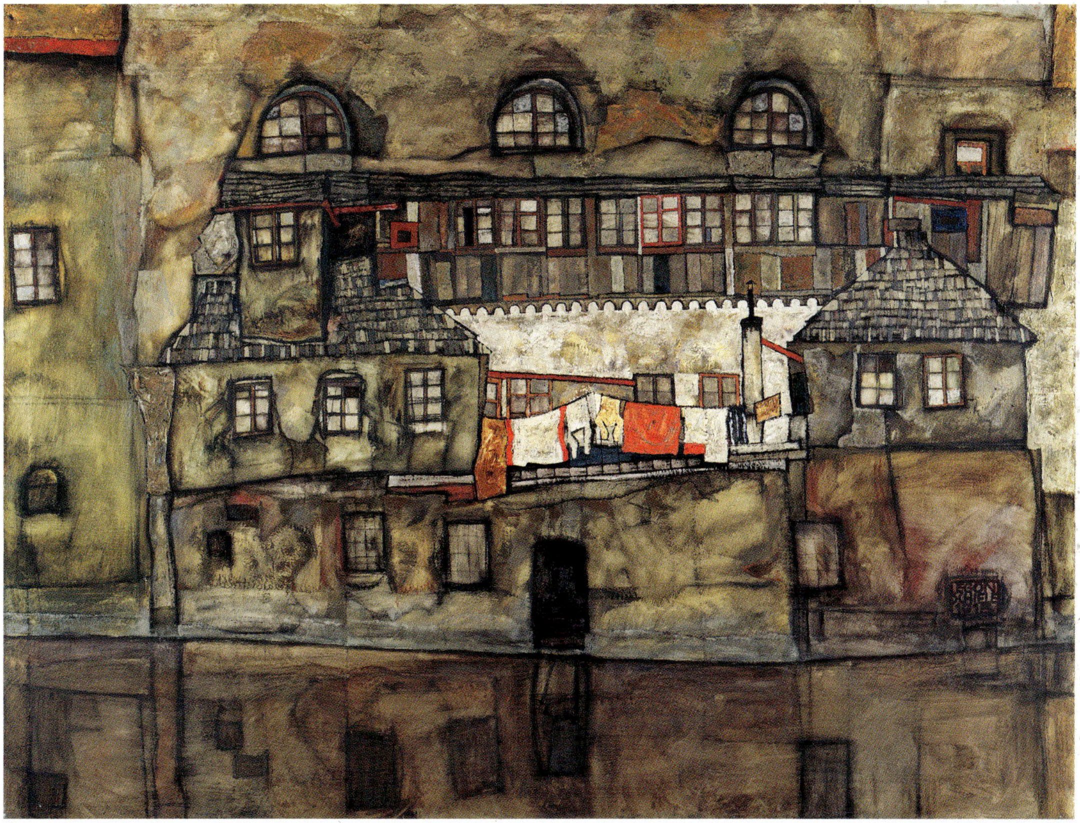

The composition, basically horizontally arranged, is enriched by passages that diverge from left to right: first, the veranda with a row of windows and the light-gray strip under the hanging laundry; and second, the river-house borderline, which in the final quarter of the painting runs convergently to the opposite section of roof. (A similar composition is found in the center section of "House with Shingle Roof" [L 262/K 295, p. 167]).

Much more significant, however, is the composition of the façades with their windows and reflections in the river. This has such a picturesque appearance that one is reminded of old house walls in nineteenth-century pictures. Yet here no romantic or sentimental mood arises. Rather, the sight of these closed windows and crumbling façades, growing moldy near the water, makes one wonder how people could live here at all. The thin, irregular lines of the bars in the unglazed windows over the river suggests the dubiousness of the protection they offer, yet at the same time recall finespun spider webs. The multiple light reflections in the windows, too, bring a touch of eeriness into the scene of decay. The three upper arched windows of St. Jost's do not so much suggest church windows as the windows of old factories, with panes divided into small squares. Unlike the glaze technique used in passages of the river and the mostly thin color layers of the house walls, the items of laundry are rendered with heavily applied paint – an intentional contrast. Still, neither the light, variegated colors of the laundry nor the whitish hue of the wall behind awaken positive associations, but rather associations with proletarian life in the suburbs.

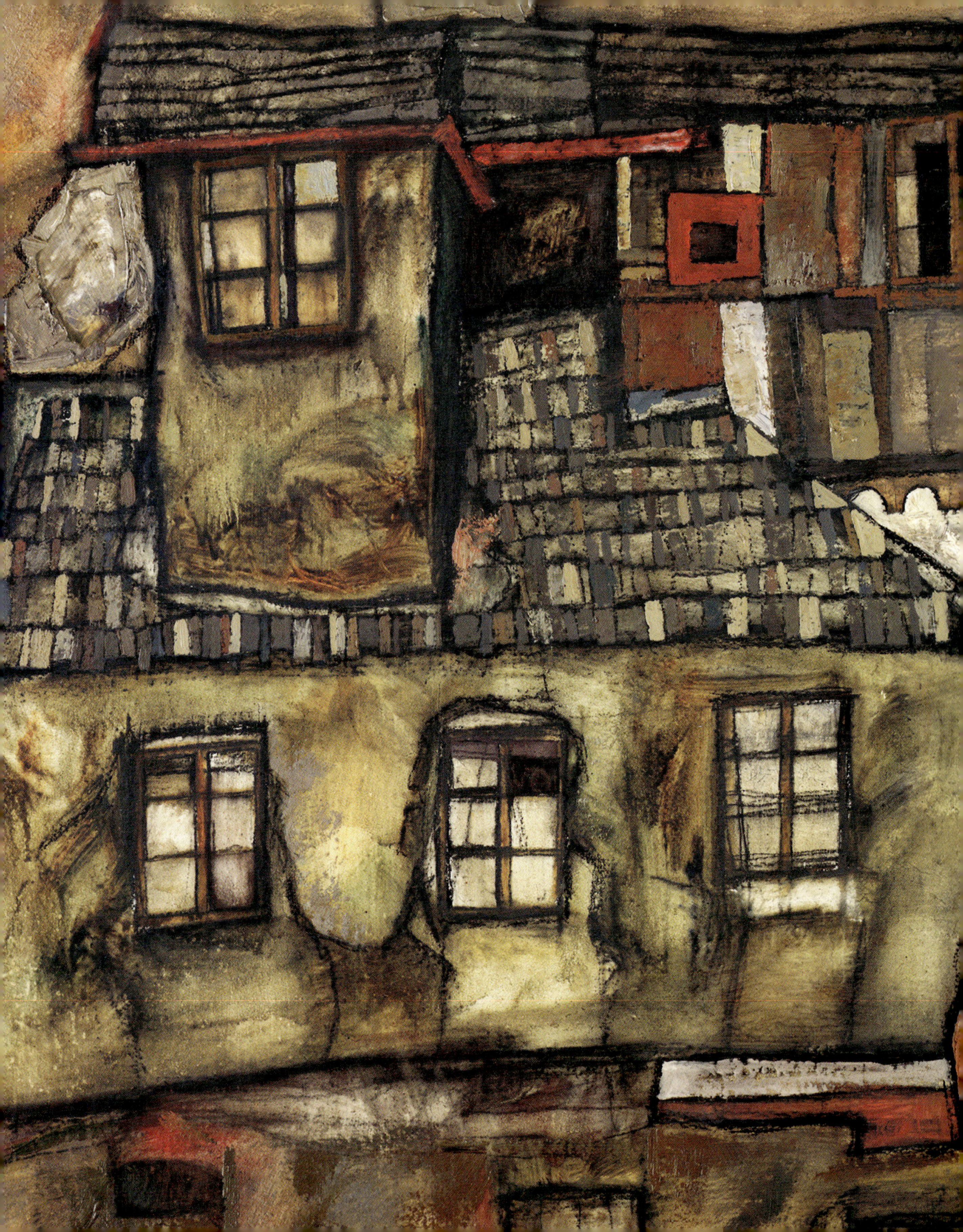

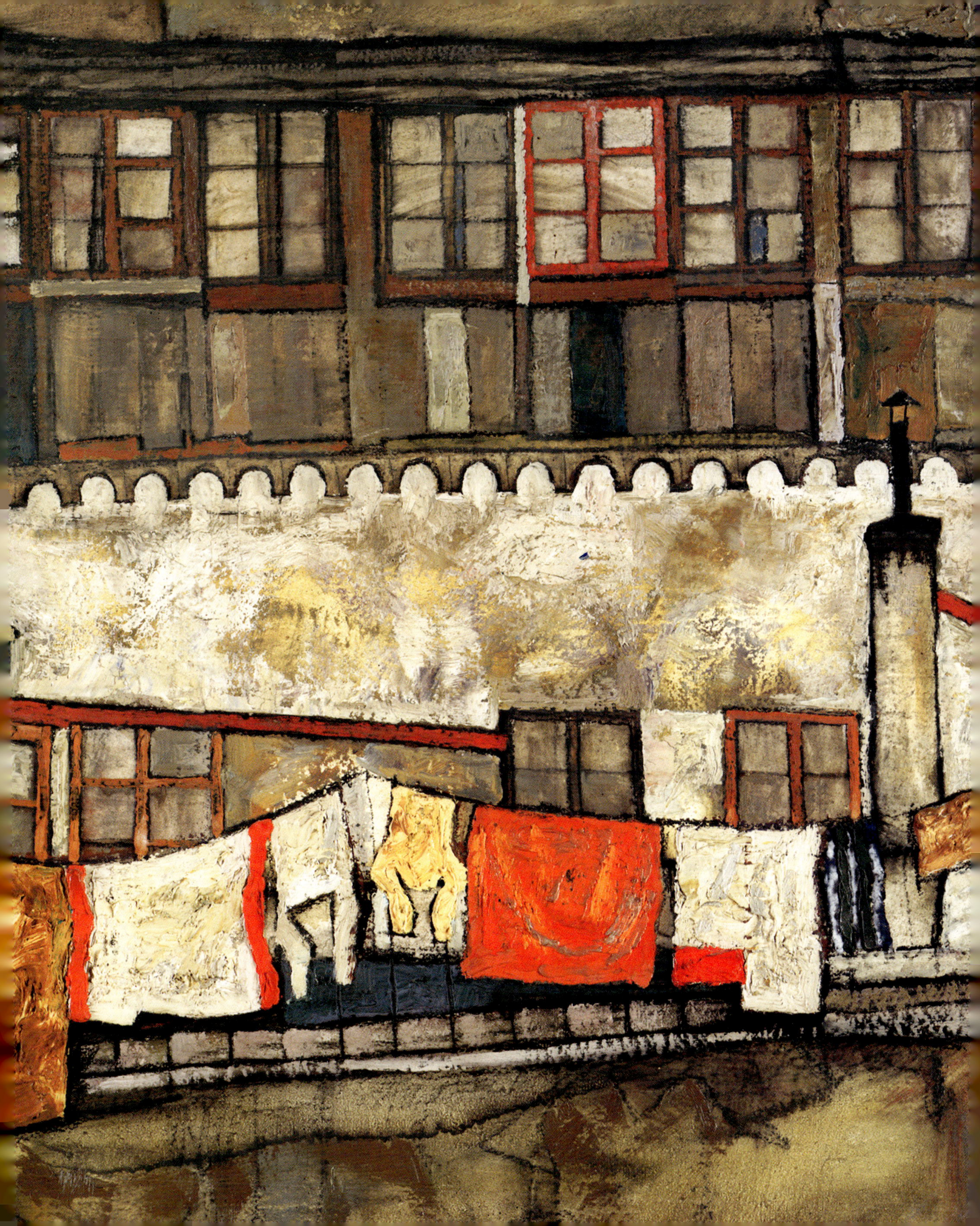

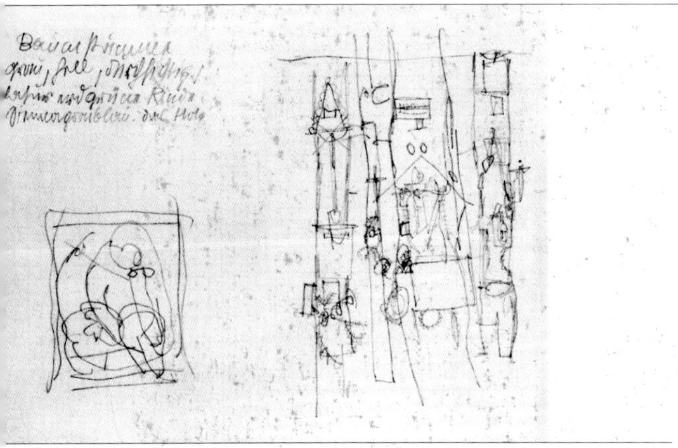

Sketch for *Shrines in the Forest*
Fifth sketchbook, 1914/15
Albertina, Vienna, ESA 322

Shrines in the Forest 1915

L 264 K 296
Oil on canvas, 100 x 120 cm
Signed and dated center right
Kunsthaus Zug, Sammlung Kamm, inv. no.: K.G 29

In one of his picture lists Schiele noted the date 1914 for "Shrines in the Forest". In view of several lapses of memory in that list, however, this should not be taken too seriously, since Schiele likewise dated the painting "Saints" to 1914 although it is identical to "Vanishing" of 1915, as he dated paintings certainly executed in the first three months of 1912, "Conversion" (I), "Agony" and "Hermits" (L 219/K 231, L 218/K 230, L 203/K 229), to 1913, and moreover in a sequence exactly opposite to their actual dates of execution.

Judging by Schiele's stylistic development, "Shrines in the Forest" ("Forest Devotions", his own title) can hardly have been finished before 1915, especially in view of the great formal analogies between the terrain textures in the lower area of this picture and those in "Vanishing" and "Death and the Girl" (L 265/K 288, L 266/K 289), which he also completed in 1915. Otherwise, however, the composition is dominated by the numerous images of saints of diverse size attached to the tree props and largely obscuring them. In terms of their varicolored, decorative treatment, these images bear little resemblance to details in other, concurrent paintings. Yet they do have a close affinity with a study for a crafts piece Schiele entitled "Design for a Pocket Bag for Edith" (K 1799). This, likewise executed in 1915, shows a reduced, sketchy version of the first state of "Mother with Two Children", which was largely finished that same year and then altered over the following years, until 1917.

"Shrines in the Forest" would appear to be a singular exception in Schiele's painting œuvre – if in an entirely different way than the equally exceptional "Meadow with Flowers and Trees" of 1910 (L 117/K 178, p. 53).

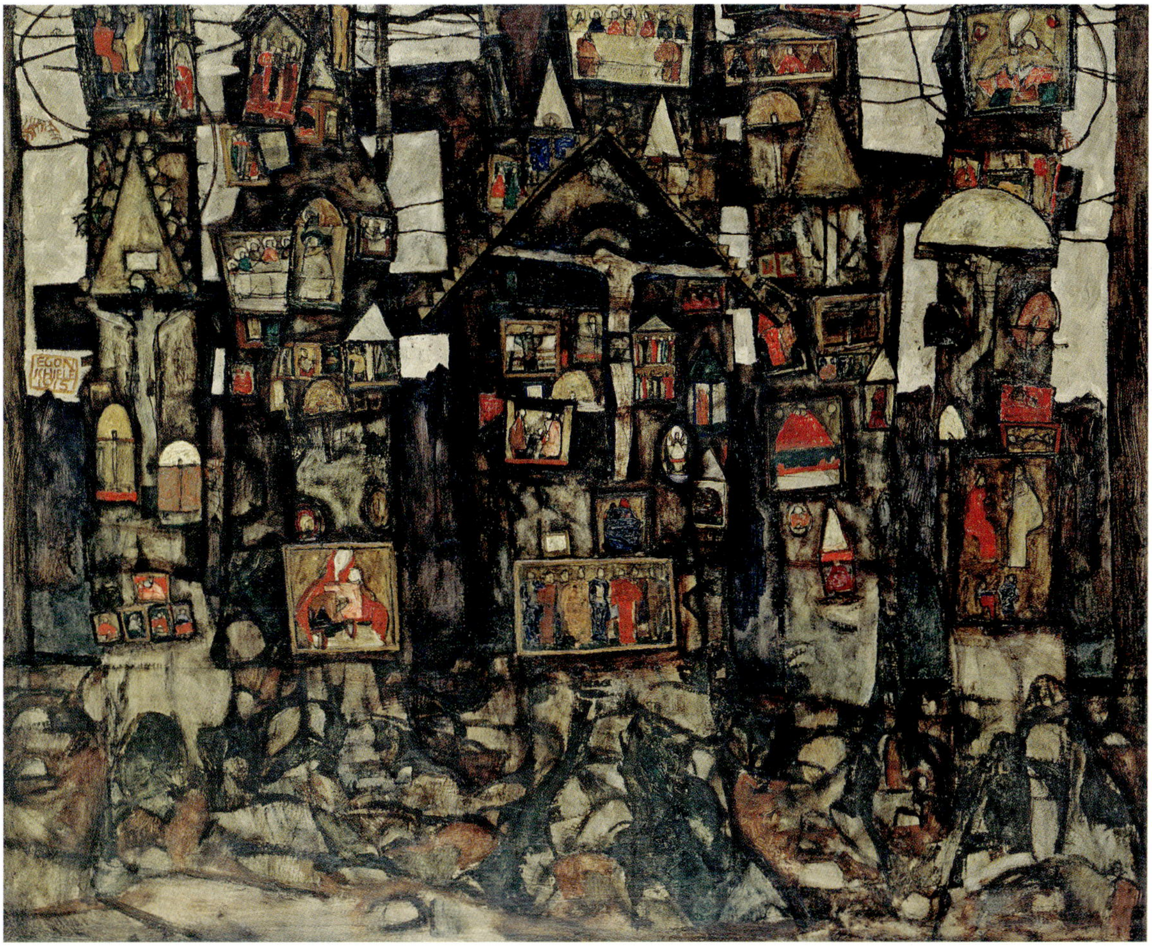
EGON
SCHIELE
1915

Row of Trees 1916

K 1861
Soft pencil on paper, 31.5 x 48.8 cm
Signed and dated lower right
Private collection

In 1916 Schiele sometimes executed drawings of both figure and landscape subjects on rather darkish brown paper – a natural color rather than one caused by exposure to light.

In the present drawing he depicted a row of trees using a very soft graphite pencil. The foremost one bears little foliage, and a few of its branches even appear dead. Through them we have a view over the countryside, if one that is no more than suggested by a few sketchily rendered fields and a group of coniferous trees at the left edge of the sheet. Yet these indications are quite sufficient to call up an idea of landscape.

Despite the nearly empty foreground, the arrangement of the tree trunks conveys an impression of receding into space. Their crowns are indicated only by a single if very agitated contour which zig-zags along the top.

By varying the pressure on the pencil, Schiele has produced lineatures that are not only graphically masterful but aptly characterize the subject.

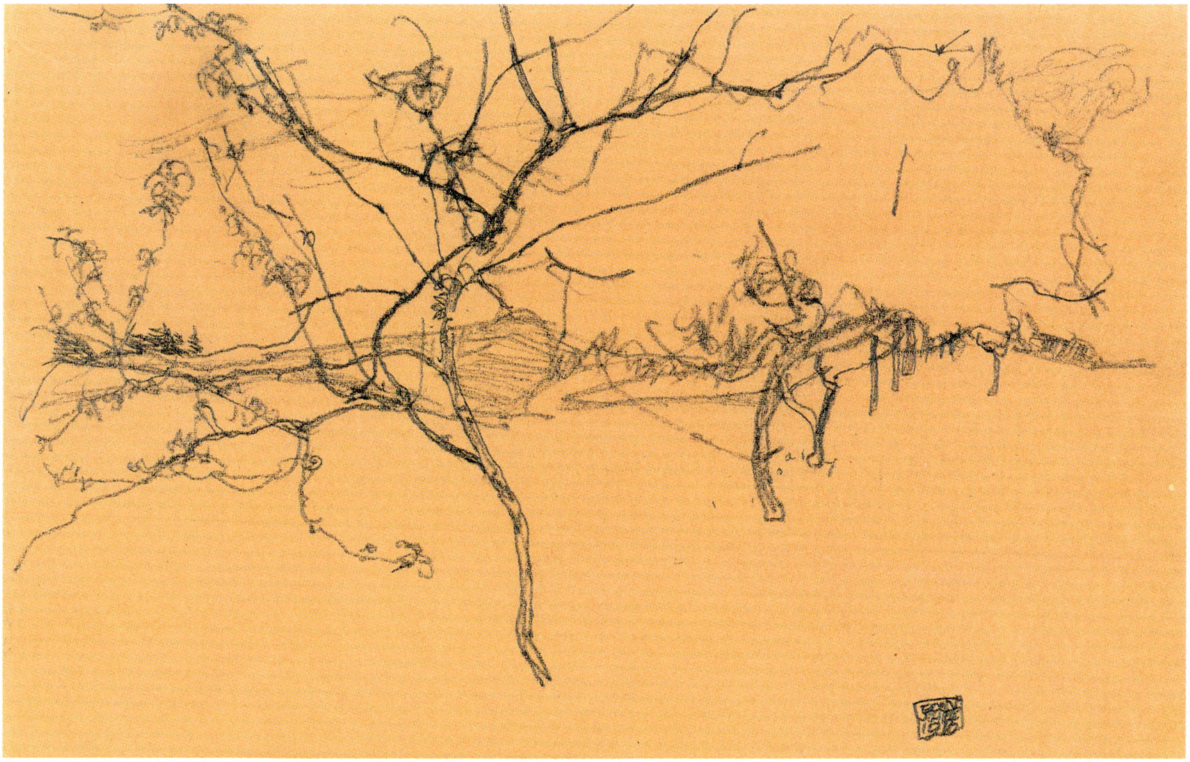

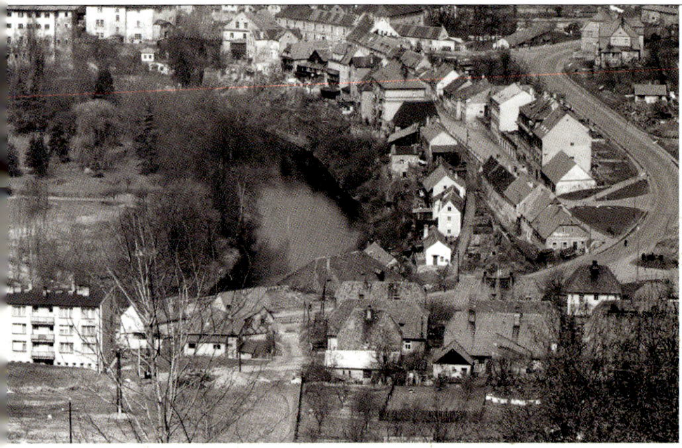

View from the Kreuzberg towards Krumau

"Town and River" (also known as "Krumau Landscape") 1916

L 268 K 298
Oil on canvas, 115 x 141 cm
Signed and dated lower left
Whereabouts unknown

It was not until three years later that Schiele used the pencil drawing of 1913 reproduced below as the basis of the painting he titled "Town and River". To facilitate its transfer to canvas he added a grid of black chalk lines.

By comparison to the 1913 drawing, the 1916 painting clearly represents an artistic decline – yet it nevertheless remains of considerably higher quality than some landscapes with houses of the following years, such as "House with Drying Laundry" or "City in the Green" (L 275/K 311, p. 195, L 280/K 313).

Despite the sketchiness of the 1913 drawing, its essential elements are spatially sufficiently defined, whereas in the painting they are largely treated in a merely ornamental way. For instance, we might try to detect spatial relationships between the river and its two banks or between the street and the small low houses below the large house at the right. Unlike the drawing, spatial relationships are lacking here. Also, the house contours – compared to those in the study and in related earlier paintings – have visibly lost expressive power. The green meadow with its decoratively arranged shrubs and trees has a veritably tapestry-like effect. The arts and crafts influence is unmistakable. The bird's-eye view, so compellingly employed in paintings of 1913 to 1915, has become merely schematic here.

Still, the juxtaposition of the blue-green meadow grounds with the bright orange and red of a few house walls and chimneys, augmented by the gray, white and purple of other façades, amounts to a quite effective color harmony.

Krumau 1913
K 1469
Pencil on paper (squared in black crayon), 32.2 x 48.2 cm
Signed and dated lower right; titled lower left 'Krumau'
Leopold Museum, Vienna, inv. no.: LM 2357

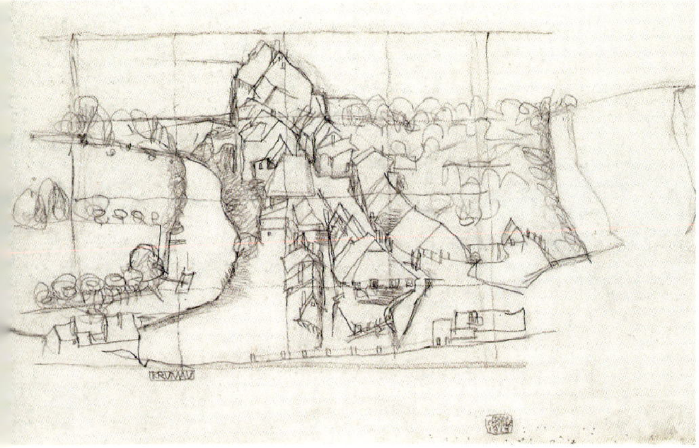

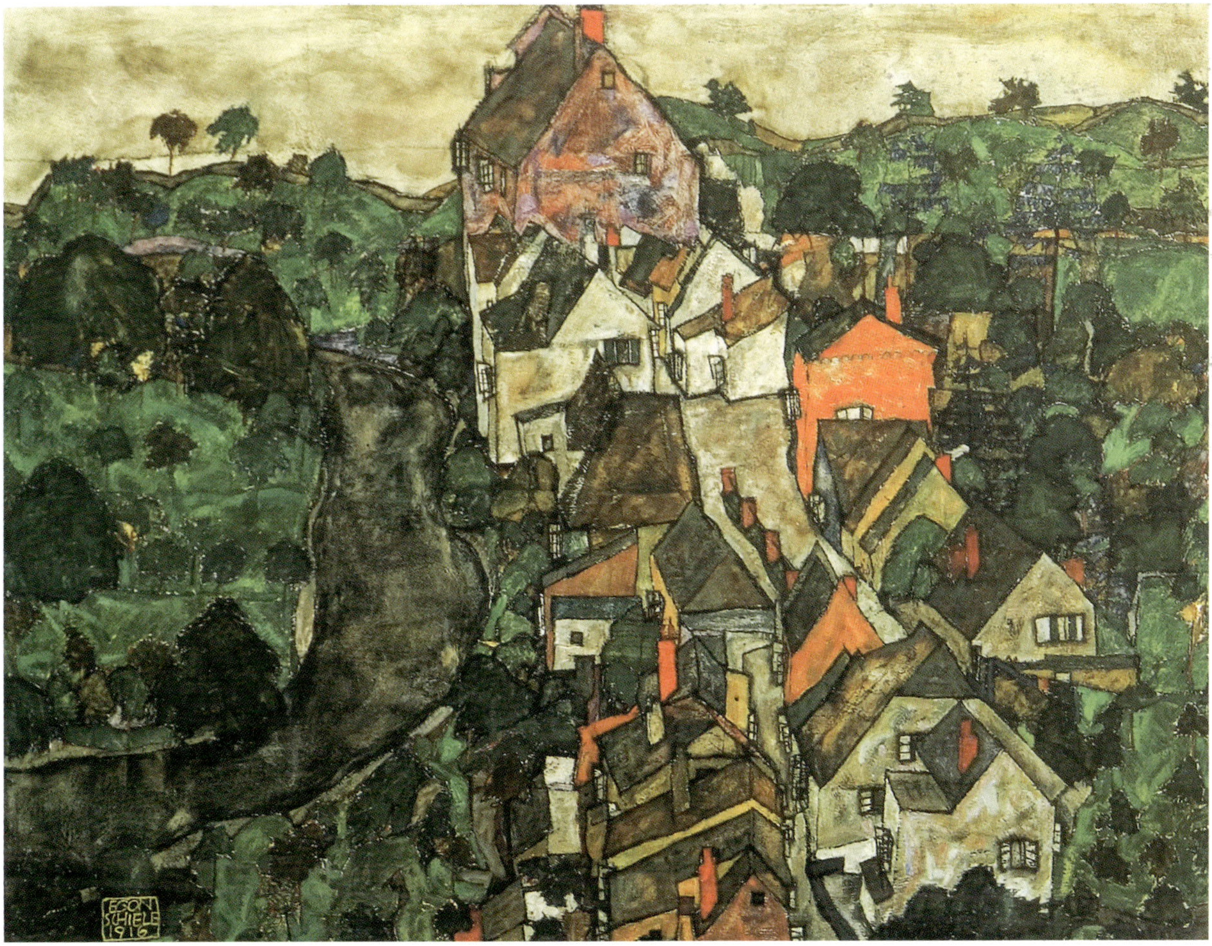
EGON
SCHIELE
1916

Street Corner 1916

K 1867
Pencil on paper, 48.3 x 31.3 cm
Signed and dated (with black crayon) lower left
Leopold Museum, Vienna, inv. no.: LM 2361

The house at the right edge is merely suggested by a roof cornice and a line leading obliquely down from it. Still, it is sufficient to make the building on the opposite side of the street appear to recede in space. In contrast to the house on the right and the adjacent ones to the left, this building is drawn in some detail.

The rough paper and very soft pencil complement the sensitive, wavy character of the lineature very well. Schiele has used stronger pressure to render this foreshortened house wall, thus conveying the impression that it stands in sunlight, while the right wall, beginning at the street corner, lies in semi-shadow. (This is confirmed by the shadows drawn on the inside of two chimney pots.)

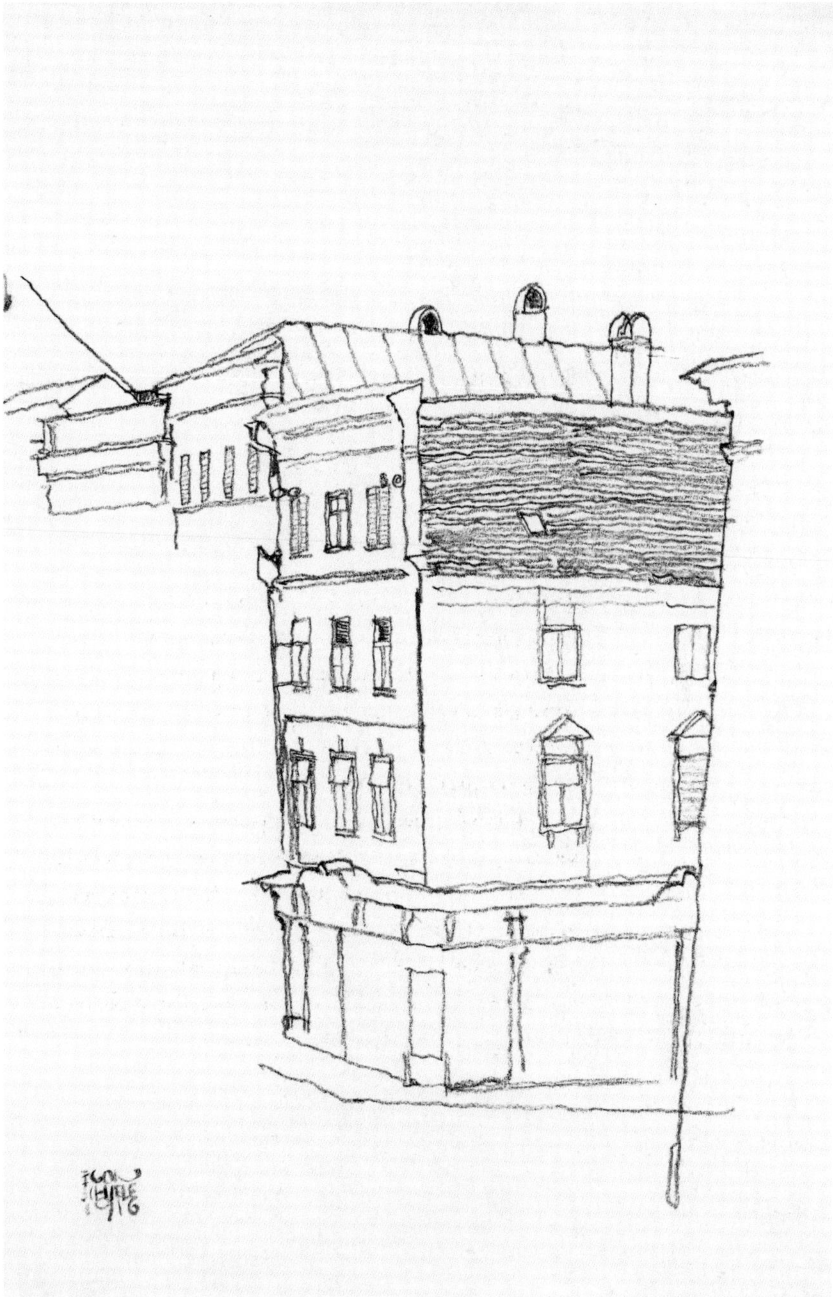
EGON
SCHIELE
1916

"Decaying Mill" (also known as "Mountain Mill") 1916

L 271 K 301
Oil on canvas, 110 x 140 cm
Signed and dated center left
Niederösterreichisches Landesmuseum St. Pölten, inv. no.: 2043

In contrast to the study drawing, here Schiele has constructed a diagonal out of the right-hand section of the mill-dam and the board bridge over the water that continues its direction. As in the study, the focal point lies at the far left. Yet it is only in the painting that the resulting diminishment in size from left to right is made apparent, and that this, together with the diagonal main axis, elicits a sense of motion – even regardless of the moving water. The sharp, irregular angle of the mill wheel and the foaming water shooting out beneath it convey an impression of demise, the destruction of the works of human hands by the forces of nature. This effect must have been conscious on Schiele's part, as indicated by his title, "Decaying Mill." Yet it is conveyed in the painting by the graphic elements alone.

The effect of decay is virtually counteracted by the saccharine color-combination of gray, pinkish-brown and orange boards and beams, some set off by bluish-green edging, and the house wall with its bluish cast shadows. While in earlier works every colored detail expressively reinforced the visual idea, here this is little in evidence. Although Schiele has depicted the moss on the boards, his treatment does not suggest its work of decomposition on the wood but merely introduces pleasing color variations with ornamental borders playing across the boards.

The foaming millrace below doubtless has its charm – in contrast, say, to the upper half of the picture with the unmossy boards. Yet there is as little connection between their color tone and the predominant olive green of the mossy area as there is between this moss green and the harsh blue-green of the water. In sum, the coloration of the picture and its unusually facile combinations reflect an "empty" manner of a type that did not occur in Schiele's earlier œuvre.

The mill Schiele drew and painted (address "3 Unternberg") stood on the right bank of the Grosse Erlauf about three kilometers downstream from Purgstall and a little over one kilometer above Mühlings (where Schiele was on duty at the officers' prisoner of war camp). Numerous notes concerning it are found in his war diary for 1916.

His entry for 7 May 1916 has likewise been associated with this mill in the previous literature. However, it actually refers to the mill near Merkenstetten, which lies far upriver from Purgstall.

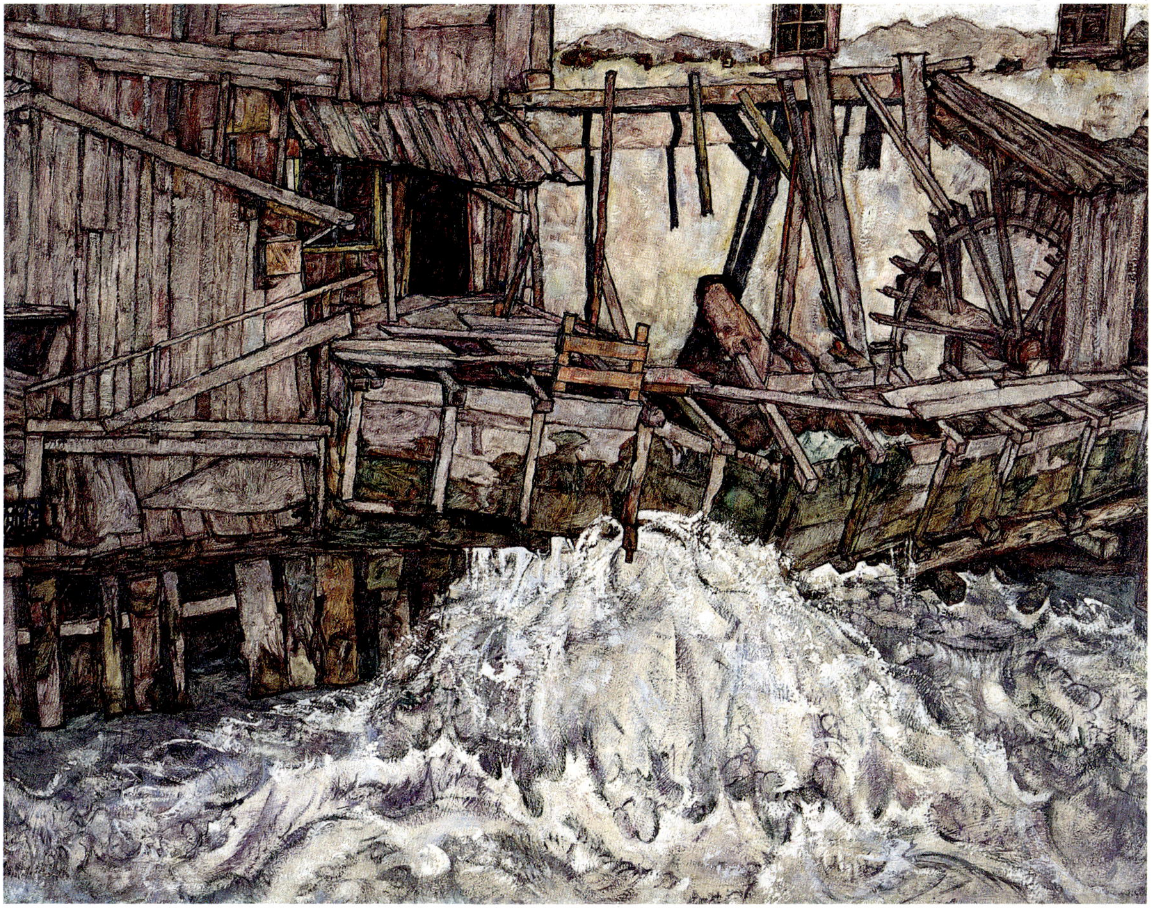

"Four Trees" 1917

L 274 K 310
Oil on canvas, 110.5 x 141 cm
Signed and dated lower right
Österreichische Galerie Belvedere, Vienna, inv. no.: 3917

This is doubtless the most successful landscape of Schiele's late period. Among gently rolling hills with a mountain chain in the distance stand four chestnut trees whose crowns with their autumn foliage stand out against an agitated sky at sunset. This is a compelling symbol of the beauty of the world, but at the same time of the natural cycle that ends in death. The leaves on all four trees have turned rust-red, and one is almost bare. Its black branches form a ghostly silhouette against the sky. The symmetrical arrangement of the trees, their verticality and the opposing horizontals of the cloud streaks in the sky underscore the melancholy mood. This stringent lineature is mitigated by the gentle, eurythmic undulations of the hills in the foreground and middle ground, which are echoed in the distant mountain range.

Hans Ankwicz-Kleehoven has argued that Hodler's "Autumn Evening," 1892, provided the model for Schiele's "Four Trees." Actually the similarity is rather superficial, relating to the motif of chestnut trees seen against a sunset. The palette of the two paintings is entirely different and evokes a quite different mood. Moreover, in Hodler's painting, unlike Schiele's, the trees stand along a road that leads in strict perspective into the distance. On the other hand, a closer analogy with "Four Trees" could be found in Hodler's "Evening Landscape," 1901, especially as regards the painting approach – if not the palette – in which a banded sky with horizontal lines is likewise found. Here the curve of a mountain crest just visible behind fir trees descends to the right, similarly to the left-hand hill in the middle ground of Schiele's picture. And in both paintings – if half obscured by trees in Hodler's – a mountain range is visible in the central declivity. Although the foreground in "Evening Landscape" is very differently treated in every respect, including linearity, the borderlines between the strip of woods and the meadows below them in the middle ground do show an affinity with certain key details in Schiele's painting.

Even more interesting aspects, however, are revealed by a comparison with Schiele's own "Setting Sun," exe-

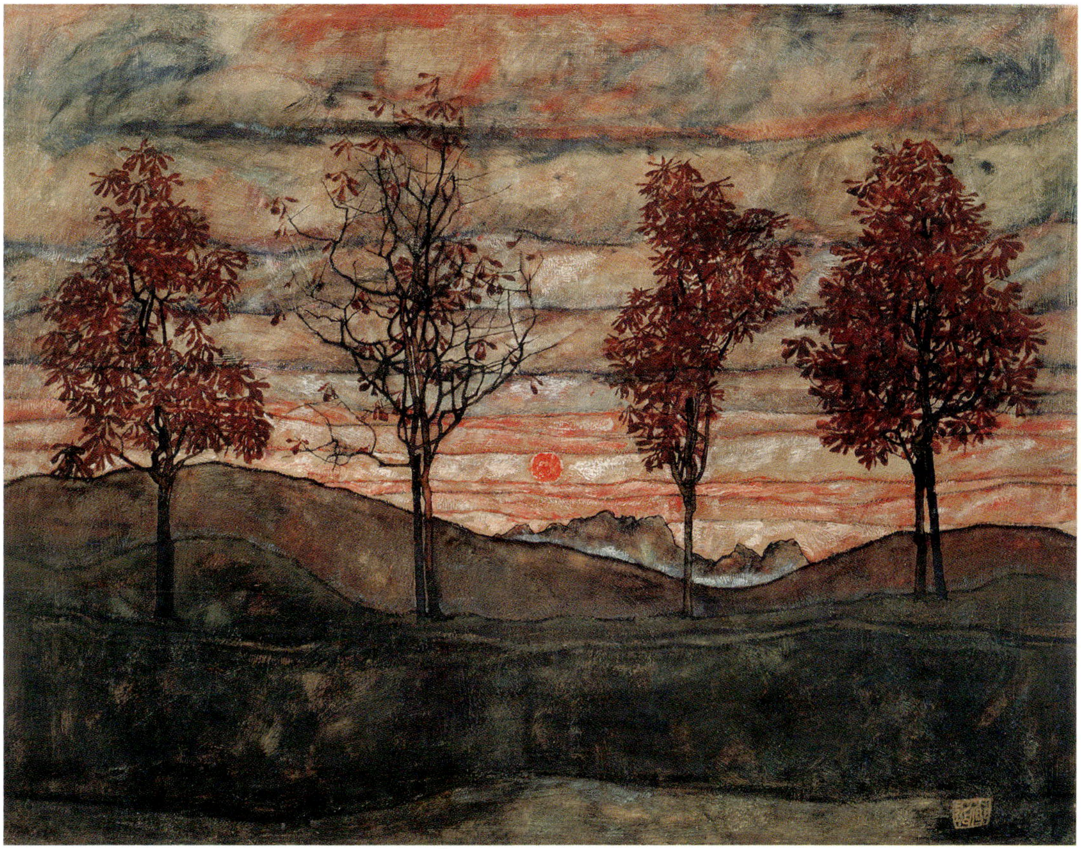

cuted four years previously (L 235/K 265, p. 123). The style of that earlier period was reflected in the considerably flatter, less naturalistic composition of the various sections of the composition.

Both works show chestnut trees in autumn against a sunset sky. While in the 1917 picture the leaves are quite homogeneously painted in, reflecting the manner – not to say mannerism – of this and other landscapes of 1917–18, each leaf on the chestnut trees of 1913 appears individually delineated, and as if petrified with cold. This corresponds very well with the sun setting into the sea and the sensitively rendered sky, quite in contrast to the relatively "wild gestural painting" used to represent the sky in the 1917 painting.

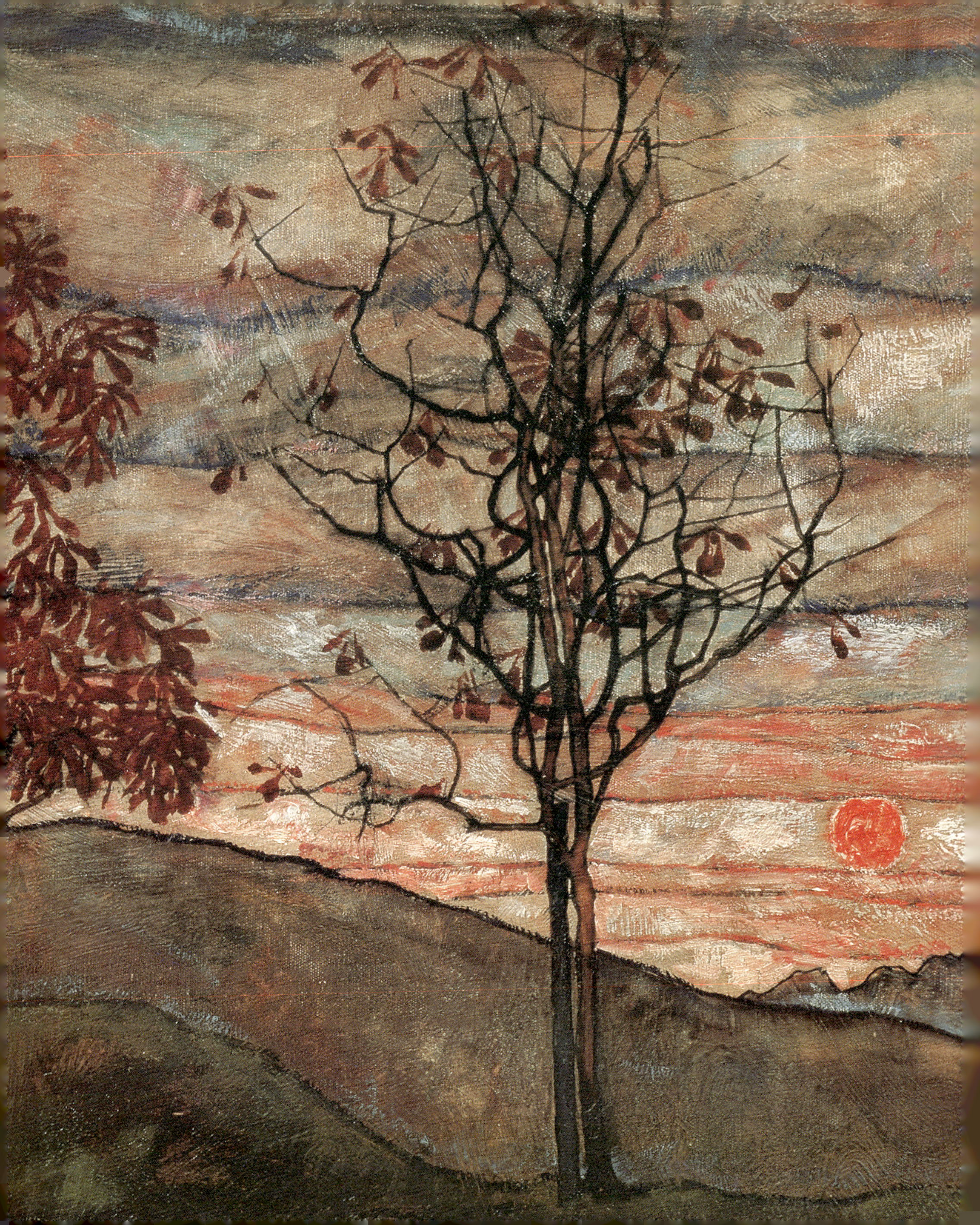

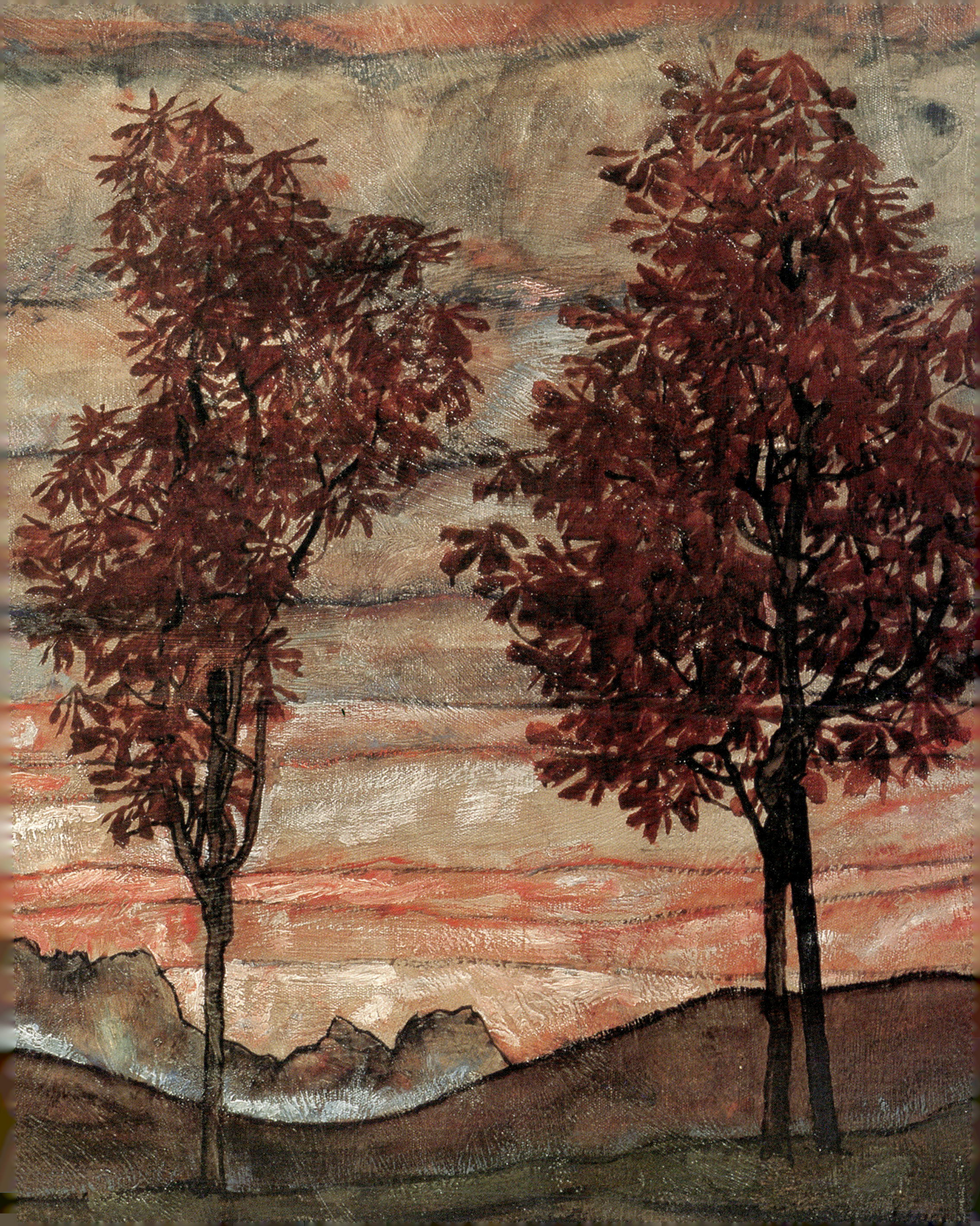

Branch in Brixlegg 1917

K 2156
Black crayon on paper, 26.8 x 43.5 cm
Signed and dated lower right;
inscribed lower right 'BRIXLEGG'
Leopold Museum, Vienna, inv. no.: LM 1400

Using black crayon applied with varying pressure, Schiele has wonderfully evoked the sunlight impinging on this house wall and its windows with open shutters.

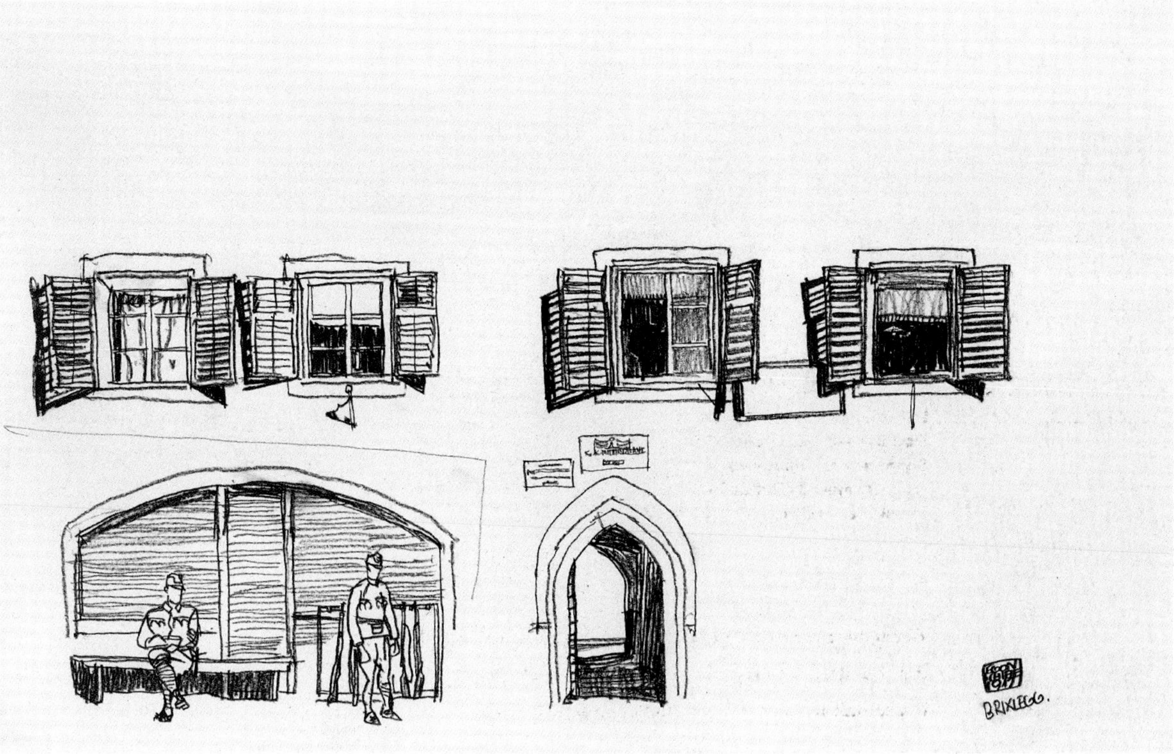
BRIXLEGG.

Old Gabled House in Krumau 1917

K 2133
Black crayon and gouache on paper, 46 x 29.9 cm
Signed and dated lower right; on the reverse inscribed with pencil 'Krumau a./d. M. vom Schlossturm'
Beginning of June 1917
Sammlung E.W.K., Bern

Like the drawing of houses with Renaissance gables on Latrongasse (K 2134, p. 191), the present work was likely executed in the first half of June 1917. Thanks to a short leave from the army, Schiele had an opportunity to visit Krumau again. It was to be his final stay in this town he so loved.

In contrast to the drawing mentioned at the outset, here the scene is depicted from the opposite point of view – from the high vantage point of Krumau Castle Tower. On the left we recognize a portion of the former Royal Hospital court, and on the right, the street-side façade of the former St. Jodocus' building. (Schiele had already depicted its Moldau-side façade and annexes in 1915, in the painting "House on a River" (L 263/K 294, p. 169)

The black chalk drawing was executed on site, and the gouache coloring added later, as was the case with almost every work on paper. The colors of the house façades do not correspond with the reality but were freely invented. Small human figures populate the street, a feature found only in Schiele's late stylistic phase.

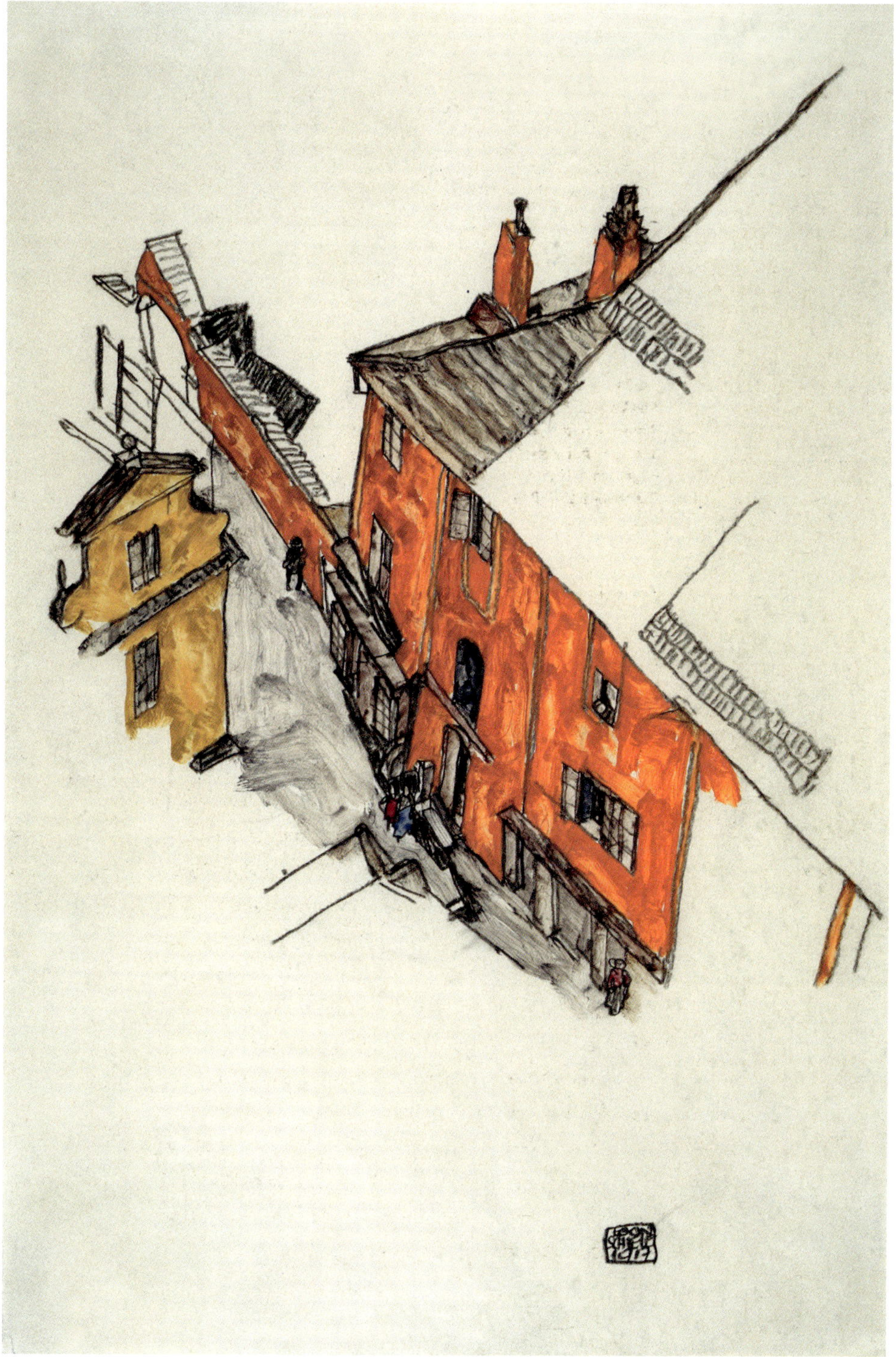

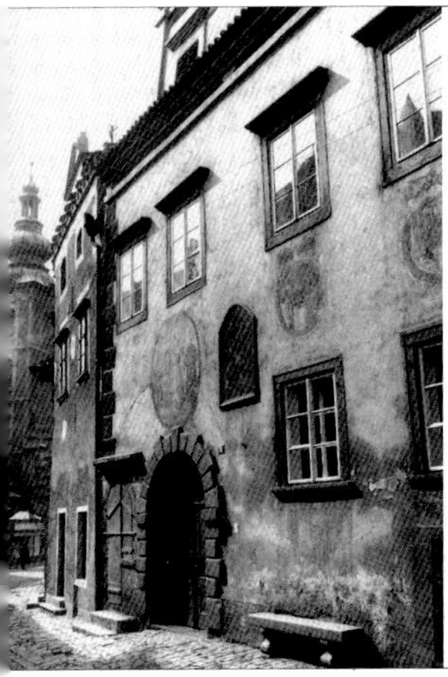

19 Latrongasse, Krumau

Old Gabled Houses in Krumau 1917

K 2134
Black crayon, 45.8 x 28.8 cm
Signed and dated lower center
Albertina, Vienna, inv. no.: 31.172

Here two houses on a bend of Latrongasse in Krumau are rendered from an oblique point of view. The one nearer the viewer is designated no. 19. Schiele has omitted the house's large gateway, but drawn the two wooden door wings of the adjacent shop, which at the time stood open. They can be identified based on the oblique board on the upper section of the right wing, and also the horizontal crossboard on the left, open flap, both of which are clearly indicated in the drawing.

From this vantage point the tower of St. Jodocus' church should be visible behind the houses on the left. However, Schiele has omitted it, likely with an eye to emphasizing the daring perspective of the house façades alone.

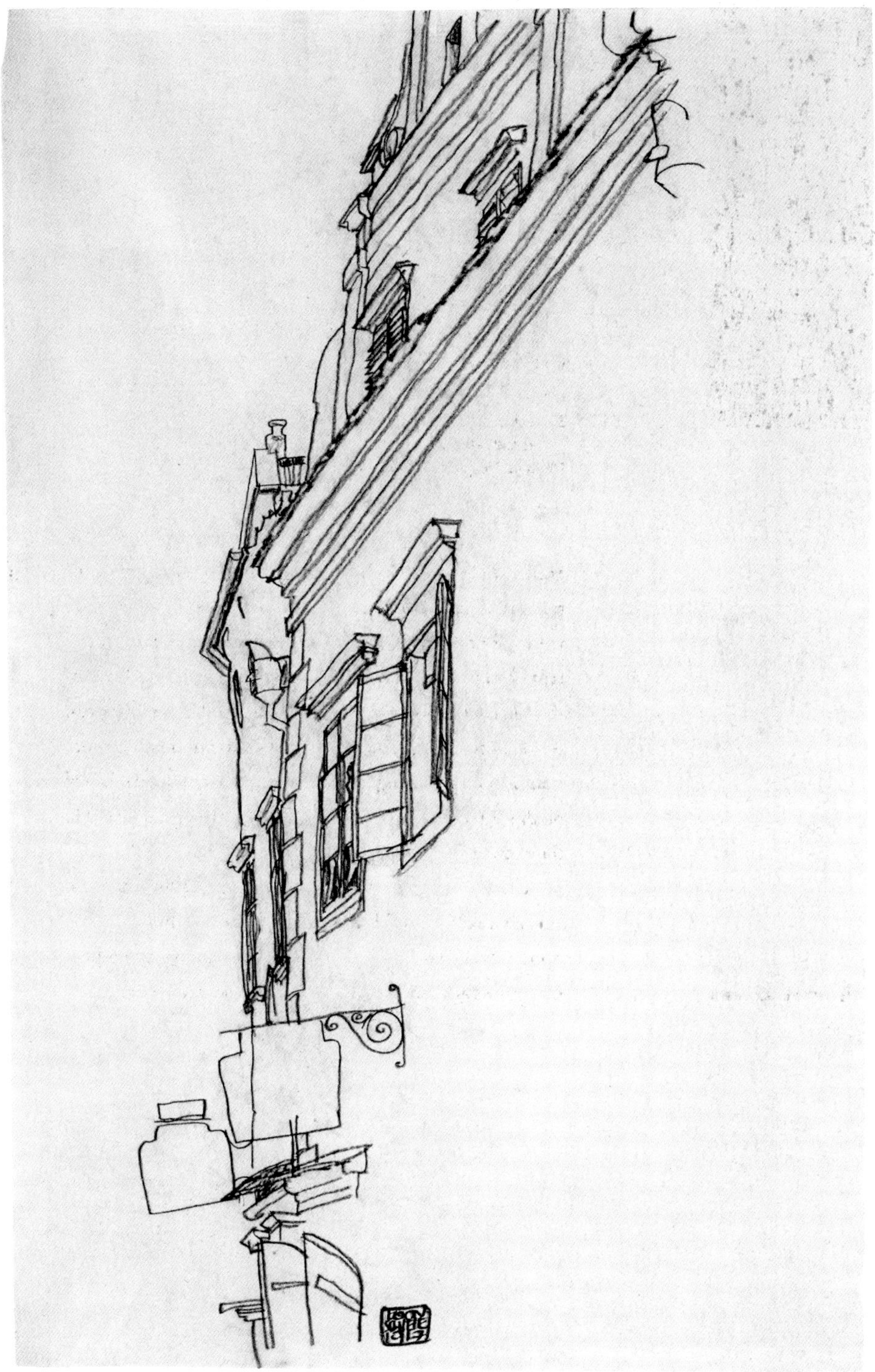

"Summer Landscape" 1917

L 281 K 312
Oil on canvas, 110.3 x 138.9 cm
Signed and dated lower left
Private collection

Here the low vantage point earlier so effectively exploited by Schiele has become merely schematic. Both in "Summer Landscape" and a painting of the same year, "Town in the Green" (L 280/K 313), the landscape with houses appears uniformly tipped up into the picture plane, which seems to recede only slightly towards the top. Only the mountain chain at the very top of the present picture, thanks to its blue tone, conveys an impression of distance.

The trees and especially the house roofs in the painting reproduced in the plate almost appear to have come from a box of toys. The drawing of trees and roofs in both paintings reflects a rather empty mannerism, which can be seen in not few of the drawings of this phase. Moreover, "Summer Landscape" contains several lemon-yellow house walls with light gray roofs above. In conjunction with a few strongly colored façades among the primarily whitish-gray ones, these may have been intended to suggest the poor or proletarian character of the dwellings. Yet this impression is not compelling – and the green of the treetops evinces only slight nuances in gradation. Moreover, their contours are almost entirely executed in the same blue. Schiele probably adopted this type of contouring in "Summer Landscape" and "Town in the Green" from Koloman Moser, yet unlike that artist, he employed it quite uniformly, making the contours appear just as mannered as the homogeneous green of the foliage.

The strip of green adjacent to the right-hand row of houses has been left undetailed. It has neither been objectively characterized nor its position in space determined.

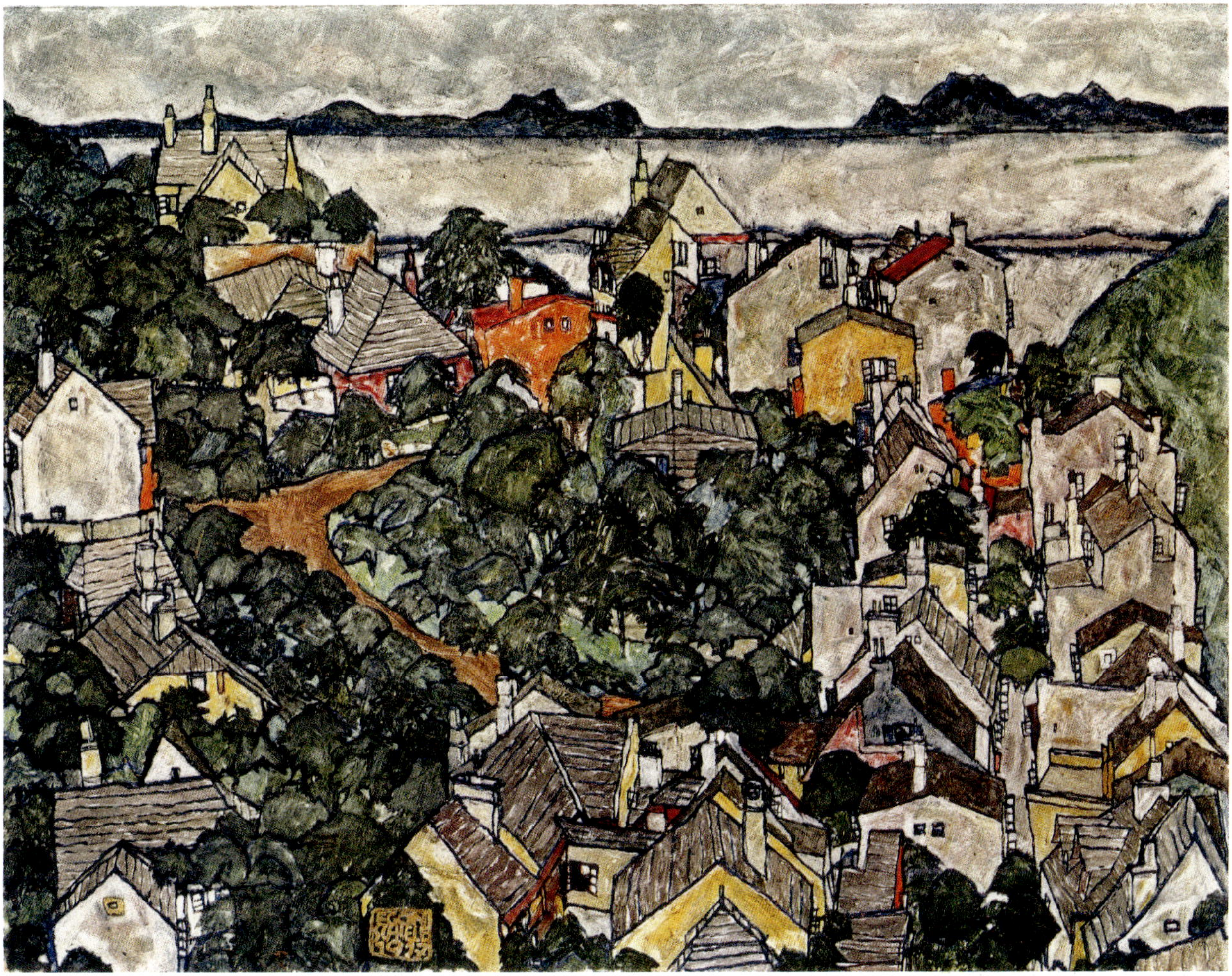

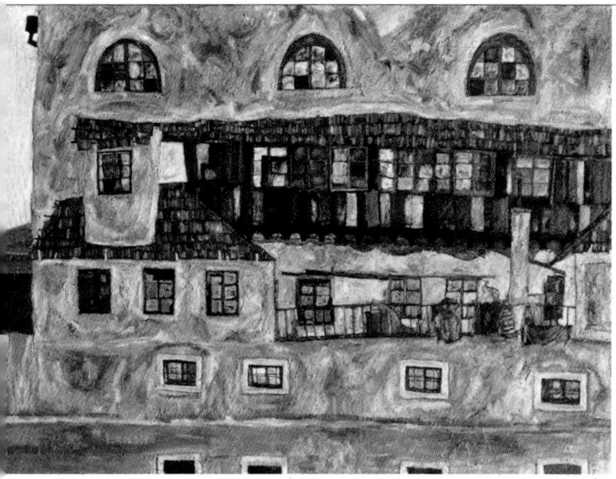

House with Drying Laundry
First version of the motif, later painted over

House with Drying Laundry 1917

L 275 K 311
Oil on canvas, 110 x 140.4 cm
Signed and dated lower right
Private collection

As the first state of this work, illustrated above, indicates, Schiele began it almost as a replica of the "House on a River" (L 263/K 294, p. 169). Yet here impasto technique predominates, while the 1915 painting evinces an alternation of opaque and glaze technique (partly contrasted, partly combined). The earlier work's sensitivity of paint handling and palette, as well as its compositional tensions, have entirely vanished from this one of 1917. For instance, there is no longer any formal reason why the balcony runs downwards to the left, whereas in the earlier picture, the grayish-white bands under the balcony found a logical correspondence in the opposing direction of the borderline between house wall and river.

Schiele replaced the uninteresting lower section of the first state with a narrow street and a clothes line. Yet how mannered it all appears. A comparison of the street lined by a strip of grass with that in the second "Town Crescent" (L 260/K 293, p. 161) reveals the lack of inventiveness in this passage of the 1917 painting. The same holds true for the quite banally rendered clothes. Although they dangle in various directions – only those above the balcony really seeming to flap in the wind – their depiction conveys a

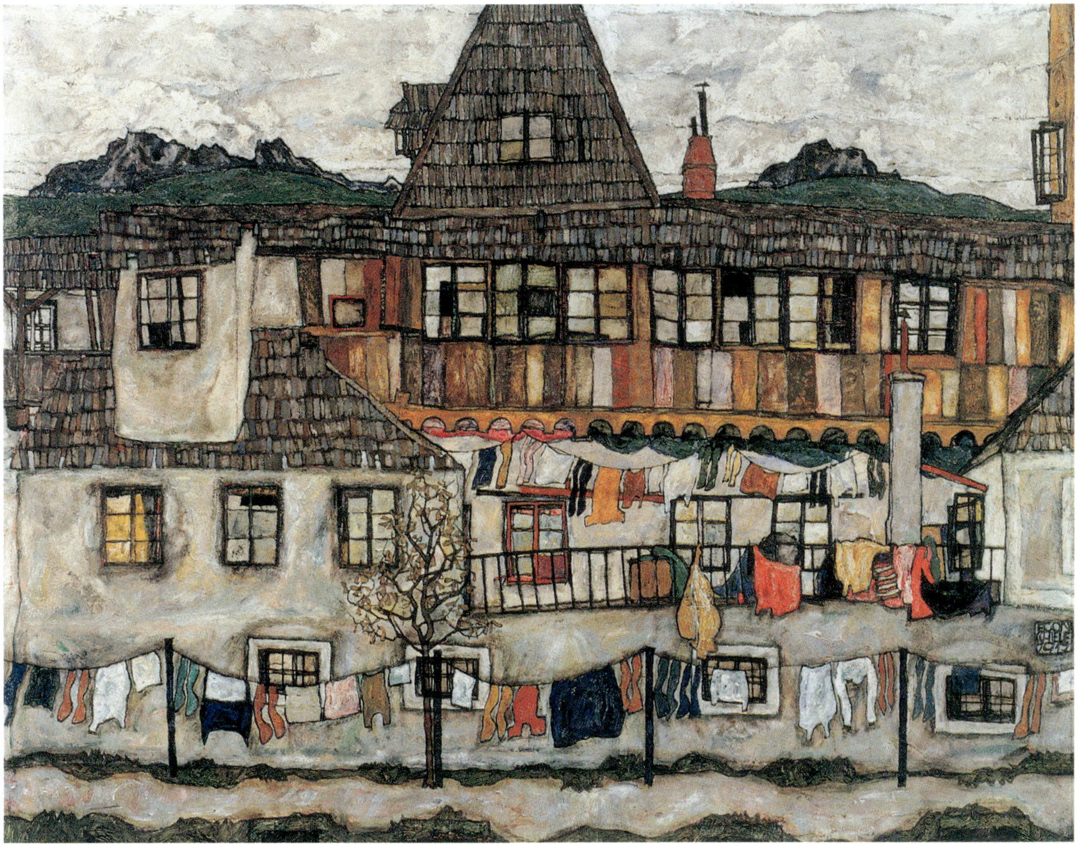

generally rather lackluster impression. In contrast, what great formal tension infused the clothes lines in the 1914 painting "Houses and Laundry" (L 251/K 283, p. 145)!

If we further compare the drawing of the tree crowns in "Setting Sun" (L 235/K 265, p. 123) with the branches and leaves of the little tree by the street here, their mannerism becomes immediately apparent. This also holds to a certain extent for the treatment of the upper sections of the picture, for instance the triangular gable roofed with shingles. Although Schiele may well have depicted this in memory of his so compellingly rendered "House with Shingle Roof" (L 262/K 295, p. 167), this time it was without inspiration. With the gable, the meadows and mountains behind, and the sky with its whitish clouds and bands, he replaced an initial depiction in this area of the wall of the former St. Jost's Church (as he had in the 1915 painting).

The enigmatic coloration of the earlier work has been supplanted by an in part blatant decorativeness, although this admittedly lends the composition a superficial coherence.

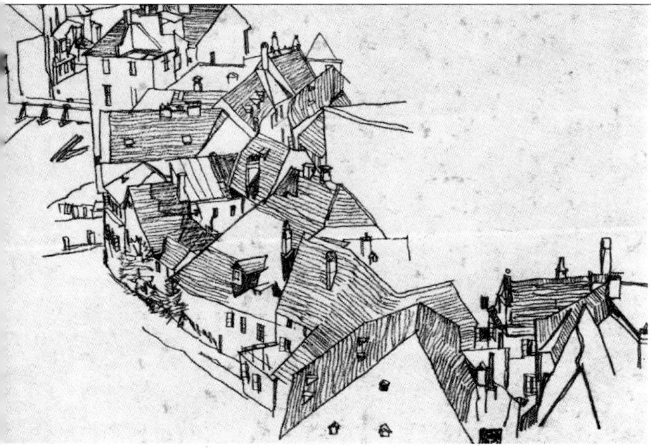

Edge of Town (Krumau Town Crescent III) 1917/18

L 284 K 331
Oil on canvas, 109.5 x 139.5 cm
Signed and dated lower center
Neue Galerie Graz am Landesmuseum Joanneum, inv. no.: I/466

The path from the first to the third painted versions of this subject led to an almost complete elimination of details surrounding the town crescent. The sparse vegetation and the tiny figures are basically negligible. Except for a rather small passage to the right of the houses, they are now contrasted to a dark background (as frequently were the human figures in portraits of these years, or the figure groups in "Family", "Three Standing Women" and "Lovers III" [L 289/K 326, L 300/K 330, L 299/K 329]).

The beginning of the crescent at the lower right, where it is cut off by the picture edge, appears loosely composed, especially by comparison with the second version. The most convincing area is the upper left end, especially the house wall with the dark, empty, as if burned out window apertures. Formally and intellectually, this building complex signifies the end of human habitation. Yet the effect of the compelling color contrast between the predominant pale yellows on the last house and the blacks of the windows is disturbed by the reddish-blue wall contours above and the blue window casements. Above all, the various bright hues used for many of the roofs and walls do not exactly amplify the notion of the edge of a town – rather, they have a rather blatant, decorative effect.

Houses in Krumau 1917
K 2135
Pencil on paper, 28.7 x 44.8 cm
Signed and dated lower right
Private collection

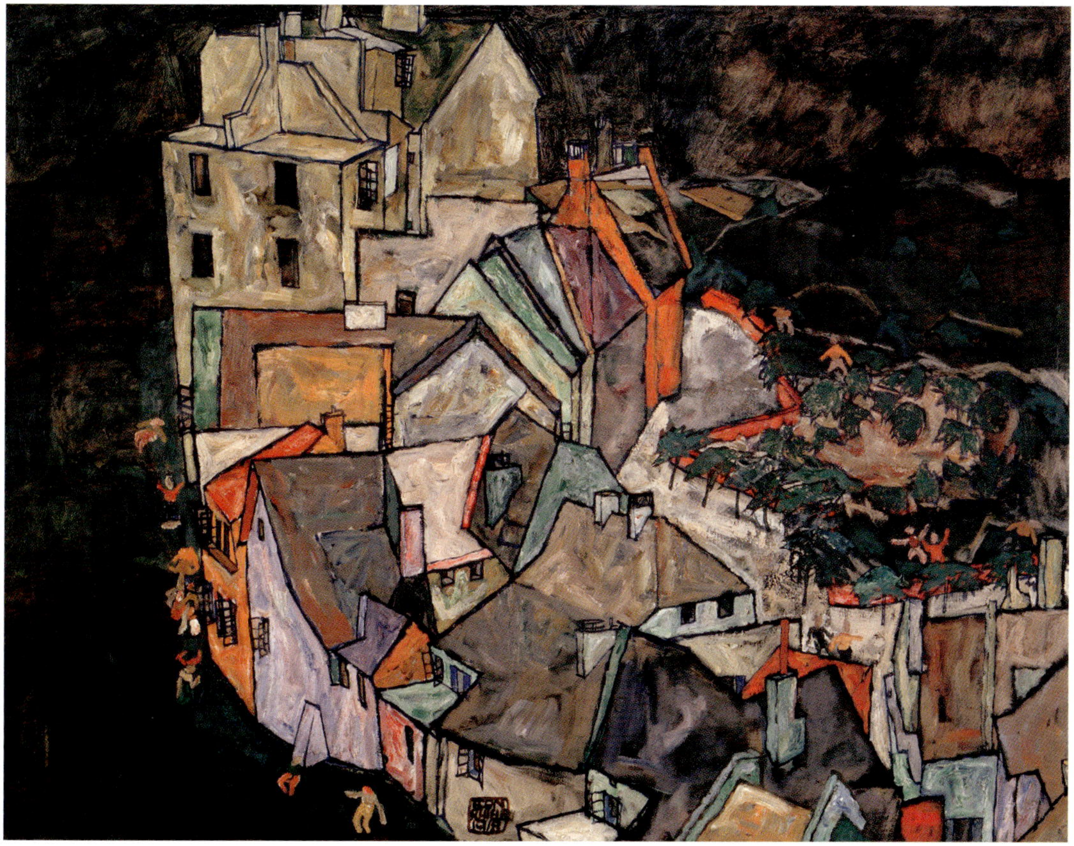

The drawing throughout and the composition of certain details are likewise not entirely convincingly handled. If we compare the three colorful roofs below the left wall of the upper building with the corresponding passage in the second version, we see that there they are spatially distinguished from one another and find a meaningful continuation in the associated walls. Here, in contrast, the three house walls have been replaced by a single one, and only the orange roof appears to lie slightly in front of the subdued dark red. Otherwise the position of the walls in space remains undefined, and they merely form an ornamentally decorative area.

Judging by the stylistic development of Schiele's painting, especially as regards the frequently garish colors and the special type of chiaroscuro employed, the present painting must have been executed between the final third of 1917 and the beginning of 1918.

For the final version of the "Town Crescent" Schiele made another pencil study (p. 196). That it, too, is rather casual and lax, may be seen from a comparison with the first drawing of the subject, done in 1914 (K 1696, p. 157).

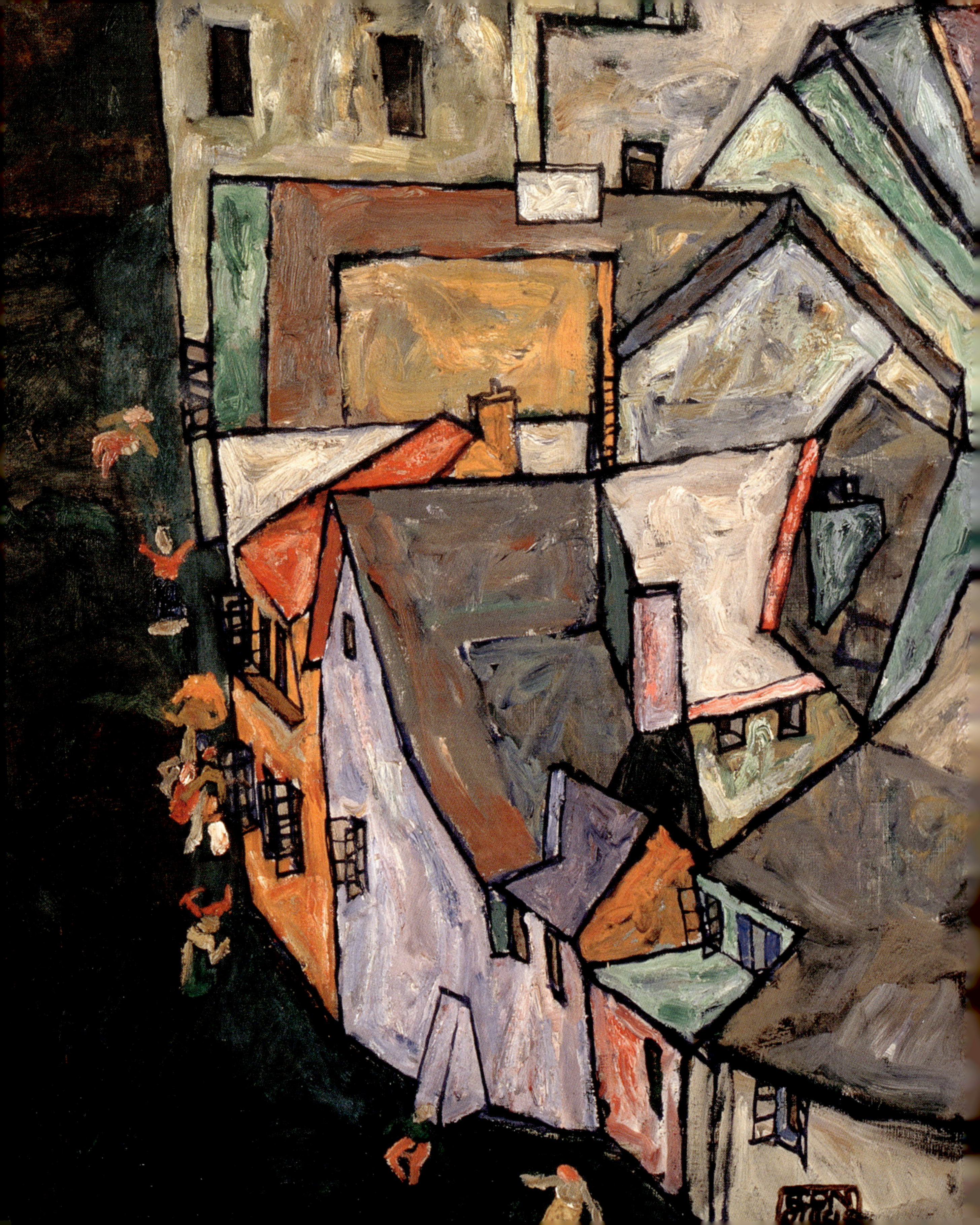

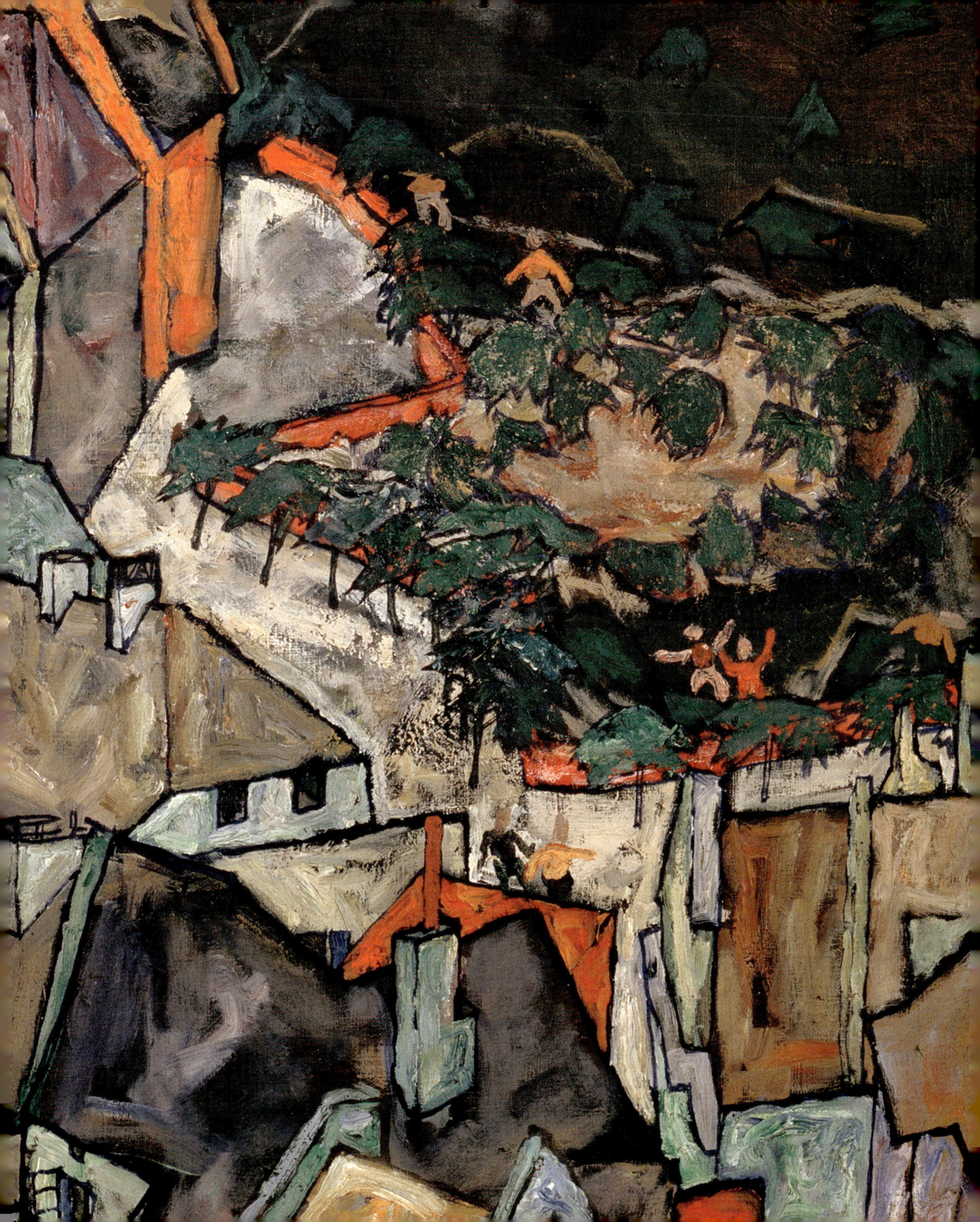

Mountain Stream 1918

L 291 K 332
Oil on canvas, 110.2 x 140.5 cm
Signed and dated lower right
Scheffenegger Family, Vienna

As in the painting "Windows," 1914 (L 252/K 284, p. 151), but in a different way, Schiele has here depicted only an excerpt from a natural scene, a mountain stream tumbling over a rocky bed. The radicality of this narrow excerpt marks an essential difference from certain works by Hodler, despite the strong influence they doubtless exerted on the present painting. At an earlier date, Hodler depicted the stones in mountain streams with linear contours, and in a picture done two years before Schiele's, gave them a similar pinkish tone. However, Hodler always included the wider natural surroundings in the composition. In his "Grindelwald Glacier," 1911, not only the course of the glacier but its source exhibit a considerable affinity with the stream in Schiele's painting.

In contrast to the decoratively mannered treatment of the ripples, the rocks are clearly and firmly contoured. Yet the pink gradations applied to them appear somewhat saccharine, especially in the original. In combination with the predominant gray and the comparatively harsh color values set in certain of the shadowed areas, these result in a rather vapid impression. Still, thanks to the cool palette and lucid graphic framework, Schiele has managed to achieve an effect of monumentality.

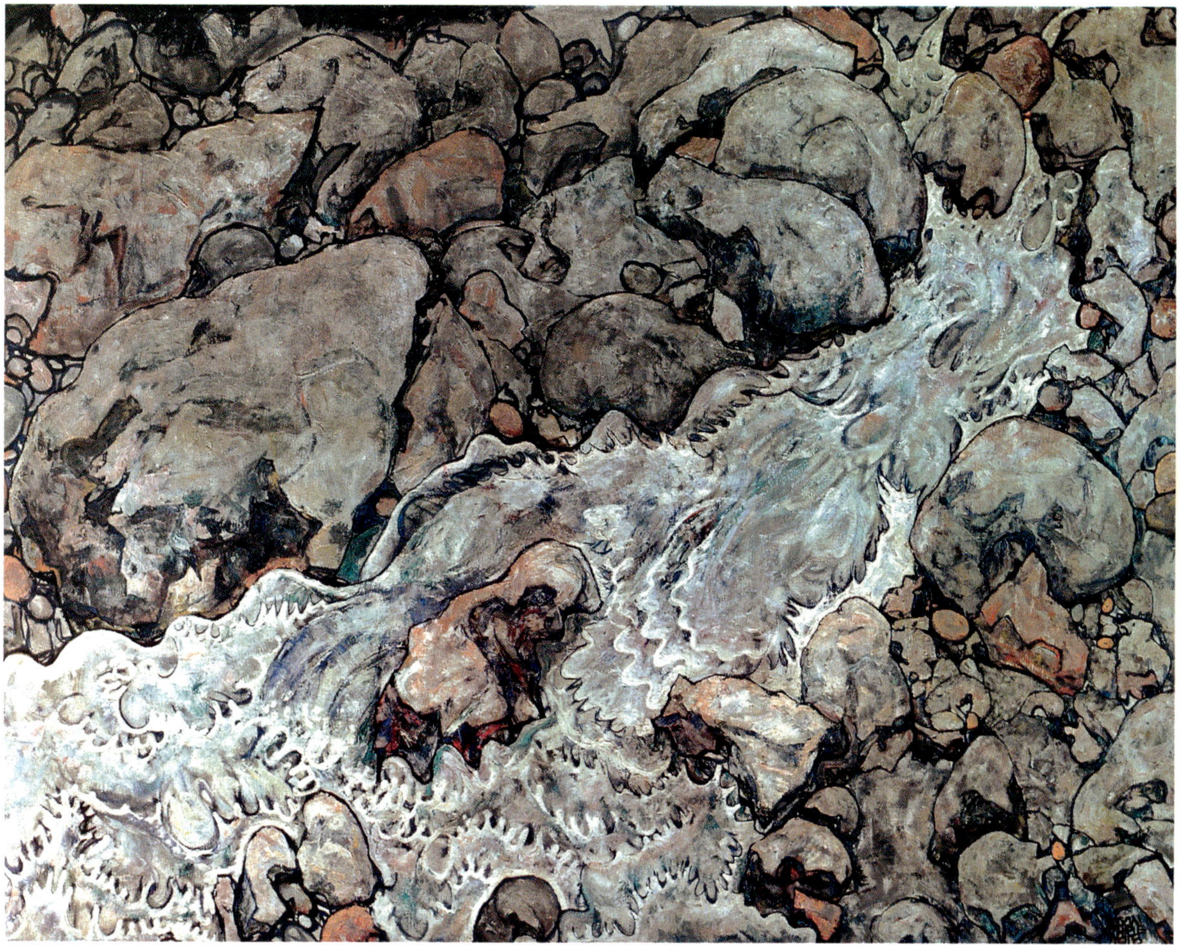

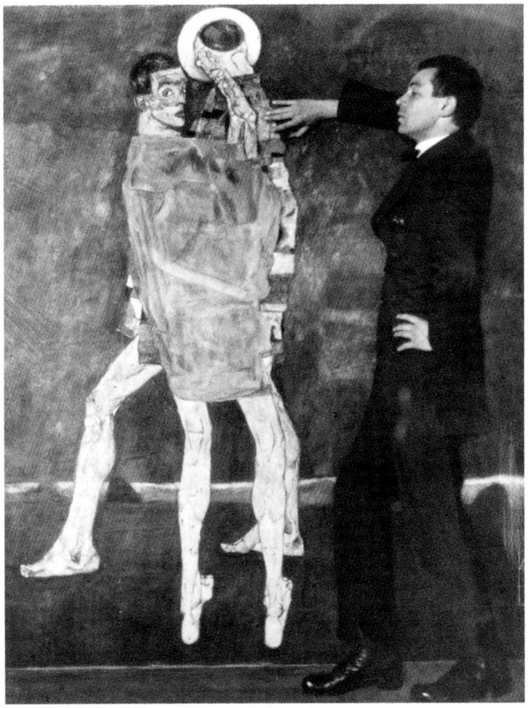
Egon Schiele in front of "The Encounter" 1914

Biography

Like so many other outstanding personalities, Schiele was one of those people of highly diverse origin and background who succumbed to the attraction of the multinational Austro-Hungarian monarchy and became part of what might be termed a thoroughly Austrian identity.

His grandfather and father actually originated from northern Germany. The latter, Friedrich Karl Schiele, was a councilor of justice in Ballenstedt, and served from 1833 to 1847 as first mayor of Bernburg, in the state of Anhalt. Although Schiele's grandfather was born in Ballenstedt, he died in Prague, in 1862. In 1844 he became a construction engineer on the Imperial and Royal (I & R) Emperor Ferdinand Northern Railway in Moravia, and subsequently built the I & R Privileged Bohemian Western Railway. In other words, Schiele's family put down roots in the Austro-Hungarian Empire two generations before his birth. His maternal grandfather, Johann Franz Soukoup, came from Krumau, then ran a construction company and acquired real estate in Vienna. His and his wife's ancestors were farmers and shopkeepers from Southern Bohemia. In contrast to the fraternal line, this side of the family was marked by considerable class differences.

In a draft biography, Schiele once colorfully described himself as "... a great-great grandson of councillor of justice Friedrich Karl Schiele ... I was ... born through a Viennese father of a lady from Krummau as mother ..." Egon Leo Adolf Schiele saw the light of the world on 12 June 1890, in Tulln an der Donau, a small town in Lower Austria. He was his parents' third child, he had two older sisters, Elvira, born in 1883, and Melanie, born in 1886. The Schieles' youngest offspring, Gertrude, known in the family as Gerti, was born in 1894. During the artist's early period Gerti often sat for him, for portraits as well as for studies from the nude.

Schiele's father was employed from 1879 as chief operations agent of the I & R State Railway in Launsdorf, Carinthia, from 1886 in the same function in Steyr, Upper Austria, and then from 1890 onwards in Tulln. He had a company apartment in the railway station, where he lived with his family.

Egon attended elementary school in Tulln from 1896 to 1900. Already as a schoolboy he made many drawings, especially of trains standing in the station or in the switching yard. At age eleven Schiele entered the Secondary Trade School in Krems, but after a poor first-semester performance required a tutor to finish the school year. In autumn 1902 his father sent him to Klosterneuburg, to attend the State Secondary and Upper School. His family soon followed, a worsening illness having forced his father to retire from service. Shortly before his marriage he had become infected with syphilis, for which the medicine of the day had no cure. This probably explains why his wife's first three children, all of them boys, were stillborn, before she gave birth to her first living child, Elvira. Yet Elvira would die at the age of ten, a circumstance for which the family records provide no explanation.

The following anecdote used to be related in the Schiele family. Once Adolf Schiele was alone in the apartment and felt a chill. So, apparently in a fit of mental derangement, he heated the stove with the valuable stocks owned by him and his wife, an incident to which the family's impoverishment was attributed. Whatever the case, Adolf Schiele likely died of progressive paralysis, one of the possible consequences of syphilis, on New Year's Day of 1905. In other words, the artist's father had no true, hereditary mental illness, and therefore cannot have passed a propensity for it on to his son – something that has often been maintained by those who judge Schiele's art negatively.

How deeply his beloved father's death affected the fourteen-year-old boy may be gathered from a letter Schiele wrote many years later to his brother-in-law, Anton Peschka. Due to the family's precarious financial situation after his father's death, guardianship of Egon was assumed by his prosperous uncle and godfather, Leopold Czihaczek, an engineer and husband of Adolf Schiele's sister.

Schiele showed little interest in normal high-school subjects, preferring to draw – not only in his spare time but during instruction, to the dismay of his teachers. In addition, he was faced with the prospect of having to repeat a school year. Still,

Czihaczek would not allow Egon to take up the career in art he desired. Like his father, his uncle wanted the boy to attend technical college. Yet when two professors at his secondary school, the drawing instructor Ludwig Karl Strauch and the Augustine choir conductor Dr. Wolfgang Pauker – as well as Max Kahrer, a Klosterneuburg artist – spoke out for an art education for Schiele, Czihaczek finally gave his blessing.

First he applied to the Vienna School of Arts and Crafts. However, the drawings Schiele submitted were thought good enough to qualify him for the Vienna Academy of Visual Arts. There, at age sixteen, Schiele passed the entrance examination in October 1906. He entered the "general painting class" taught by Prof. Christian Griepenkerl, and ardently launched himself into his new tasks. Yet soon the relationship with his teacher, a diehard advocate of the Historical Revival style seen in Vienna's Ringstrasse, began to deteriorate. In his spare time Schiele visited exhibitions of French Impressionists and Austrian Secessionists in the new Vienna Secession building, designed by Art Nouveau architect Joseph Maria Olbrich. His experience of this innovative art inspired a series of *plein air* landscapes, which began to show a progressive, quite unacademic style, especially in the latter half of 1907. In addition, during that year and the following year Schiele travelled with his younger sister Gerti to Trieste, where interesting oil studies of harbor motifs emerged.

In 1907 Schiele left his mother's Vienna apartment and moved into his first studio, in Vienna's second district. The following year saw his first participation, with ten works, in a public exhibition, held in the Imperial Hall of the Augustine Choir Chapter in Klosterneuburg.

Nevertheless, during his three years at the academy Schiele's teachers continued to give him lower grades in every subject than, say, his fellow student (and future brother-in-law) Anton Peschka, despite the fact that Peschka's artistry was no match for Schiele's. The reason for this poor evaluation was likely Schiele's obviously increasing interest in avant-garde directions of which his academic professors disapproved. This culminated in a documented outbreak on the part of the arch-reactionary Griepenkerl: "The devil crapped this Schiele in my school!" Schiele reputedly sought out Gustav Klimt as early as 1907, but this is no more than a widespread legend. In all probability he did not make Klimt's aquaintance until 1909, on the occasion of the second "Kunstschau" (an opinion shared by Christian Nebehay).

In other words, Schiele had good reason to leave the academy. Yet the generally accepted assumption that he took this step together with like-minded students in April 1909, has proven incorrect. Schiele could not possibly have left the academy at that point in time, for the following, quite plausible reason: According to the then valid regulations of the Vienna Academy of Visual Arts, students who had successfully completed a triennial period were granted the right to one-year voluntary military service. This put them on a level with high-school graduates, who, instead of the three years required of the "common man", had to serve only one. Now, Schiele did not complete his triennium until the end of the academic year 1908–09, as evidenced by a certificate dated 3 July 1909. If he had left the academy at an earlier point, he would not have received this certificate. In other words, his withdrawal from the academy must have occurred later.

It was only then that Schiele joined with like-minded colleagues, including Anton Faistauer, Rudolf Kalvach, Sebastian Isepp and Franz Wiegele, to found the "Neukunstgruppe", or New Art Group. Another member was the theater-scene painter Erwin Dominik Osen, who temporarily exerted a not inconsiderable influence on Schiele. Somewhat later, the group was joined by Albert Paris Gütersloh and Hans Böhler.

That same year, 1909, four of Schiele's works were included in the second summer exhibition of the Kunstschau. Known as the "Internationale Kunstschau 1909", the show was improvised by Josef Hoffmann on the vacant lot where the Vienna Concert House now stands. Gustav Klimt was president of the exhibition committee. This significant show already included paintings and sculptures by internationally acclaimed artists, such as, to name only a few, Ernst Barlach, Pierre Bonnard, Paul Gauguin and Vincent van Gogh – the last-named represented by eleven paintings, including "Bedroom in Arles". This work was acquired at the time by the collector Carl Reininghaus, a friend of Schiele's, in whose home the young artist was surely able to view it. Van Gogh's "Bedroom" inspired him to depict his own room in Neulengbach in 1911.

During the exhibition Schiele also met the architect Josef Hoffmann, through whom he made contact with the Wiener Werkstätte. In 1910 this arts and crafts workshop published three, today highly sought-after postcards based on Schiele's fashion designs. In 1910–11 he submitted numerous further designs to the Wiener Werkstätte, all of which were rejected, for reasons that are hard to understand today. Likewise thanks to Hoffmann's aid, Schiele was able to participate in the 1910 "Viennese Hunting Exhibition", with a large-format nude of an adolescent girl, the present whereabouts of which is unfortunately unknown. At the exhibition opening, this work aroused the disapproval of Emperor Franz Josef. Otto Wagner, in contrast, found it so appealing that he acquired the preliminary study for it, directly from Schiele (now in the Vienna Museum).

According to a report by Roessler, Wagner encouraged Schiele to paint life-size portraits of well-known personalities, saying he would sit to Schiele himself. However, after only a few sessions the architect lost patience with the process. Since his head was finished, Wagner suggested that the young artist do the body from another model. But Schiele dismissed the idea for artistic reasons, and later cut the head out of the canvas and offered it to Roessler at a very low price (the portrait was since lost). At any rate, that year Schiele was able to create significant portraits of many other personalities, including Poldi Lodzinsky, Erwin von Graff, Arthur Roessler, Oskar Reichel, Eduard Kosmack, and the young Herbert Rainer.

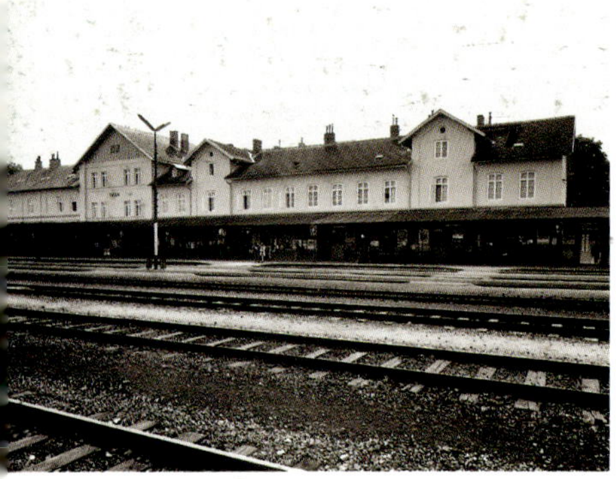

Railway station building in Tulln

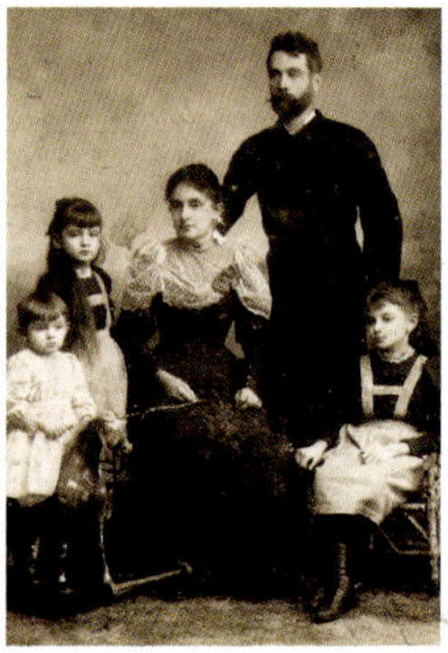

The artist's parents, Marie and Adolf Schiele, with Egon, Melanie and Elvira, 1893

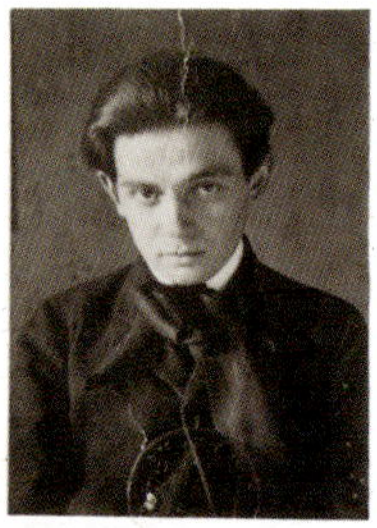

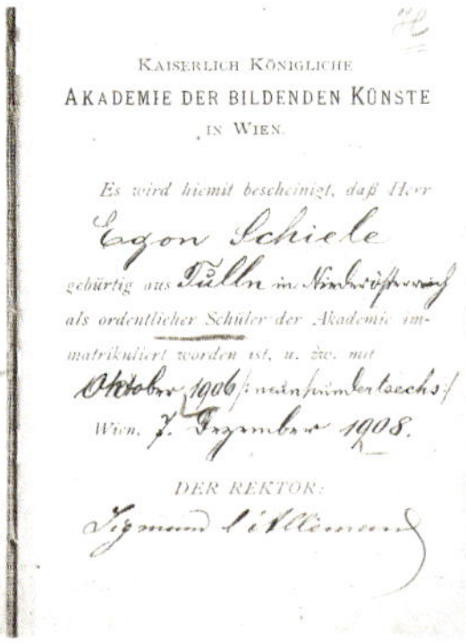

KAISERLICH KÖNIGLICHE
AKADEMIE DER BILDENDEN KÜNSTE
IN WIEN

Es wird hiemit bescheinigt, daß Herr
Egon Schiele
gebürtig aus Tulln in Niederösterreich
als ordentlicher Schüler der Akademie immatrikuliert worden ist, u. zw. mit
Oktober 1906 (neunzehnhundertsechs)
Wien, 7. Dezember 1908.

DER REKTOR:
Sigmund L'Allemand

Attendance record of the Akademie der bildenden Künste, Vienna, 1908

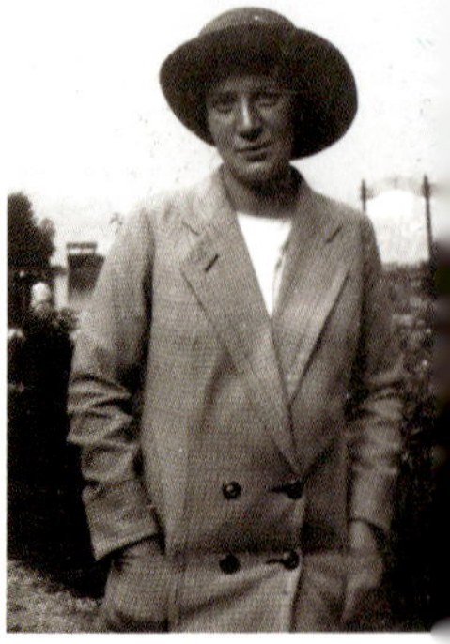

Wally Neuzil in Altmünster, 1913

By 1910, at the age of only twenty, Schiele had found his personal style and with it his artistic independence. His merciless revelations of the seamy side and pitfalls of human existence could not help but run counter to the extreme aestheticism of Art Nouveau. Not until Schiele and a second Austrian expressionist, Kokoschka, were the 'tragic and ugly' discovered as worthy of depiction and made accessible for twentieth-century art. In their portraits of the decisive early years, both artists cultivated an approach that relied largely on dark, subtly nuanced colors that had little in common with the purposely primitive palette of German Expressionism. Against Kokoschka's comparatively painterly approach, Schiele set an emphasis on structure and texture, which became just as apparent in the portraits of 1910 mentioned above, as in the nudes of that year – whether on canvas or paper. Of the four nudes on canvas, measuring about 1.5 meters square, only a seated male nude has survived (Leopold Museum, Vienna).

In the phase of 1911–12 the painterly aspect came increasingly to the fore, as seen in numerous watercolors and small paintings on wood, such as "Krumau at Night", "Krumau Town Hall", and "Dead City" (III). Yet like all of Schiele's later townscapes, these were by no means conceived as panoramas in the sense of veduta painting. Although the majority of motifs were taken from medieval Krumau, Schiele condensed them into a new unity, heightened them to fantastic visions. Their allegorical character was echoed in the three renderings of sunflowers Schiele produced in 1910, 1911 and 1914.

The years 1911 and 1912 also brought forth expressive landscapes, including the anthropomorphic depiction of a "Small Tree in Late Autumn", "Landscape with Ravens", "Calvary", and "Autumn Tree in Turbulent Air". The first publications on the artist appeared in 1911, authored by the poet and painter Albert Paris Gütersloh (pen-name of Albert Conrad Kiehtreiber) and the art writer Arthur Roessler. That same year saw Schiele's first participation in a group exhibition, at the prestigious Galerie Miethke in Vienna – which, however, ended without notable financial gain for the young artist.

Generally speaking, his artistic breakthrough in 1910 remained largely unaccompanied by public recognition. The few collectors who had been introduced to Schiele by Roessler acquired his works only hesitantly. The sole exception was Heinrich Benesch (father of the later director of the Albertina), who, however, had met Schiele not through Roessler but after an exhibition at the Choir Chapter in Klosterneuburg. The paintings by various artists on view there included "Sunflower", 1910. Benesch was so taken with it that he soon looked up the artist, and subsequently became the most persistent collector of his drawings and watercolors in particular. (The majority of these are now in the Albertina Museum, Vienna.) Benesch, a railway official, could not afford to buy oils in any great number, but he did manage to unite three outstanding works in his collection: "Landscape with Ravens", "Mourning Woman", and "Calvary" (all now in the Leopold Museum).

Wishing to put Vienna behind him, Schiele moved with his model, Wally, to Krumau, his mother's birthplace, where he hoped to settle permanently. There, in addition to studies of nudes on paper, numerous paintings of Krumau motifs in mysteriously shimmering colors emerged, including those mentioned above.

This fruitful activity, however, was soon interrupted. The narrow-minded local people could not stomach his cohabitation with Wally or his occasional requests to young Krumau girls to model for him in the nude. Schiele had to leave Krumau, and moved to Neulengbach, a small town outside Vienna. Here he produced pioneering works, such as "Landscape with Ravens", "The Hermits", "Mourning Woman", "Autumn Tree in Turbulent Air", and "Cardinal and Nun". The last-named picture, according to a letter from the Munich Secession dated 10 March 1912, was selected for that group's spring exhibition. At the beginning of the year Schiele had already been invited by the Munich artists association "Sema" to contribute to a portfolio of lithographs by numerous artists, including Paul Klee and Alfred Kubin. There Schiele's first print appeared, a powerful pen-and-brush lithograph of himself in the nude.

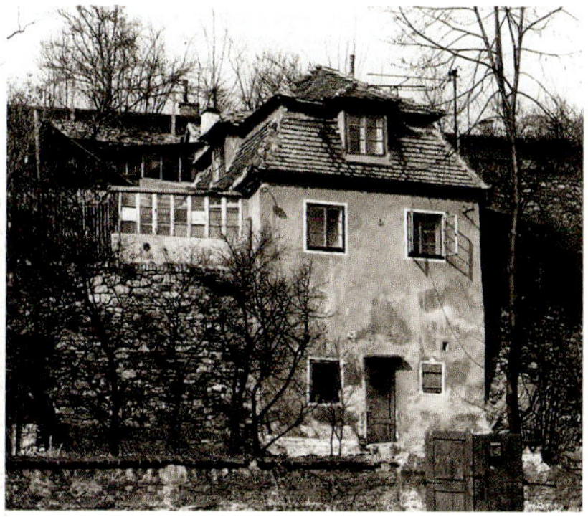

Schiele's studio and residence in Krumau

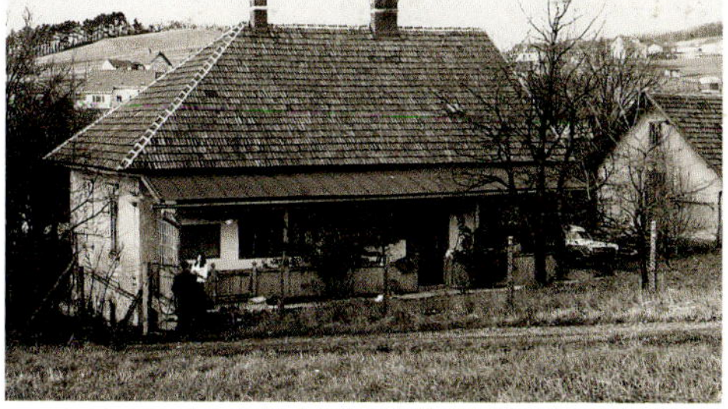

Schiele's studio and apartment in Neulengbach

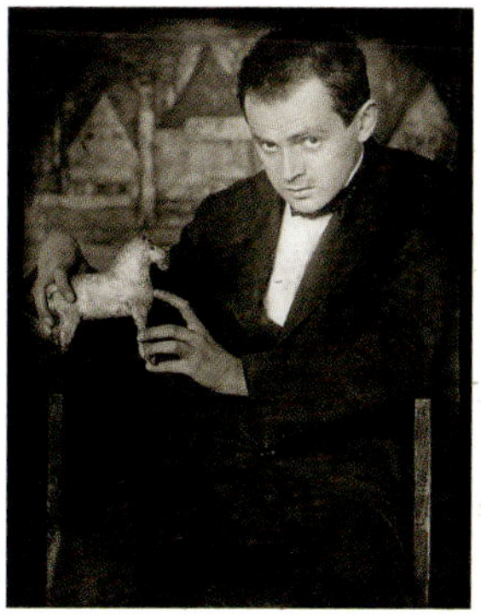

Egon Schiele with wooden horse, 1914

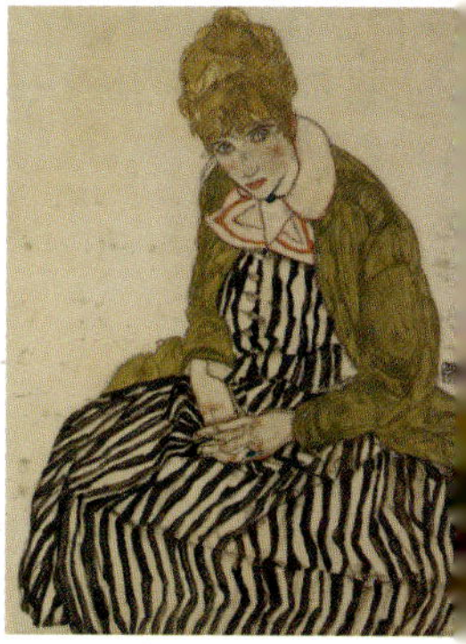

"Edith Schiele in a Striped Skirt" 1915
Pencil and gouache on paper, 51 x 40 cm
Signed and dated right center
Leopold Museum, Vienna, inv. no.: 4147

Also in spring 1912, the Munich dealer Goltz showed Schiele works alongside those of Der Blaue Reiter, but was unable to sell more than a few. Immediately thereafter, Karl Ernst Osthaus mounted a representative exhibition at his Museum Folkwang in Hagen, Westphalia. This favorable if modest development was abruptly interrupted when Schiele was taken into investigative custody on 13 April. The main charge against him, seduction of a minor, proved unsubstantiated. Yet because children occasionally saw studies of nudes in his studio, and this was considered to represent "a dissemination of indecent drawings", the court sentenced Schiele to three days' arrest (which his longer investigative custody already covered). At the close of the trial, the judge actually publicly burned a depiction of a nude that had been confiscated from Schiele's studio. All of this was a profound shock for the artist. He didn't wish to write about it because it disgusted him too much, Schiele confided in a letter. (In 1922, four years after the artist's death, Roessler would publish "Aufzeichnungen", or Notes, supposedly made by Schiele in jail. Actually they were Roessler's invention.)

After his release from prison Schiele spent several days in Trieste and drew and painted boats and ships in the harbor. In July 1912, seven Schiele oils, including the biographically significant "Hermits", were shown at the "Hagenbund" in Vienna. The artist acquired a new patron and collector, the art-loving innkeeper Franz Hauer. On 26 July he received 900 crowns for three paintings from him.

Schiele travelled to Munich, Lindau and Bregenz, where he stayed for a protracted period. From there he made an excursion to Zurich. At the prestigious "International Sonderbund Exhibition", held from 25 May to 30 September 1912 in Cologne, Schiele was represented with three works.

In November, back in Vienna, the artist found a suitable studio at 101 Hietzinger Hauptstrasse, which he would retain until his death. Since Schiele was among the few Austrian artists he truly admired, Klimt introduced him to one of his most prosperous collectors, the industrialist August Lederer. Before and after the Christmas holidays in 1912–13, Lederer invited Schiele to Györ, Hungary, to portray his son, Erich. The boy would later become Schiele's scholar.

The year 1913 again found Schiele travelling extensively. He went several times to the Wachau region, where he made studies of the town of Stein an der Donau. These provided the basis for two large-format versions of the subject, done in the studio. Schiele also travelled to Krumau and to Munich, where, as in the previous year, he participated in the spring exhibition of the Munich Secession. Shortly thereafter, at the beginning of summer, Galerie Goltz mounted a great review of his œuvre. Later Schiele spent time in Villach and Tarvis. He had a falling-out with Roessler, not being prepared to give him his important painting "Setting Sun" in exchange for a few nineteenth-century firearms and Fiji arrows. Yet since his art and person were continually under attack at that time and he needed at least one critic on his side, Schiele ended up giving Roessler the painting. As a "modest" return he received a ten-day invitation to Altmünster am Traunsee, and, to Roessler's chagrin, took his girlfriend Wally along. After that, likewise with Wally, Schiele went to Sattendorf on Lake Ossiach, where several successful studies emerged (including the superb drawing "Old Gable" [see p. 131], now in the Leopold Museum).

In 1913 Schiele was accepted into the Bund Österreichischer Künstler, or League of Austrian Artists, of which Klimt was president. That same year he was able to participate in the "Grosse Deutsche Kunstausstellung", or Great German Art Exhibition, in Düsseldorf, and in the "International Black and White Exhibition" held by the Vienna Secession. Also in 1913, Schiele became a contributor to "Die Aktion", a "weekly for politics, literature and art". Edited by Franz Pfemfert, the journal published both drawings and prose poems by Schiele. In 1916 "Die Aktion" devoted an entire issue to him (no. 35/36), which in addition to reproductions of drawings contained his woodcut, "Bathing Men". (Along with "Der Sturm", "Die Aktion" was one of the key German periodicals of the day in the fields of cultural policy and modern art.)

In 1914 works by Schiele were on view at the Werkbund Exhibition in Dresden, Hamburg, Munich and Cologne, but also outside of Germany and the Austro-Hungarian monarchy – in Rome (International Secession), Brussels and Paris. However, Schiele's art enjoyed little more than a *succès d'estime* among foreign audiences at that time.

In summer 1914 he produced six drypoint etchings. And sessions with the photographer Anton Josef Trçka resulted in a series of highly idiosyncratic photoportraits. In the person of Heinrich Böhler, cousin of the painter Hans Böhler, Schiele gained a prosperous collector, and a new scholar as well – if only for about a year and a half.

The year 1913 marked the beginning of Schiele's involvement with Cubism, of which he soon developed a highly personal version. Cases in point are the second large-format painting of "Stein on the Danube", 1913, "Krumau on the Moldau", 1914, and above all, "Blind Mother", 1915, the second "Town Crescent", "House with Shingle Roof", the depiction of the façade of St. Jost's Church on the left bank of the Moldau, and two large figurative works, "Floating Away" and "Death and the Girl".

The year 1915 had begun with a remarkable overview exhibition at Galerie Guido Arnot in Vienna. Watercolors and drawings by the artist were also on view at the Kunsthaus in Zurich.

On 17 July, Schiele married Edith Harms, daughter of the locksmith Johann Harms, a native of Hannover, who owned the house diagonally opposite Schiele's studio. Only four days later, on the 21st, Schiele had to report for military duty, and was initially stationed in Prague, then he was transferred to Neuhaus in Bohemia. His wife followed him on each move, living in hotel rooms. Before 20 July, Schiele was transferred to Vienna, where he was able to resume his artistic activity. His wife sat for him for the superb "Portrait of Edith Schiele in a Striped Skirt", which was preceded by a few wonderful studies. At this period Schiele was on guard duty, charged with escorting Russian prisoners, and he occasionally depicted them in drawings.

At the end of the year Schiele was invited by the Berlin Secession to participate in the important "Wiener Kunstschau" exhibition, which took place in January-February 1916 in Berlin. As we gather from one of the artist's letters, his "Floating Away", 1915, was juxtaposed in the foyer with Klimt's "Death and Life", 1911/15. In addition to numerous drawings, two large paintings by Schiele were on view: "Death and the Girl" and "Mother with Two Children" which he would considerably rework until 1917.

Schiele kept a war diary from 8 March to 30 September 1916. At the time he was permitted to spend his off-duty hours in his Hietzing street studio. He was able to finish the paintings "City and River" and "Town of Mödling" – which would be destroyed by fire in the Second World War. Then he began a portrait of his father-in-law. Here Schiele succeeded in transcending mere portraiture to create a universal symbol of age.

On 1 May 1916, the artist was detailed to Upper Austria, to a prisoner of war camp for Russian officers. He made drawings both of Russian and Austrian officers there. During his few off-duty hours Schiele was able to complete only two relatively large-format paintings, one of an old watermill, which he very aptly titled "Decaying Mill". In a later flood the painted mill would in fact suffer the fate Schiele had predicted for its original.

In 1917 Schiele was able to return to Vienna, where he was employed in the I & R Supply Stores for Members of the Army in the Field. Subsequently this institution would commission him to record in drawings not only its headquarters in Vienna but its branches scattered throughout the Austro-Hungarian Empire. These drawings were intended for a festschrift, whose publication, however, was precluded by the end of the war. In 1917 Schiele and Albert Paris Gütersloh were entrusted with organizing a war exhibition in the Vienna Prater. Schiele was represented in the Munich Secession exhibition in the Crystal Palace, as well as in shows in Amsterdam, Stockholm and Copenhagen, held from late 1917 to early 1918.

In the final phase of his career, from about the middle of 1916 to his death in 1918, Schiele abandoned his expressive style in favor of a more naturalistic approach, if one in which certain mannerisms became apparent. Still, in early 1918 he achieved a new breakthrough, with "Family", "Pair of Crouching Women", "Three Standing Women", and his final "Lovers". These new depictions left Expressionism far behind. Schiele, considerably younger than Picasso and Braque, had not developed his "Cubism" until five years after their pioneering achievement. Yet the classical character of his new renderings of volumes in space was years in advance of Picasso.

In October, the bookdealer Richard Lányi published a first portfolio containing twelve original-size black and white photogravures of Schiele drawings with watercolor wash. Two issues of the journal "Der Anbruch – Flugblätter aus der Zeit", for December 1917 and January 1918, carried a reproduction of a Schiele drawing on the cover. The third issue contained Schiele's obituary for Klimt, who died on 6 February 1918. The following day Schiele had made three drawings of the dead artist, whose beard had been shaven, in the Pathological Anatomy.

For the March 1918 exhibition of the Vienna Secession, the group put its main room at Schiele's disposal. Here he displayed nineteen large paintings and twenty-nine drawings, some with watercolor wash. This exhibition brought his first truly meaningful success, in both an artistic and a financial respect. That same month the Gesellschaft für vervielfältigende Kunst, or Association for Art Reproductions, asked Schiele to submit a colored design for a nude or a landscape. Although he sent them only black and white works, they were outstanding ones: an expressive head, "Portrait of Paris Gütersloh", and a lovely nude of a reclining young girl. Both works, however, were rejected. Members of the selection committee, Dr. Arpad Weixlgärtner, Dr. Franz Martin Haberditzl, Dr. Jung and the painter Harlfinger, found them not "exemplary of the special character and strengths" of Schiele's art. These gentlemen's misjudgement

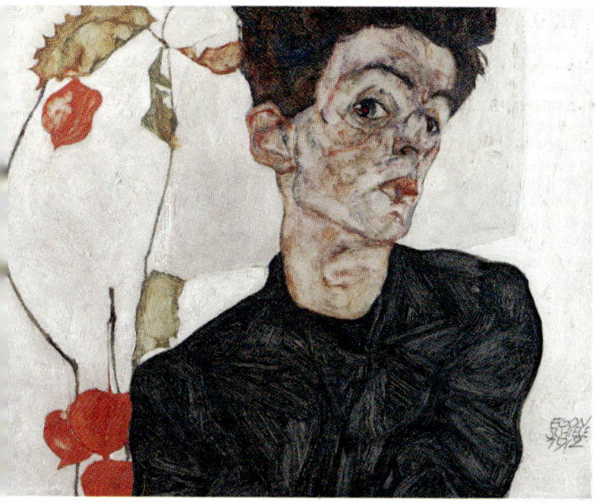

Self-portrait with Chinese Lantern Plant 1912
Leopold Museum, Vienna, inv. no.: LM 454

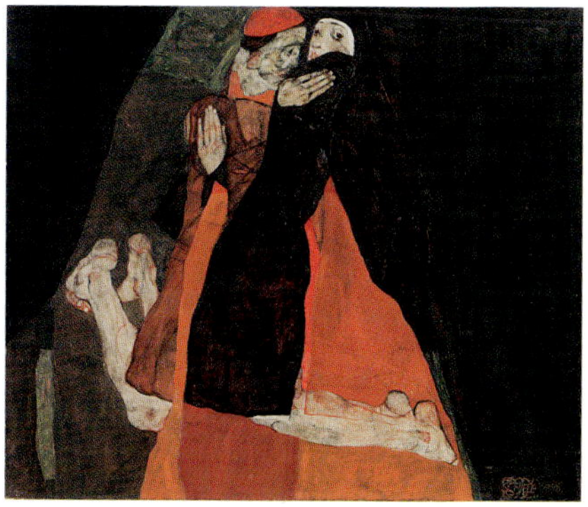

Cardinal and Nun (Tenderness) 1912
Leopold Museum, Vienna, inv. no.: LM 455

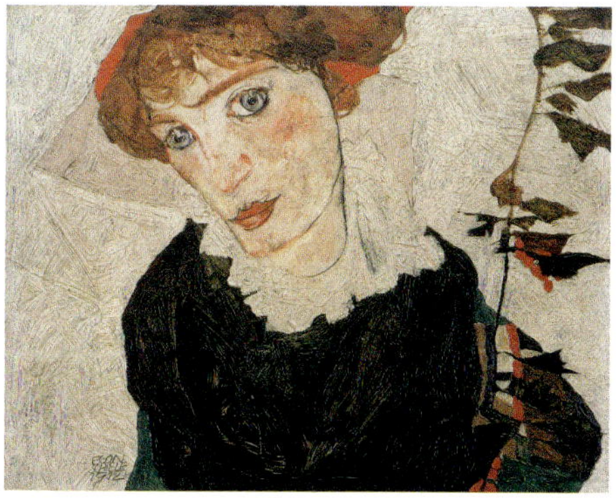

Portrait of Wally Neuzil 1912
Leopold Museum, Vienna, inv. no.: LM 453

seems all the crasser in view of the fact that the association considered the mediocre works of a now entirely forgotten artist more worthy of reproduction than Schiele's.

Four paintings and a number of drawings by Schiele were included in the exhibition "Ein Jahrhundert Wiener Malerei", or A Century of Viennese Painting, held in May-June at the Kunsthaus Zurich.

After Klimt's decease and Kokoschka's departure from Vienna, Schiele became the intellectual leader of progressive art in Austria. At that period the Art Association for Bohemia in Prague offered to display about 200 graphic works of his in the context of their "Art Group", a show that subsequently took place at the Künstlerhaus Rudolphinum in Prague. As we may gather from one of Schiele's letters, his wife, who was six months pregnant, had been in bed since 19 October with Spanish influenza, which was then raging throughout Europe. Nine days later, on 28 October at eight o'clock in the morning, she died. Schiele had made two drawings of her the evening before. These were to be his final works. Afflicted with the same illness, the artist succumbed at one o'clock in the morning of 31 October. He was twenty-eight years old.

As many passages in his letters indicate, despite the enmity of his backward contemporaries Schiele was quite conscious of the important place he held in emergent modern art. Yet there was an aphorism he repeated again and again, with slight variations: "Art cannot be modern. Art is eternal". This was the view of one of the major avant-garde artists of the twentieth century. His independence, both in drawing and painting, was extreme. Otto Benesch, director of the Albertina from 1947 to 1961, called Schiele one of the most brilliant draughtsmen of all time. His graphic gifts doubtless surpassed those of any Austrian or German Expressionist. None of them was capable, as he was, of conveying with a contour not only the outline but the volume of an object or figure – and beyond that, often the emotions these motifs aroused in him. Schiele is today justifiably considered to be one of the great innovators in visual art.

Bibliography

Significant publications about Egon Schiele, chronologically listed

Books and magazines

1913/16 *Die Aktion* (published by Franz Pfemfert in Berlin "Wochenschrift für Politik, Literatur und Kunst"), also includes drawings and prose-poems by Schiele; 1916 as nos. 35/36 a separate Schiele-issue, which moreover included his woodcut "Badende Männer" (Bathing Men).

1921 Arthur Roessler, publisher, *Briefe und Prosa von Egon Schiele*; Verlag Buchhandlung Richard Lányi, Vienna

1930 Otto Nirenstein [later Kallir], *Egon Schiele, Persönlichkeit und Werk*, includes 140 plates of Schiele's paintings; Paul Zsolnay Verlag, Berlin – Vienna – Leipzig; the second edition appeared in 1966 by the same publishers: Otto Kallir, *Egon Schiele, Œuvre-Katalog der Gemälde*, with contributions by Otto Benesch and Thomas Messer, includes 180 plates

1958 Otto Benesch: "Egon Schiele und die Graphik des Expressionismus", with 19 illustrations from Schiele's works, in: *Continuum, zur Kunst Österreichs in der Mitte des 20. Jahrhunderts*, Verlag Brüder Rosenbaum, Vienna

1959 Rudolf Leopold: "Egon Schiele. Ein Genie aus Österreich", essay with 13 illustrations, in: *BP Querschnitt*, issue 1

1961 Erwin Mitsch: *Egon Schiele, Zeichnungen und Aquarelle*, with 64 illustrations; Verlag Galerie Welz, Salzburg

1968 Werner Hofmann: *Egon Schiele. Die Familie;* Philipp Reclam Verlag, Stuttgart

1968/69 Johannes Dobai: "Egon Schiele 'Jüngling vor Gott Vater kniend'", essay with 19 illustrations, in: *Schweizerisches Institut für Kunstwissenschaft*, Zürich, yearbook 1968/69

1972 Rudolf Leopold: *Egon Schiele, Gemälde, Aquarelle, Zeichnungen;* includes, inter alia, curriculum vitae, catalogue raisonné of his paintings, Schiele's recognition – admirers and opponents of his art, as well as the first motif location study of his paintings; Residenz Verlag, Salzburg (Engl. edition, Abrams, New York, 1973)

1974 Alessandra Comini: *Egon Schiele's Portraits*, Berkely, University of California

1979 Christian Nebehay: *Egon Schiele, 1890 bis 1918, Leben, Briefe, Gedichte*; Residenz Verlag, Salzburg

1988 *Egon Schiele und seine Zeit, Österreichische Malerei und Zeichnung von 1900 bis 1930, Aus der Sammlung Leopold*, catalog for the exhibition in the Kunsthaus Zürich, in Kunstforum Vienna, in the Hypo-Kulturstiftung Kunsthalle, Munich, and in the Von-der-Heydt-Museum, Wuppertal; Prestel, Munich and elsewhere.

1990 Jane Kallir: *Egon Schiele, The Complete Works, including a Biography and a Catalogue Raisonné*; Abrams, New York (Expanded edition: Abrams, New York, 1998)

1995 Rudolf Leopold: *Egon Schiele, Die Sammlung Leopold*, catalog for the exhibition in the Kunsthalle Tübingen, in the K20 Kunstsammlung Nordrhein-Westfalen, Düsseldorf, and in the Hamburger Kunsthalle; DuMont, Cologne

1999 *Menschenbilder, Egon Schiele und seine Zeit*, catalog for the exhibition in the Tiroler Landesmuseum Ferdinandeum, Innsbruck; DuMont, Cologne

2001 *Meisterwerke aus der Sammlung Leopold*, catalog for the opening of the Leopold Museum; Leopold Museum Privatstiftung, Vienna, and DuMont, Cologne

2004 Kimberley A. Smith: *Between Ruin and Renewal, Egon Schiele's Landscapes*; Yale University Press, New Haven and London

Portfolio editions

1912 *Sema-Portfolio:* contains *15 original lithographs* by members of the 'Sema' arts union, including a nude self-portrait by Egon Schiele, a lithography in quill and brush style; Delphin-Verlag, Munich

1917 *Zeichnungen – Egon Schiele*: 12 black and white phototype copies of Schiele's sheet drawings in original scale, with an introduction and an index, both signed by Schiele in Indian ink, 400 copies; Verlag Buchhandlung Richard Lányi, Vienna

1920 *Egon Schiele, Handzeichnungen,* 4 color phototype copies of watercolored drawings und 11 black and white phototypes of pure drawings in original scale; Verlag Ed. Strache, Vienna – Prague – Leipzig

Undated (probably 1950) *Egon Schiele als Zeichner*: 16 illustrations in color offset printing and 8 illustrations in monochrome gravure; introduction by Otto Benesch; Österreichische Staatsdruckerei, Vienna

1968 *Egon Schiele, Aquarelle und Zeichnungen*; published by Walter Koschatzky, selected and edited by Erwin Mitsch: 64 reproductions in color phototype; also appeared in bookform; Verlag Galerie Welz, Salzburg

1985 *Egon Schiele: Blätter aus Privatbesitz, Teil 1,* introduction by Rudolf Leopold; Akademische Druck- und Verlagsanstalt, Graz

1986 *Egon Schiele: Blätter aus Privatbesitz, Teil 2*, introduction by Rudolf Leopold; Akademische Druck- und Verlagsanstalt, Graz